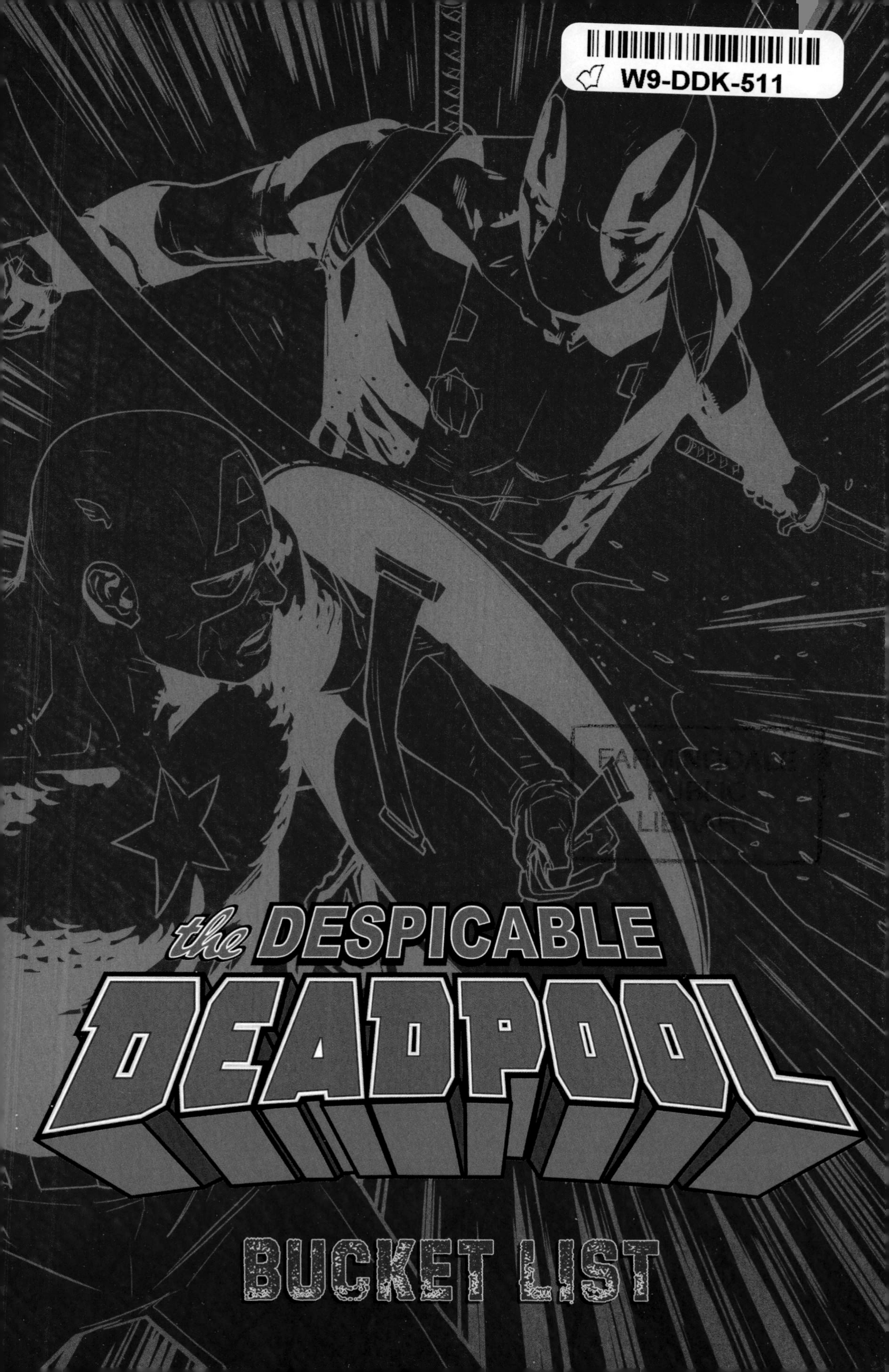
the DESPICABLE
DEADPOOL
BUCKET LIST

the DESPICABLE DEADPOOL

BUCKET LIST

WRITER
Gerry Duggan

DESPICABLE DEADPOOL #292-293, #295-296

PENCILER
Matteo Lolli

INKERS
Matteo Lolli (#292, #295-296) &
Christian Dalla Vecchia (#293)

COLOR ARTIST
Ruth Redmond

DESPICABLE DEADPOOL #294

ARTIST
Scott Koblish

COLOR ARTIST
Ruth Redmond

LETTERER
VC's Joe Sabino

LETTERER
*Mike Hawthorne &
Nathan Fairbairn*

ASSISTANT EDITOR
Annalise Bissa

EDITOR
Jordan D. White

DEADPOOL CREATED BY ROB LIEFELD & FABIAN NICIEZA

COLLECTION EDITOR JENNIFER GRÜNWALD
ASSISTANT EDITOR CAITLIN O'CONNELL
ASSOCIATE MANAGING EDITOR KATERI WOODY
EDITOR, SPECIAL PROJECTS MARK D. BEAZLEY

VP PRODUCTION & SPECIAL PROJECTS JEFF YOUNGQUIST
SVP PRINT, SALES & MARKETING DAVID GABRIEL
BOOK DESIGNER ADAM DEL RE

EDITOR IN CHIEF C.B. CEBULSKI
CHIEF CREATIVE OFFICER JOE QUESADA
PRESIDENT DAN BUCKLEY
EXECUTIVE PRODUCER ALAN FINE

DESPICABLE DEADPOOL VOL. 2: BUCKET LIST. Contains material originally published in magazine form as DESPICABLE DEADPOOL #292-296. First printing 2018. ISBN 978-1-302-90995-6. Published by MARVEL WORLDWIDE, INC., a subsidiary of MARVEL ENTERTAINMENT, LLC. OFFICE OF PUBLICATION: 135 West 50th Street, New York, NY 10020. Copyright © 2018 MARVEL. No similarity between any of the names, characters, persons, and/or institutions in this magazine with those of any living or dead person or institution is intended, and any such similarity which may exist is purely coincidental. Printed in Canada. DAN BUCKLEY, President, Marvel Entertainment; JOHN NEE, Publisher; JOE QUESADA, Chief Creative Officer; TOM BREVOORT, SVP of Publishing; DAVID BOGART, SVP of Business Affairs & Operations, Publishing & Partnership; DAVID GABRIEL, SVP of Sales & Marketing, Publishing; JEFF YOUNGQUIST, VP of Production & Special Projects; DAN CARR, Executive Director of Publishing Technology; ALEX MORALES, Director of Publishing Operations; SUSAN CRESPI, Production Manager; STAN LEE, Chairman Emeritus. For information regarding advertising in Marvel Comics or on Marvel.com, please contact Vit DeBellis, Custom Solutions and Integrated Advertising Manager, at vdebellis@marvel.com. For Marvel subscription inquiries, please call 888-511-5480. Manufactured between 3/16/2018 and 4/23/2018 by SOLISCO PRINTERS, SCOTT, QC, CANADA.

292 – Part One: "Deadpool vs. Stevil Rogers"

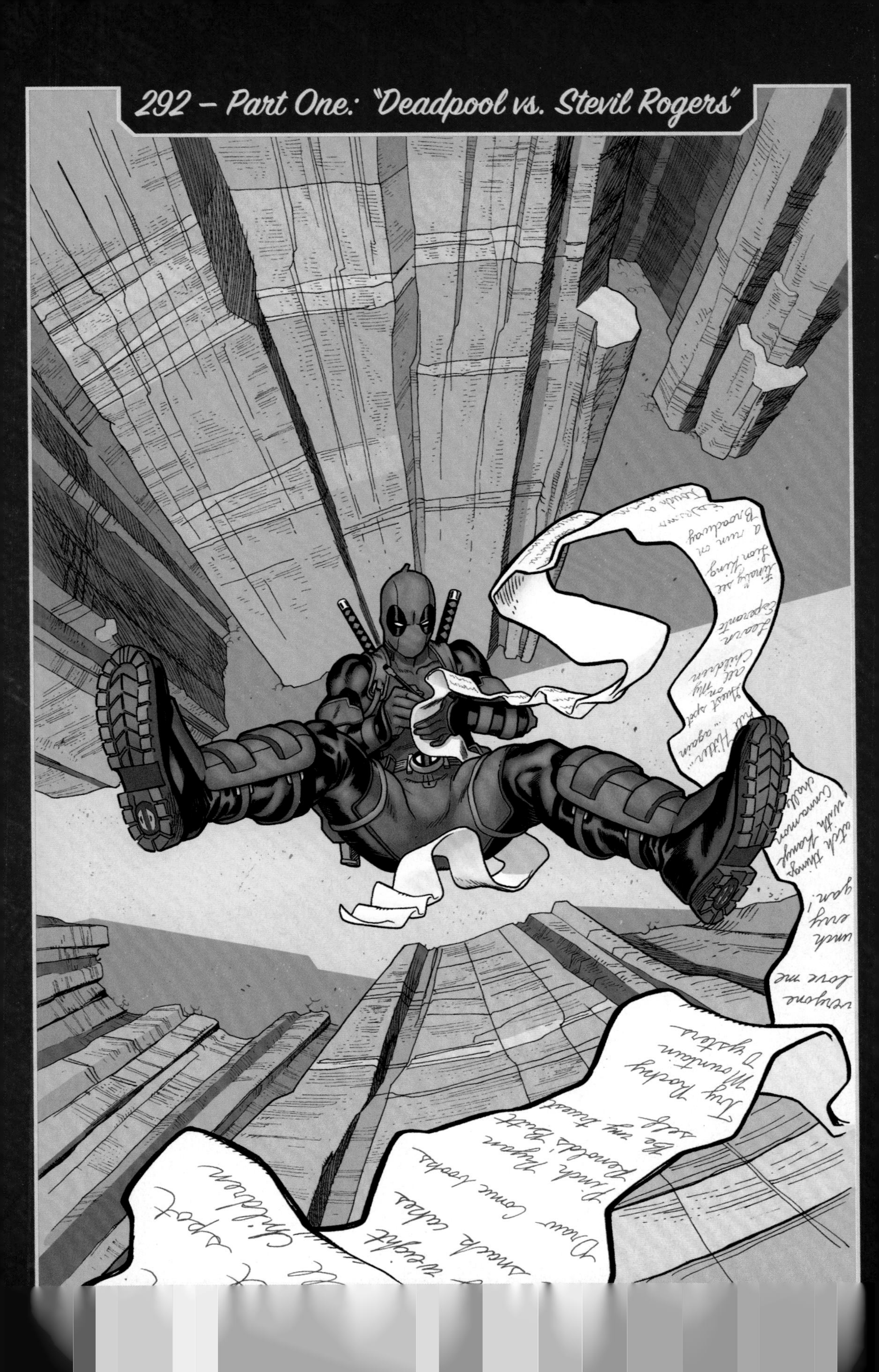

POSSIBLY THE WORLD'S MOST SKILLED MERCENARY, DEFINITELY THE WORLD'S MOST ANNOYING, WADE WILSON WAS CHOSE AS PART OF A TOP-SECRET GOVERNMENT PROGRAM THAT ACCIDENTALLY GAVE HIM A HEALING FACTOR ALLOWING HIM TO HEA FROM ANY WOUND. FOR A TIME, WADE TRIED TO BE A HERO, THROWING IN WITH THOSE WHO INSPIRED HIM: AVENGERS, X-MEN SPIDER-MEN. ALL HE GOT FOR HIS EFFORTS WAS PAIN. FORGET THAT NOISE. NOW, HE'S BACK TO BEING WHAT HE DOES BEST...

the DESPICABLE DEADPOOL

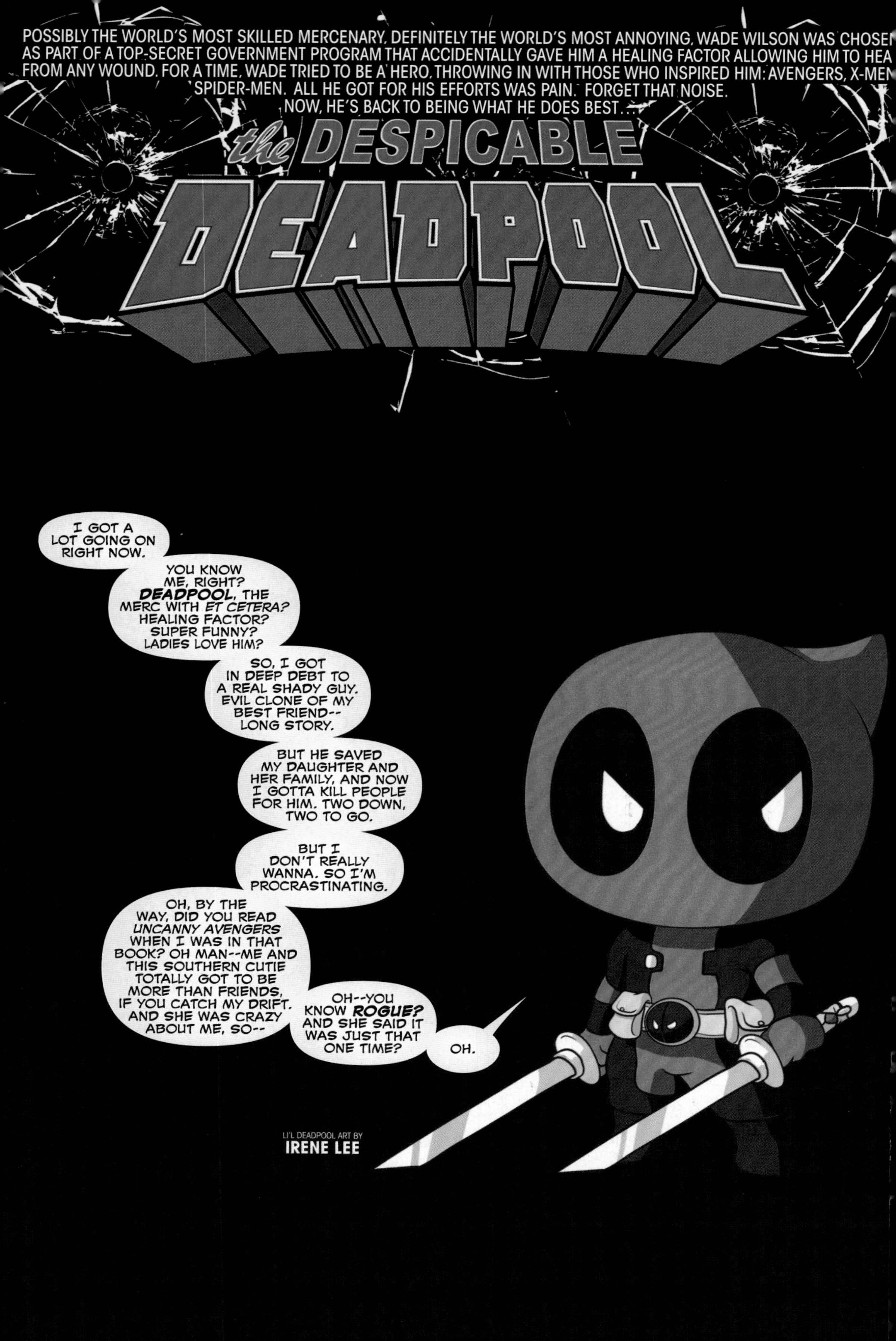

I GOT A LOT GOING ON RIGHT NOW.
YOU KNOW ME, RIGHT? **DEADPOOL**, THE MERC WITH *ET CETERA?* HEALING FACTOR? SUPER FUNNY? LADIES LOVE HIM?
SO, I GOT IN DEEP DEBT TO A REAL SHADY GUY. EVIL CLONE OF MY BEST FRIEND-- LONG STORY.
BUT HE SAVED MY DAUGHTER AND HER FAMILY, AND NOW I GOTTA KILL PEOPLE FOR HIM. TWO DOWN, TWO TO GO.
BUT I DON'T REALLY WANNA. SO I'M PROCRASTINATING.
OH, BY THE WAY, DID YOU READ *UNCANNY AVENGERS* WHEN I WAS IN THAT BOOK? OH MAN--ME AND THIS SOUTHERN CUTIE TOTALLY GOT TO BE MORE THAN FRIENDS, IF YOU CATCH MY DRIFT. AND SHE WAS CRAZY ABOUT ME, SO--
OH--YOU KNOW **ROGUE?** AND SHE SAID IT WAS JUST THAT ONE TIME?
OH.

LI'L DEADPOOL ART BY
IRENE LEE

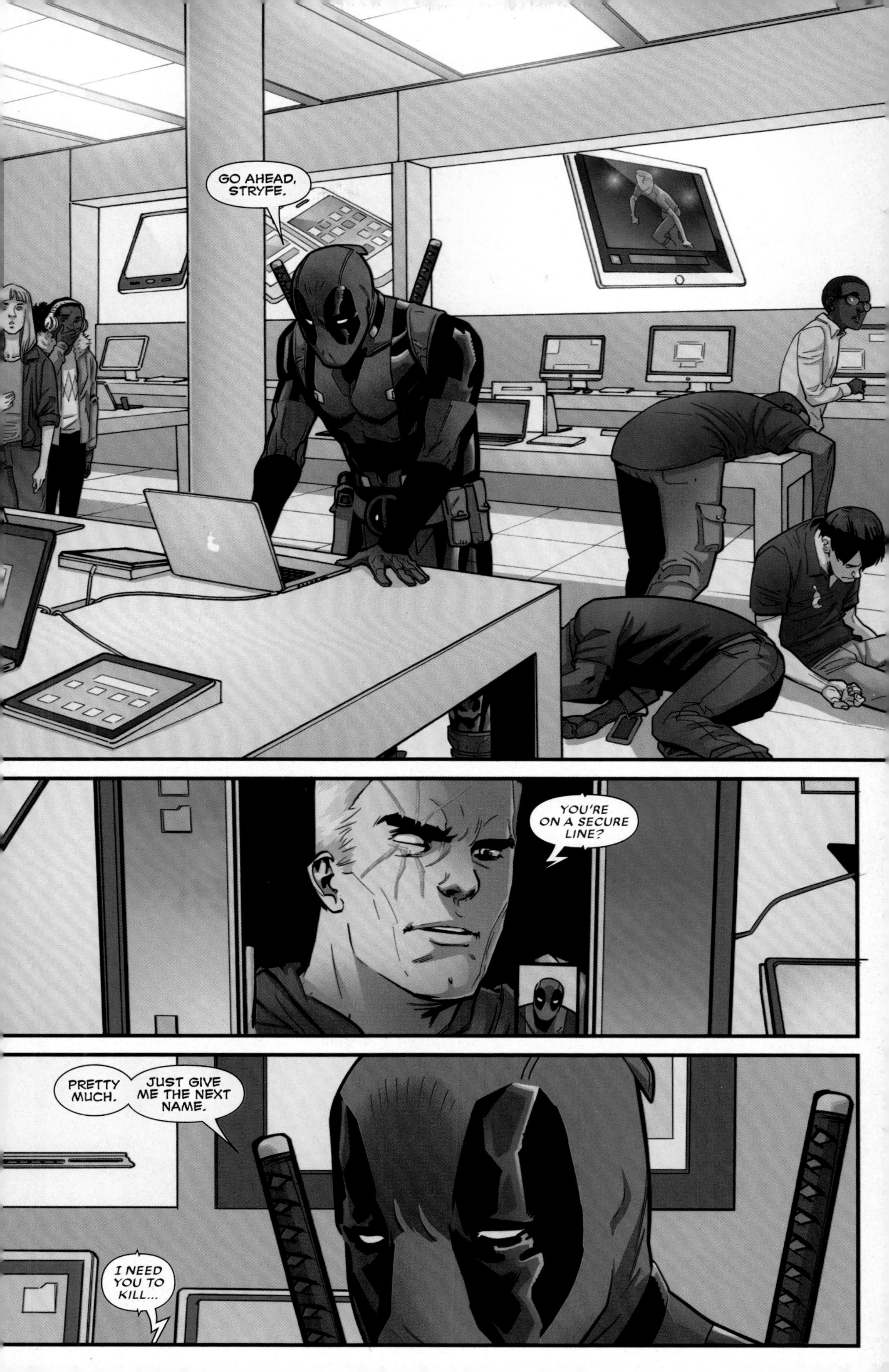
GO AHEAD, STRYFE.
YOU'RE ON A SECURE LINE?
PRETTY MUCH.
JUST GIVE ME THE NEXT NAME.
I NEED YOU TO KILL...

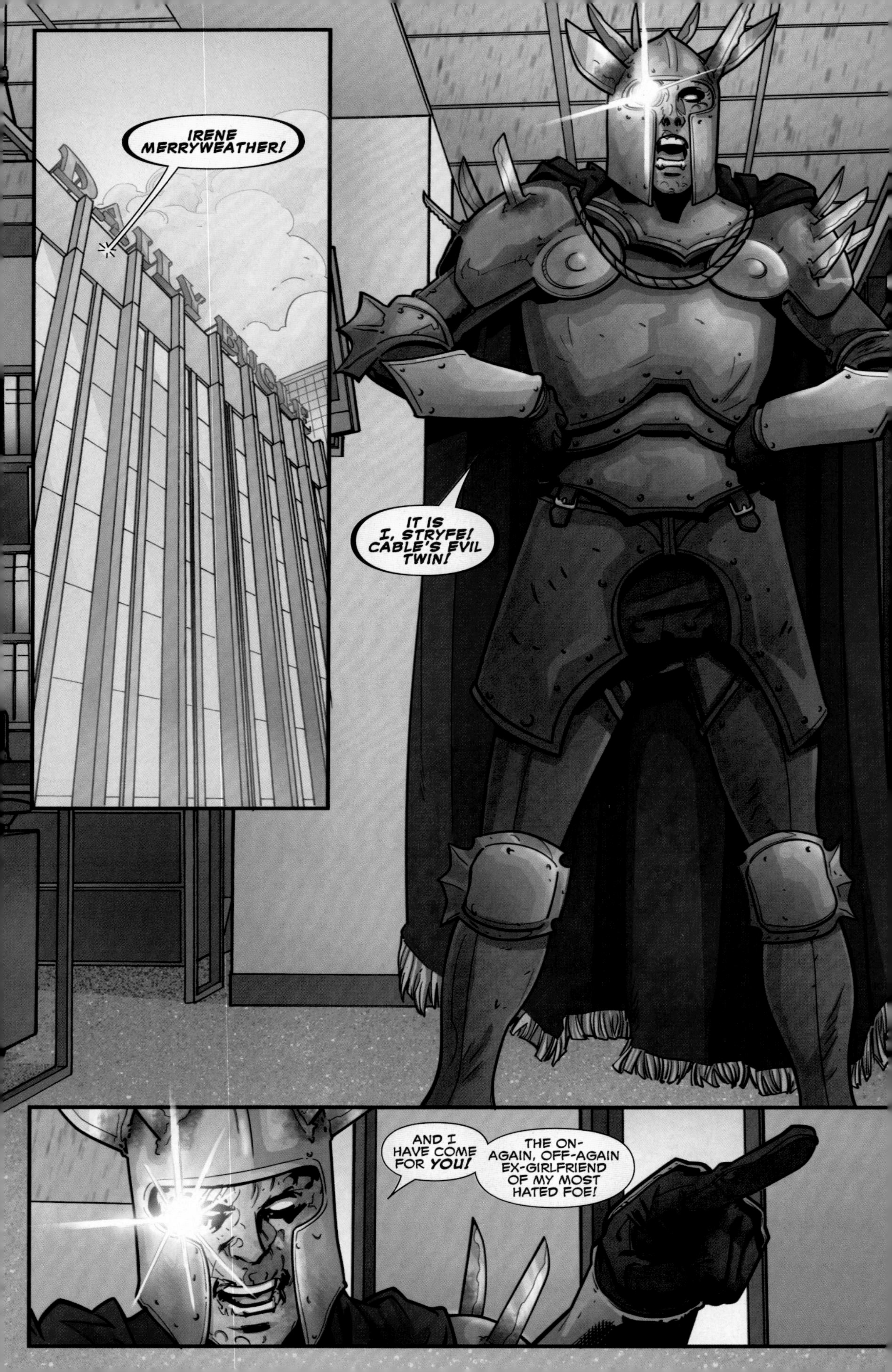
IRENE MERRYWEATHER!
IT IS I, STRYFE! CABLE'S EVIL TWIN!
AND I HAVE COME FOR YOU!
THE ON-AGAIN, OFF-AGAIN EX-GIRLFRIEND OF MY MOST HATED FOE!

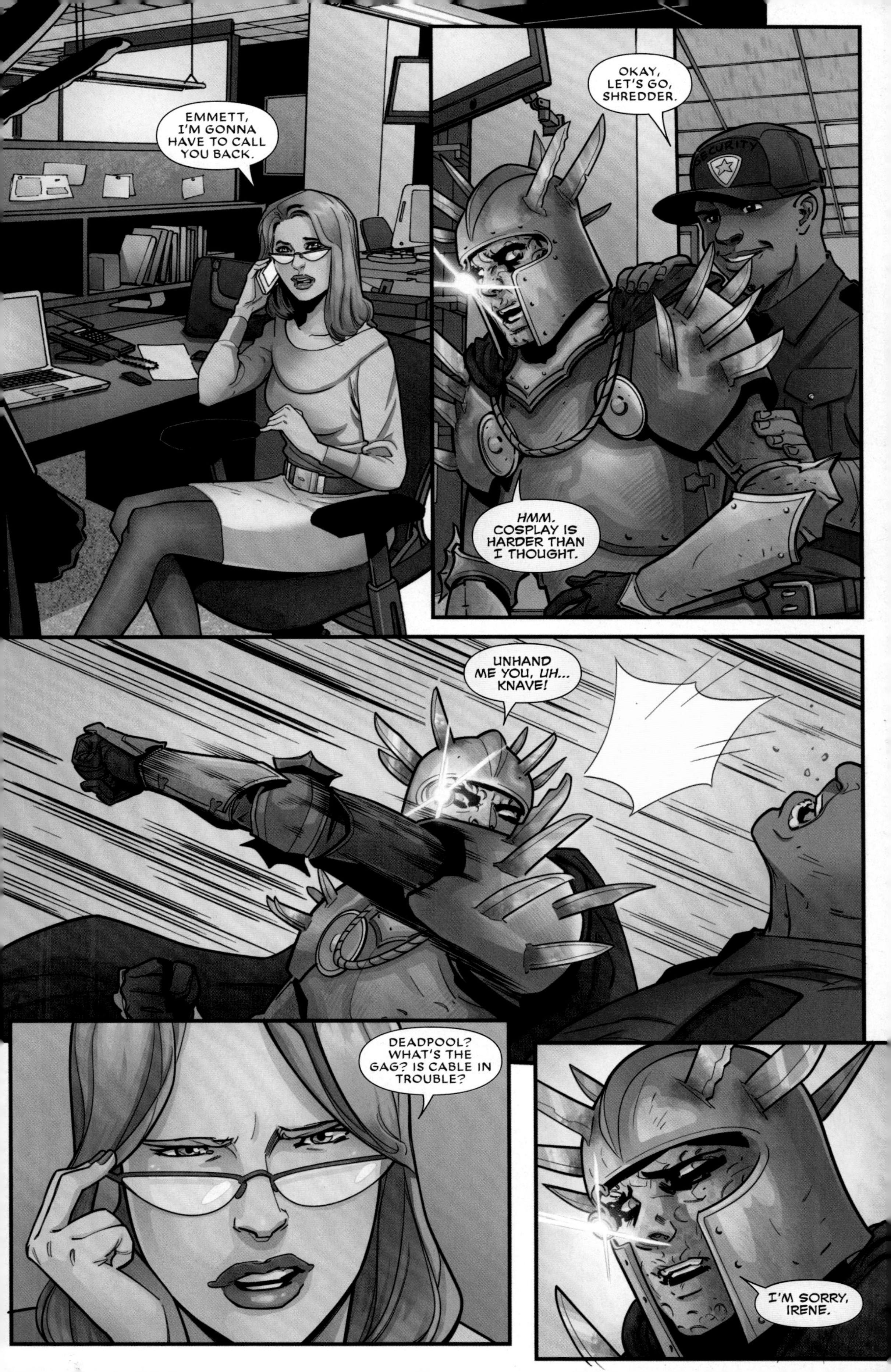
EMMETT, I'M GONNA HAVE TO CALL YOU BACK.
OKAY, LET'S GO, SHREDDER.
HMM. COSPLAY IS HARDER THAN I THOUGHT.
UNHAND ME YOU, UH... KNAVE!
DEADPOOL? WHAT'S THE GAG? IS CABLE IN TROUBLE?
I'M SORRY, IRENE.

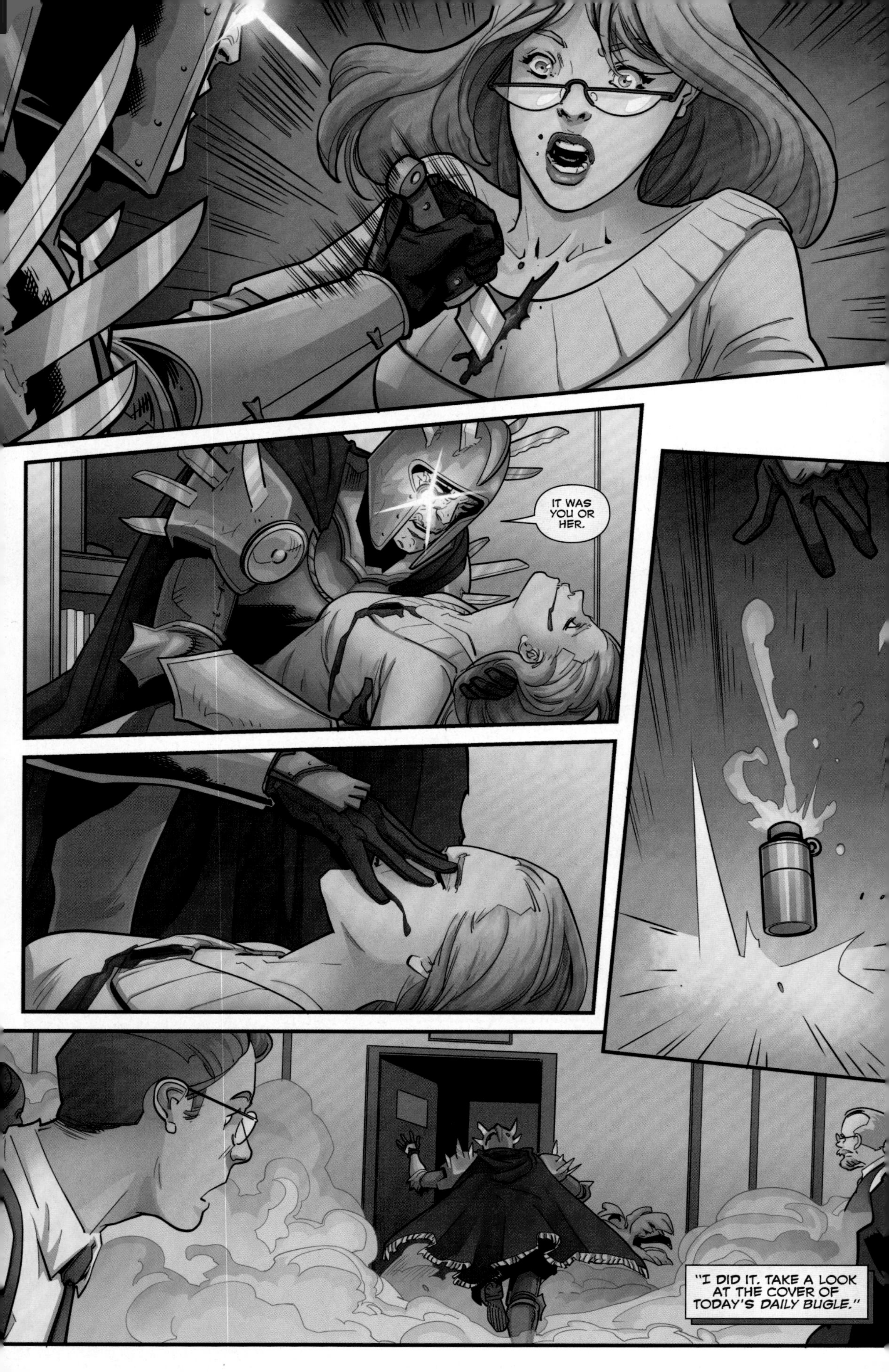
IT WAS YOU OR HER.
"I DID IT. TAKE A LOOK AT THE COVER OF TODAY'S DAILY BUGLE."

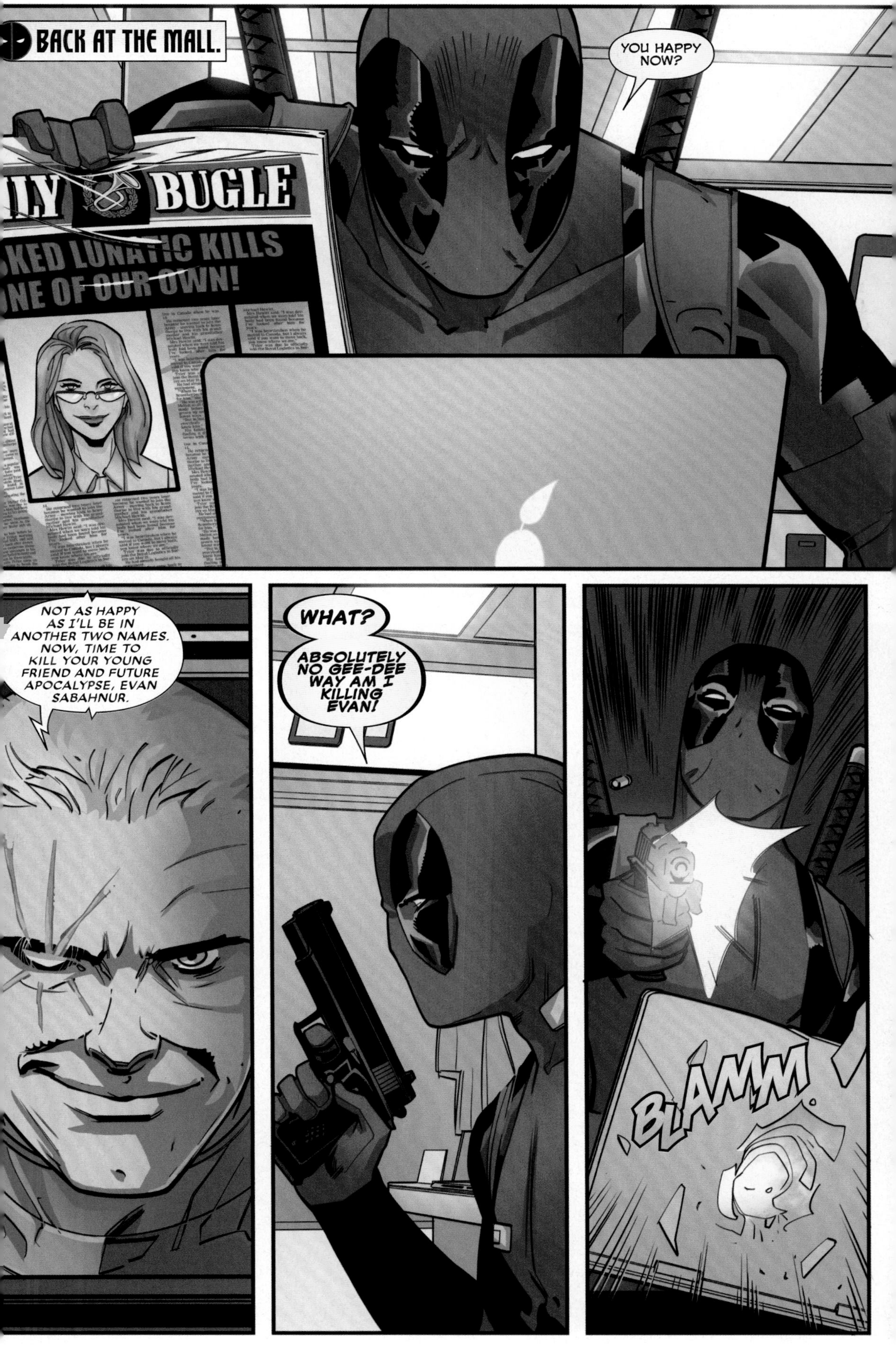
BACK AT THE MALL.
BUGLE
LUNATIC KILLS
OF OUR OWN!
YOU HAPPY NOW?
NOT AS HAPPY AS I'LL BE IN ANOTHER TWO NAMES. NOW, TIME TO KILL YOUR YOUNG FRIEND AND FUTURE APOCALYPSE, EVAN SABAHNUR.
WHAT?
ABSOLUTELY NO GEE-DEE WAY AM I KILLING EVAN!
BLAMM

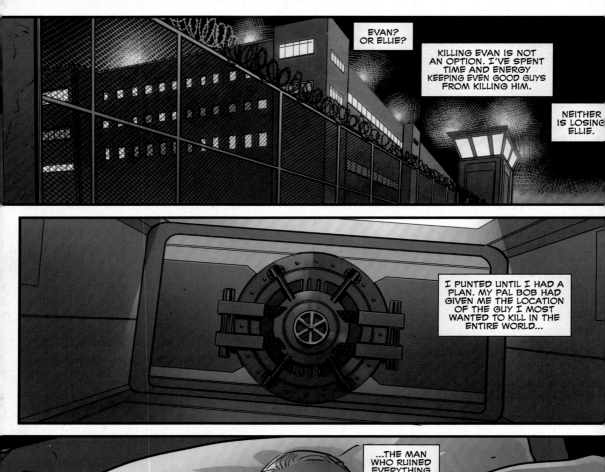

EVAN? OR ELLIE?

KILLING EVAN IS NOT AN OPTION. I'VE SPENT TIME AND ENERGY KEEPING EVEN GOOD GUYS FROM KILLING HIM.

NEITHER IS LOSING ELLIE.

I PUNTED UNTIL I HAD A PLAN. MY PAL BOB HAD GIVEN ME THE LOCATION OF THE GUY I MOST WANTED TO KILL IN THE ENTIRE WORLD...

...THE MAN WHO RUINED EVERYTHING FOR ME.

3396068

WAKEY-WAKEY, *STEVIL ROGERS.*

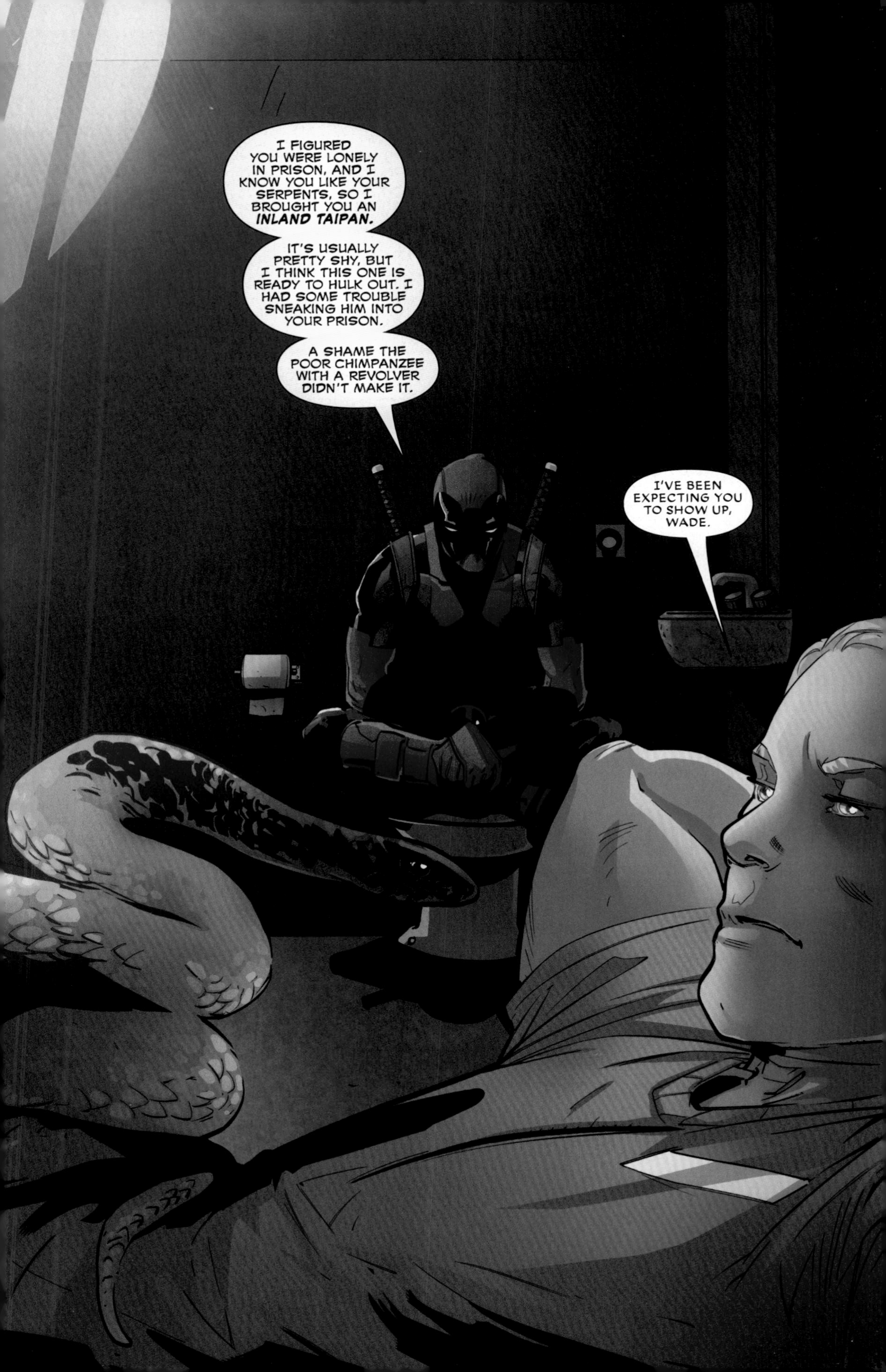
I FIGURED YOU WERE LONELY IN PRISON, AND I KNOW YOU LIKE YOUR SERPENTS, SO I BROUGHT YOU AN INLAND TAIPAN.
IT'S USUALLY PRETTY SHY, BUT I THINK THIS ONE IS READY TO HULK OUT. I HAD SOME TROUBLE SNEAKING HIM INTO YOUR PRISON.
A SHAME THE POOR CHIMPANZEE WITH A REVOLVER DIDN'T MAKE IT.
I'VE BEEN EXPECTING YOU TO SHOW UP, WADE.

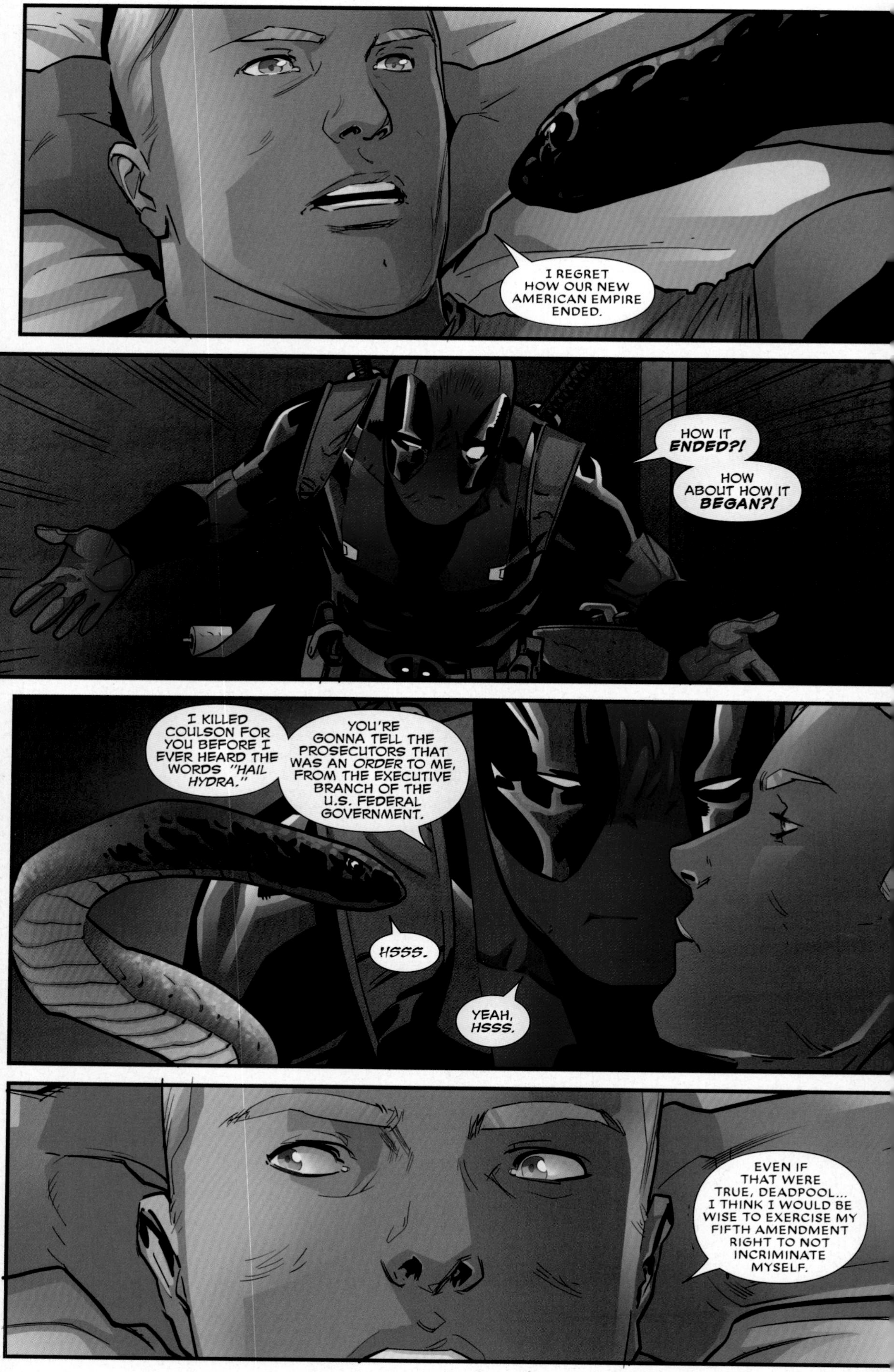
I REGRET HOW OUR NEW AMERICAN EMPIRE ENDED.
HOW IT ENDED?!
HOW ABOUT HOW IT BEGAN?!
I KILLED COULSON FOR YOU BEFORE I EVER HEARD THE WORDS "HAIL HYDRA."
YOU'RE GONNA TELL THE PROSECUTORS THAT WAS AN ORDER TO ME, FROM THE EXECUTIVE BRANCH OF THE U.S. FEDERAL GOVERNMENT.
HSSS.
YEAH, HSSS.
EVEN IF THAT WERE TRUE, DEADPOOL... I THINK I WOULD BE WISE TO EXERCISE MY FIFTH AMENDMENT RIGHT TO NOT INCRIMINATE MYSELF.

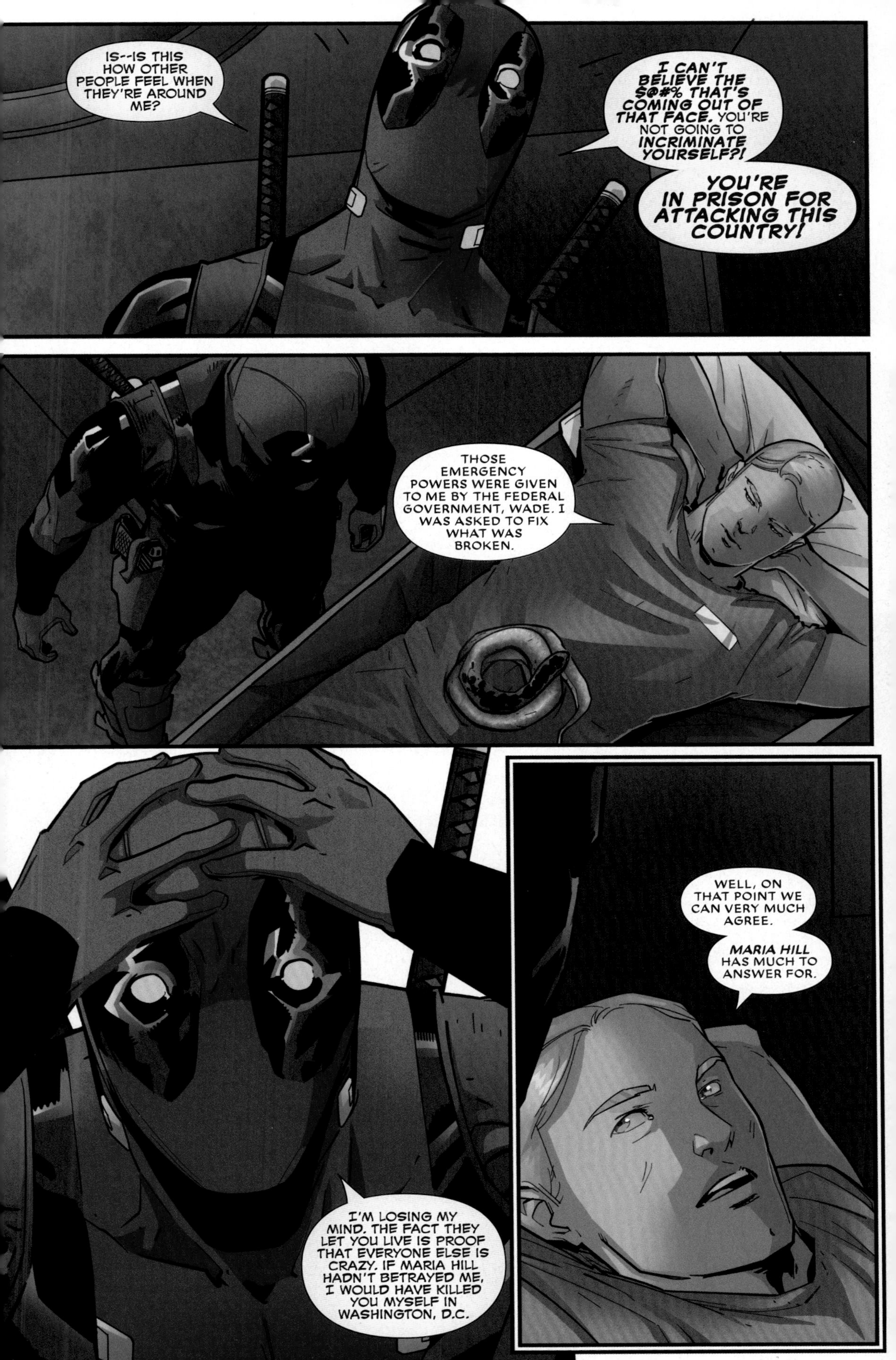
IS--IS THIS HOW OTHER PEOPLE FEEL WHEN THEY'RE AROUND ME?
I CAN'T BELIEVE THE $@#% THAT'S COMING OUT OF THAT FACE. YOU'RE NOT GOING TO INCRIMINATE YOURSELF?!
YOU'RE IN PRISON FOR ATTACKING THIS COUNTRY!
THOSE EMERGENCY POWERS WERE GIVEN TO ME BY THE FEDERAL GOVERNMENT, WADE. I WAS ASKED TO FIX WHAT WAS BROKEN.
I'M LOSING MY MIND. THE FACT THEY LET YOU LIVE IS PROOF THAT EVERYONE ELSE IS CRAZY. IF MARIA HILL HADN'T BETRAYED ME, I WOULD HAVE KILLED YOU MYSELF IN WASHINGTON, D.C.
WELL, ON THAT POINT WE CAN VERY MUCH AGREE.
MARIA HILL HAS MUCH TO ANSWER FOR.

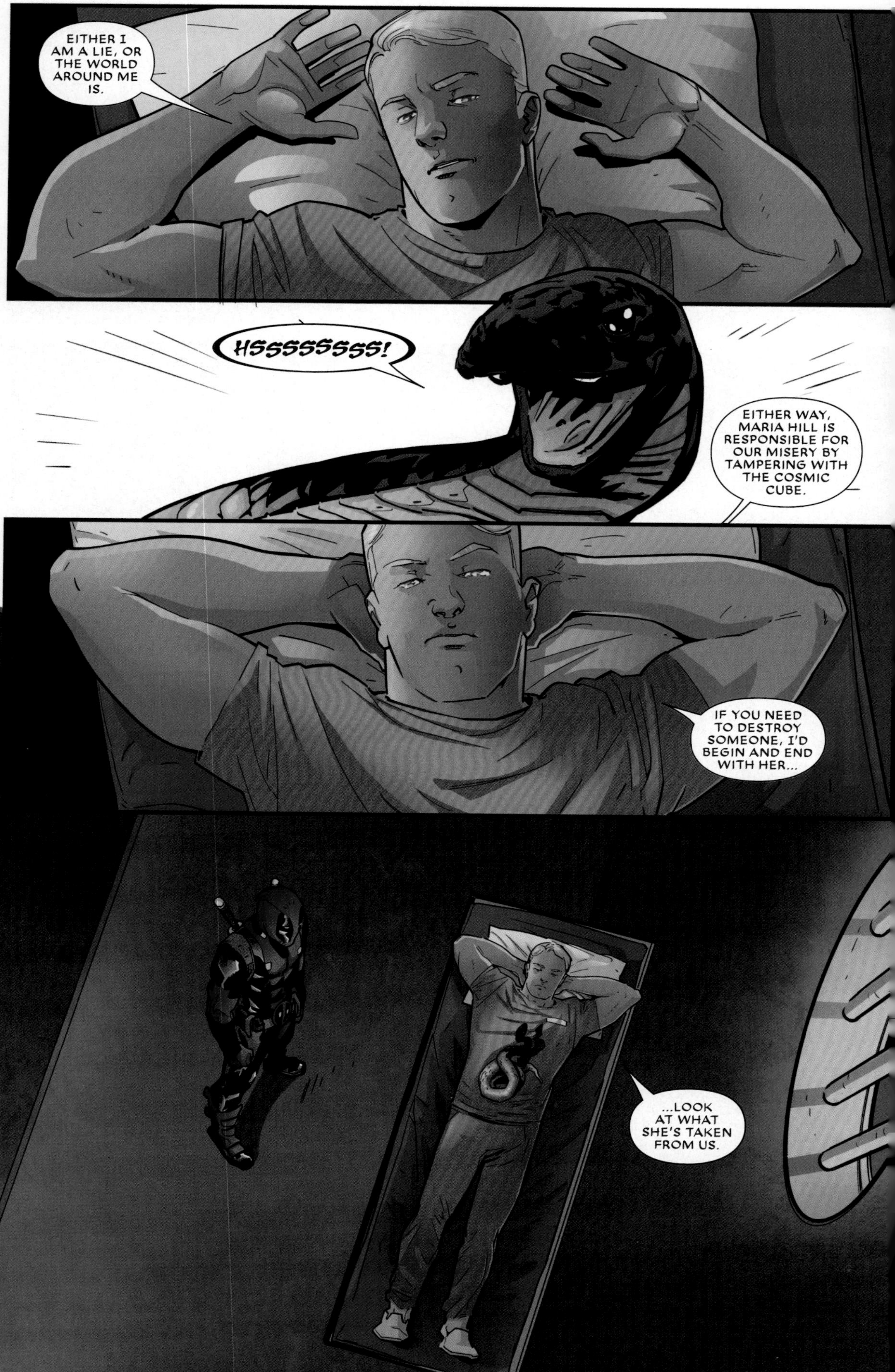
EITHER I AM A LIE, OR THE WORLD AROUND ME IS.
HSSSSSSSS!
EITHER WAY, MARIA HILL IS RESPONSIBLE FOR OUR MISERY BY TAMPERING WITH THE COSMIC CUBE.
IF YOU NEED TO DESTROY SOMEONE, I'D BEGIN AND END WITH HER...
...LOOK AT WHAT SHE'S TAKEN FROM US.

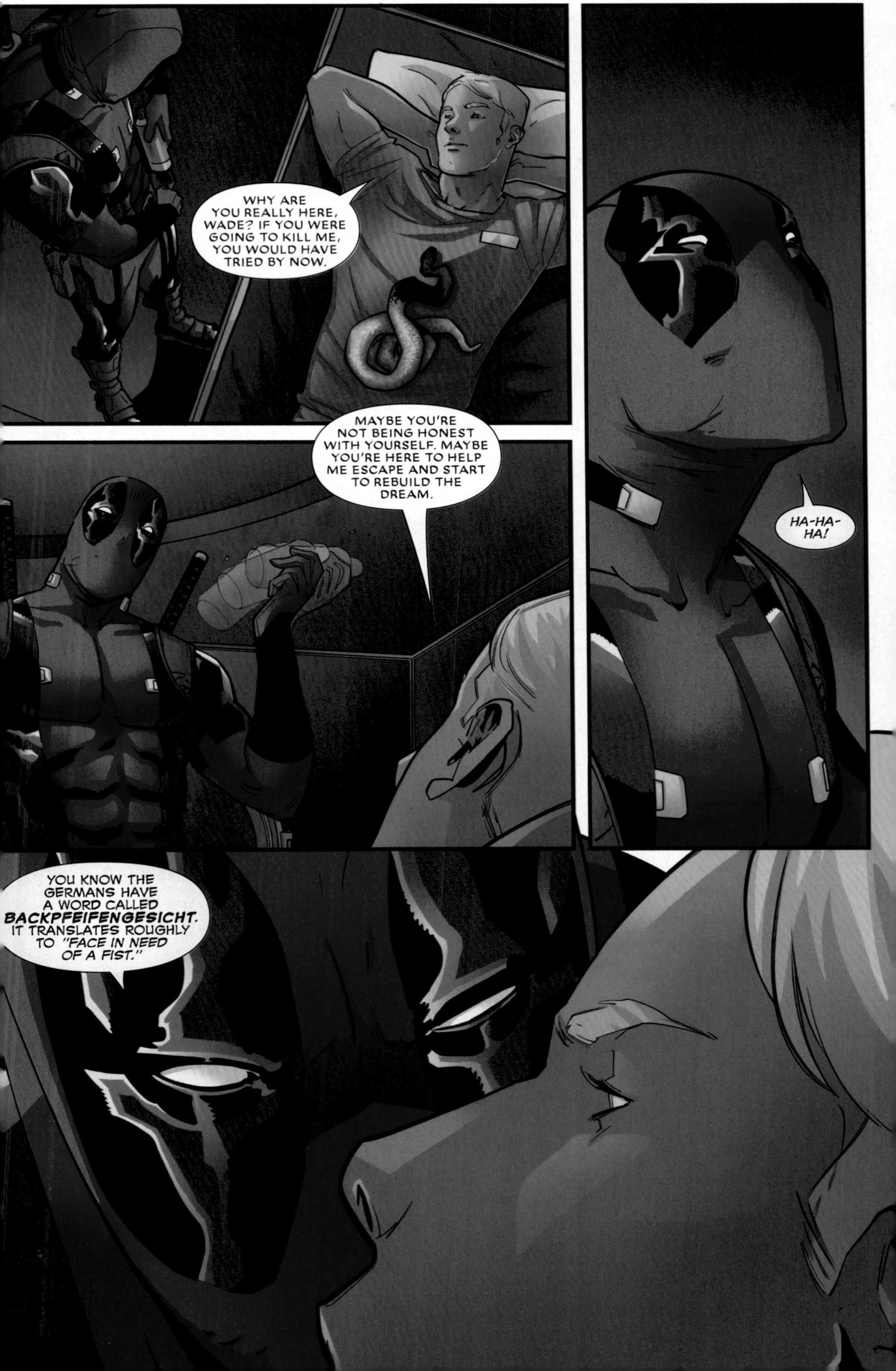
WHY ARE YOU REALLY HERE, WADE? IF YOU WERE GOING TO KILL ME, YOU WOULD HAVE TRIED BY NOW.
MAYBE YOU'RE NOT BEING HONEST WITH YOURSELF. MAYBE YOU'RE HERE TO HELP ME ESCAPE AND START TO REBUILD THE DREAM.
HA-HA-HA!
YOU KNOW THE GERMANS HAVE A WORD CALLED **BACKPFEIFENGESICHT**. IT TRANSLATES ROUGHLY TO "FACE IN NEED OF A FIST."

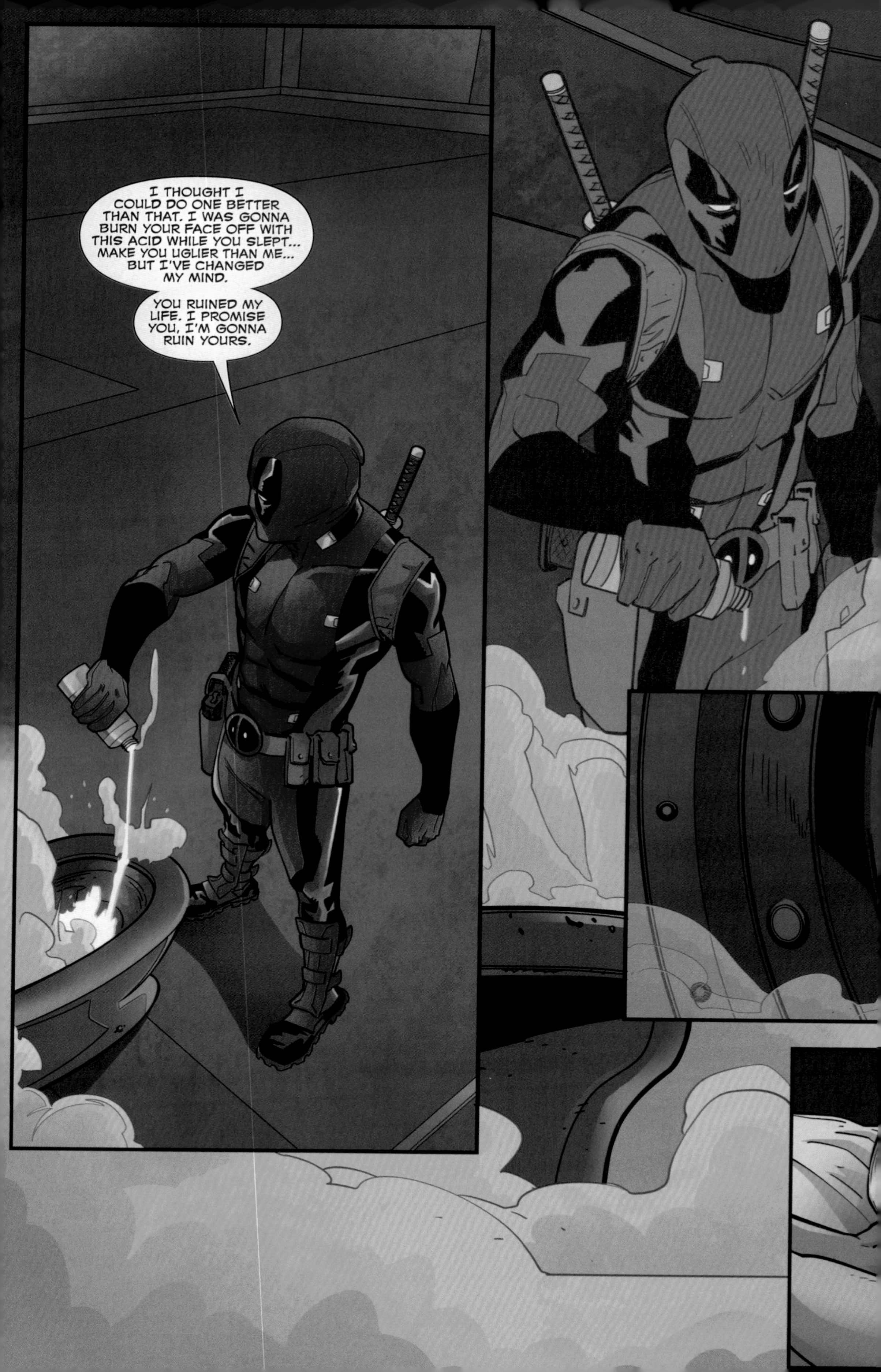
I THOUGHT I COULD DO ONE BETTER THAN THAT. I WAS GONNA BURN YOUR FACE OFF WITH THIS ACID WHILE YOU SLEPT... MAKE YOU UGLIER THAN ME... BUT I'VE CHANGED MY MIND.
YOU RUINED MY LIFE. I PROMISE YOU, I'M GONNA RUIN YOURS.

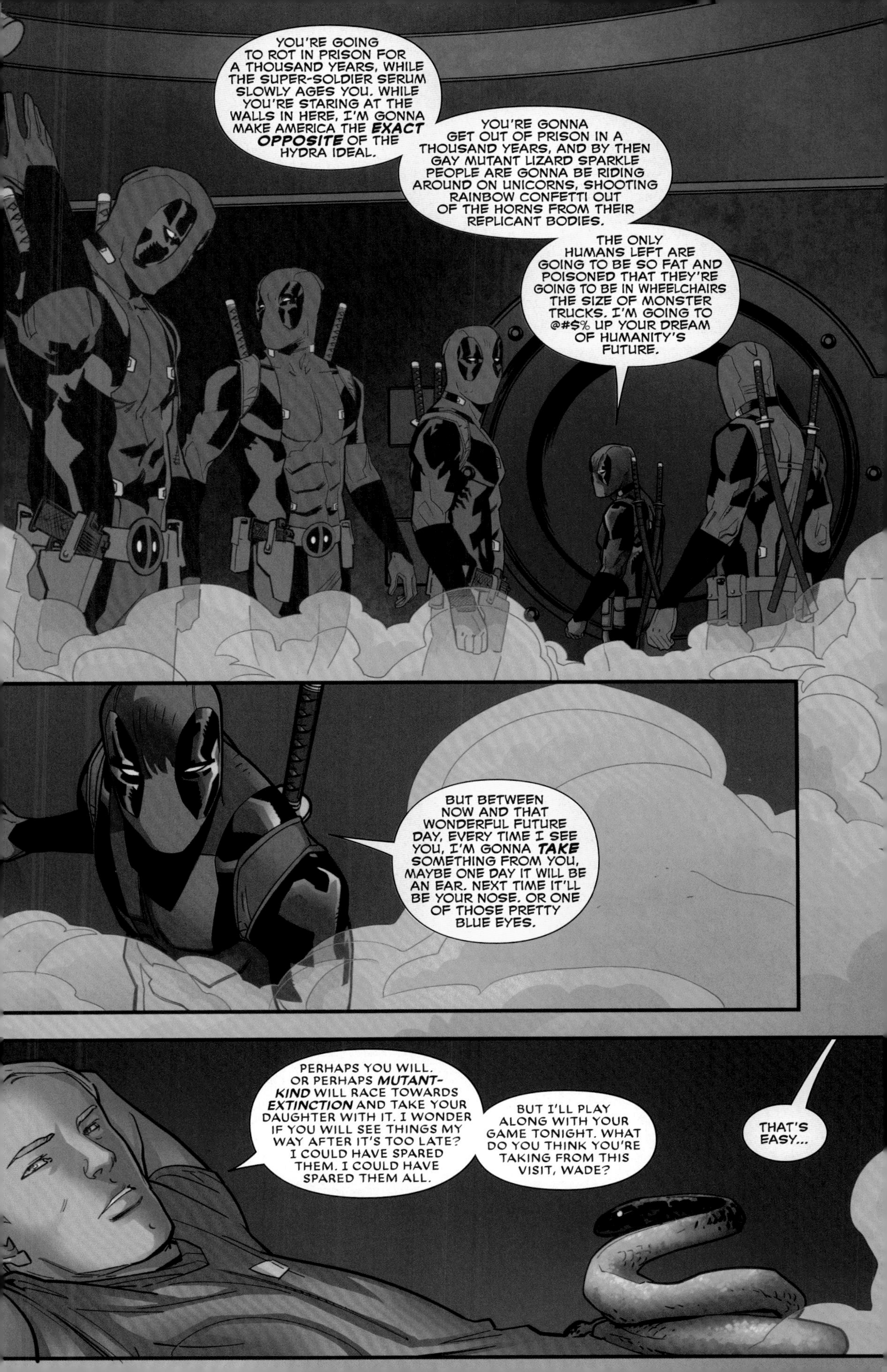
YOU'RE GOING TO ROT IN PRISON FOR A THOUSAND YEARS, WHILE THE SUPER-SOLDIER SERUM SLOWLY AGES YOU. WHILE YOU'RE STARING AT THE WALLS IN HERE, I'M GONNA MAKE AMERICA THE EXACT OPPOSITE OF THE HYDRA IDEAL.
YOU'RE GONNA GET OUT OF PRISON IN A THOUSAND YEARS, AND BY THEN GAY MUTANT LIZARD SPARKLE PEOPLE ARE GONNA BE RIDING AROUND ON UNICORNS, SHOOTING RAINBOW CONFETTI OUT OF THE HORNS FROM THEIR REPLICANT BODIES.
THE ONLY HUMANS LEFT ARE GOING TO BE SO FAT AND POISONED THAT THEY'RE GOING TO BE IN WHEELCHAIRS THE SIZE OF MONSTER TRUCKS. I'M GOING TO @#$% UP YOUR DREAM OF HUMANITY'S FUTURE.
BUT BETWEEN NOW AND THAT WONDERFUL FUTURE DAY, EVERY TIME I SEE YOU, I'M GONNA TAKE SOMETHING FROM YOU, MAYBE ONE DAY IT WILL BE AN EAR. NEXT TIME IT'LL BE YOUR NOSE. OR ONE OF THOSE PRETTY BLUE EYES.
PERHAPS YOU WILL. OR PERHAPS MUTANT-KIND WILL RACE TOWARDS EXTINCTION AND TAKE YOUR DAUGHTER WITH IT. I WONDER IF YOU WILL SEE THINGS MY WAY AFTER IT'S TOO LATE? I COULD HAVE SPARED THEM. I COULD HAVE SPARED THEM ALL.
BUT I'LL PLAY ALONG WITH YOUR GAME TONIGHT. WHAT DO YOU THINK YOU'RE TAKING FROM THIS VISIT, WADE?
THAT'S EASY...

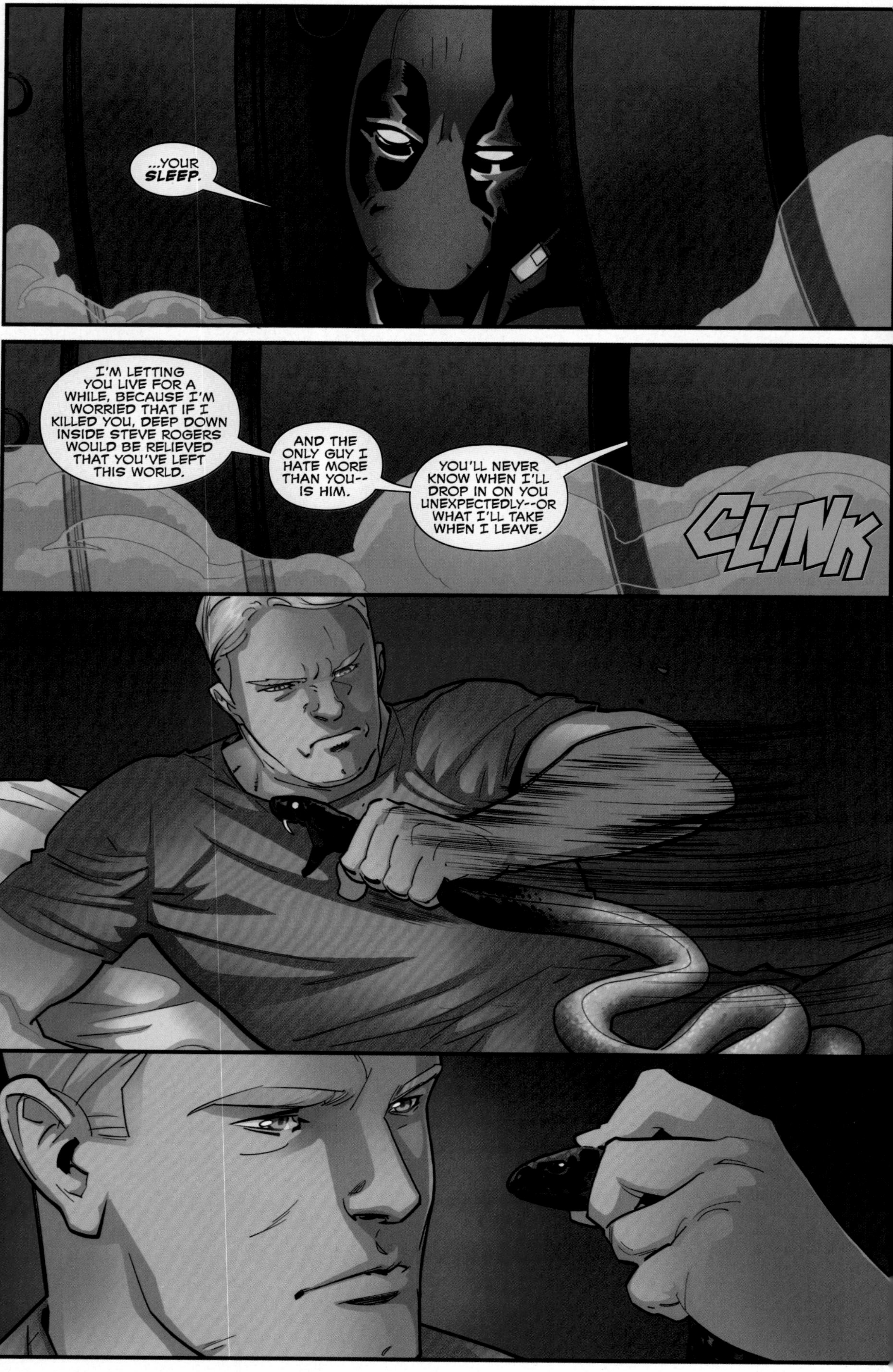
...YOUR SLEEP.
I'M LETTING YOU LIVE FOR A WHILE, BECAUSE I'M WORRIED THAT IF I KILLED YOU, DEEP DOWN INSIDE STEVE ROGERS WOULD BE RELIEVED THAT YOU'VE LEFT THIS WORLD.
AND THE ONLY GUY I HATE MORE THAN YOU-- IS HIM.
YOU'LL NEVER KNOW WHEN I'LL DROP IN ON YOU UNEXPECTEDLY--OR WHAT I'LL TAKE WHEN I LEAVE.
CLINK

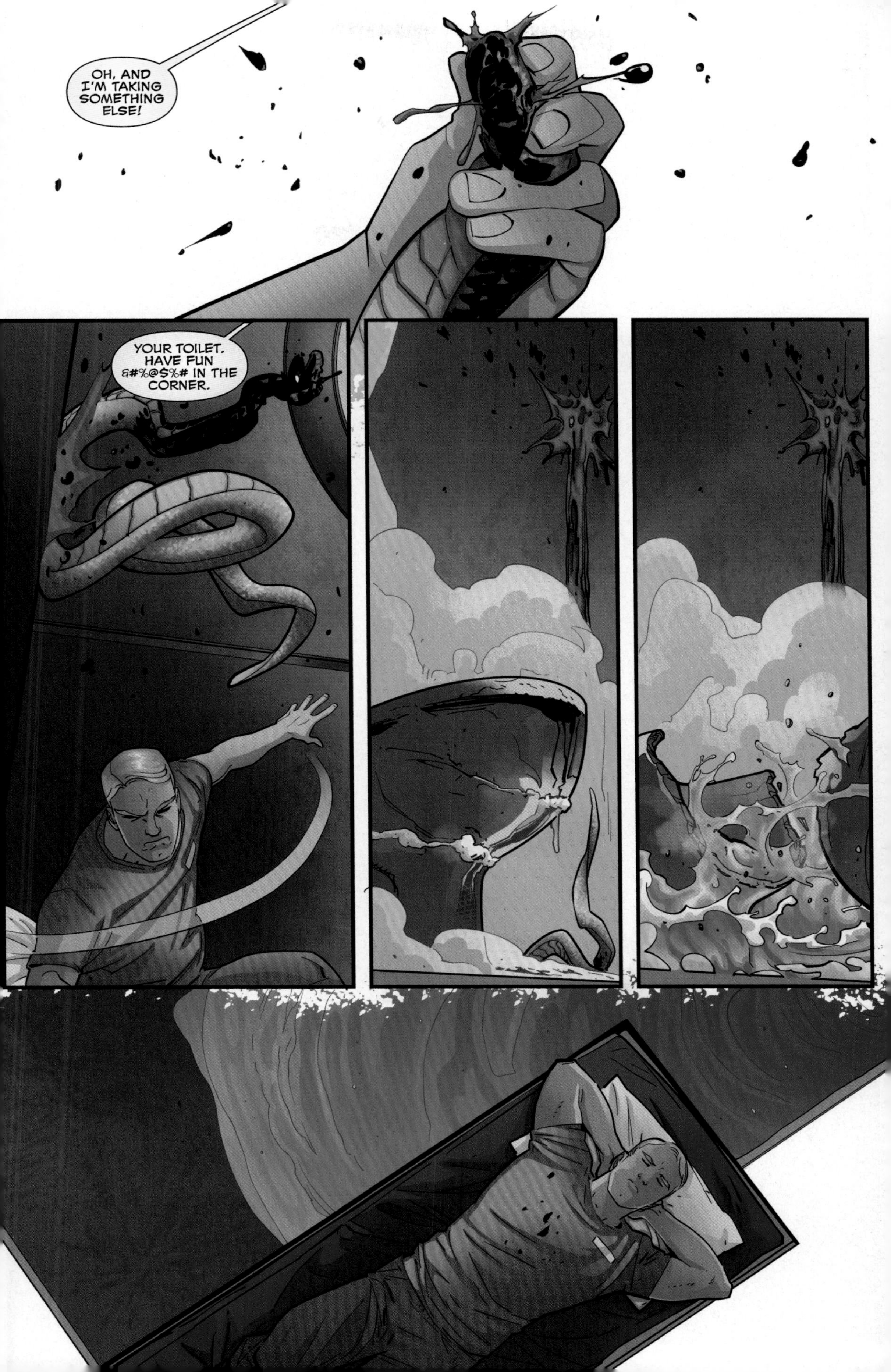
OH, AND I'M TAKING SOMETHING ELSE!
YOUR TOILET. HAVE FUN &#%@$%# IN THE CORNER.

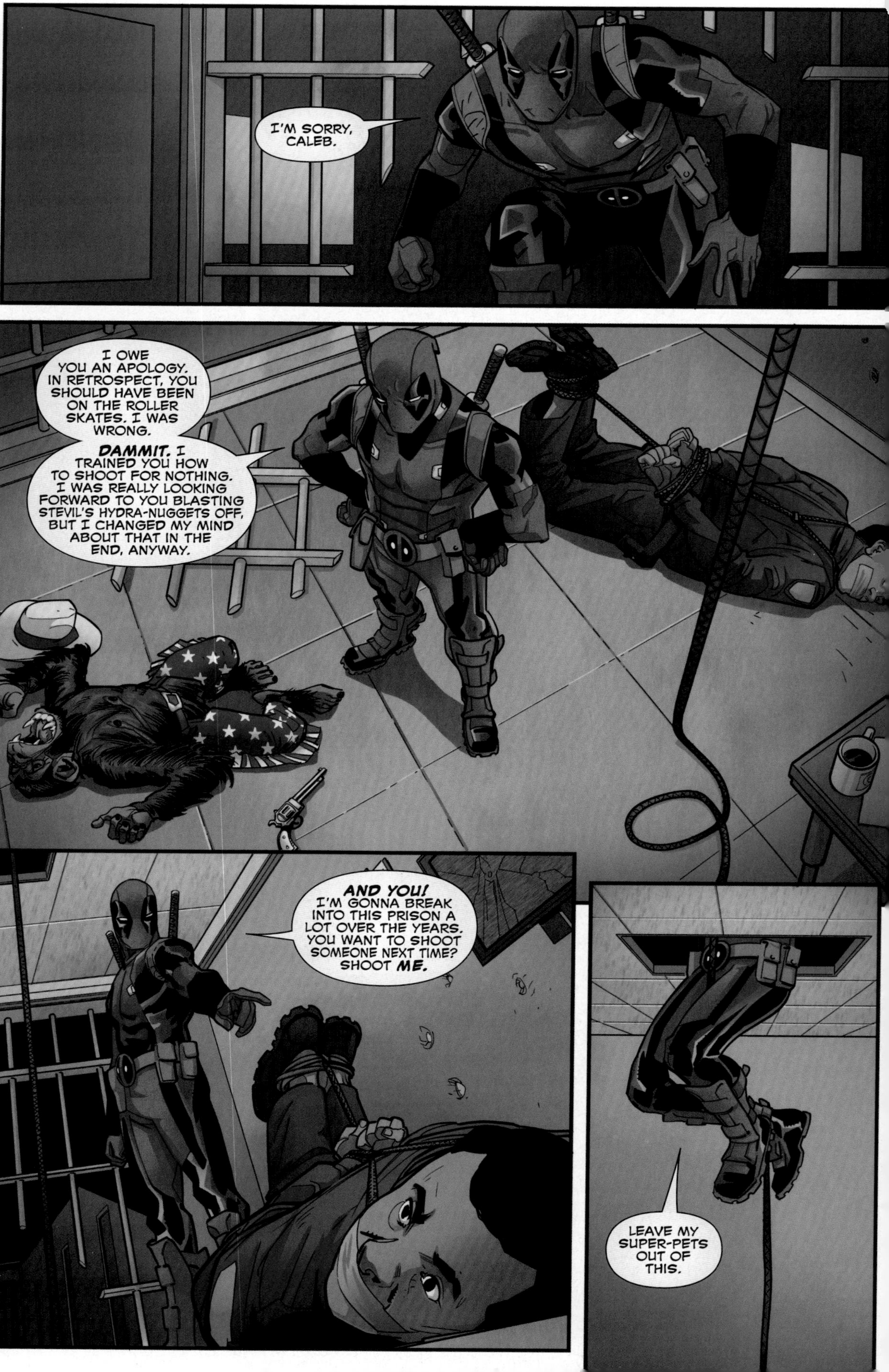
I'M SORRY, CALEB.
I OWE YOU AN APOLOGY. IN RETROSPECT, YOU SHOULD HAVE BEEN ON THE ROLLER SKATES. I WAS WRONG.
DAMMIT. I TRAINED YOU HOW TO SHOOT FOR NOTHING. I WAS REALLY LOOKING FORWARD TO YOU BLASTING STEVIL'S HYDRA-NUGGETS OFF, BUT I CHANGED MY MIND ABOUT THAT IN THE END, ANYWAY.
AND YOU! I'M GONNA BREAK INTO THIS PRISON A LOT OVER THE YEARS. YOU WANT TO SHOOT SOMEONE NEXT TIME? SHOOT ME.
LEAVE MY SUPER-PETS OUT OF THIS.

YOU KNOW WHAT? TAKING THE NIGHT OFF AND BLOWING OFF SOME STEAM AND MELTING MY ENEMY'S ONLY TOILET REALLY WORKED TO CLEAR MY MIND.

I GOT AN IDEA HOW TO DO EVAN.

EVERYTHING IS GONNA BE OKAY FROM NOW ON.

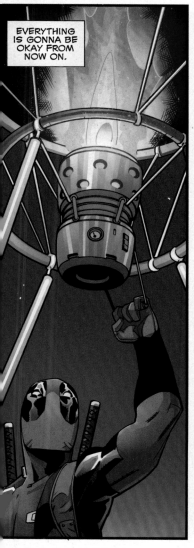

UP, UP AND AWAY!

UP! UP! ... C'MON.

WHAT THE--?!

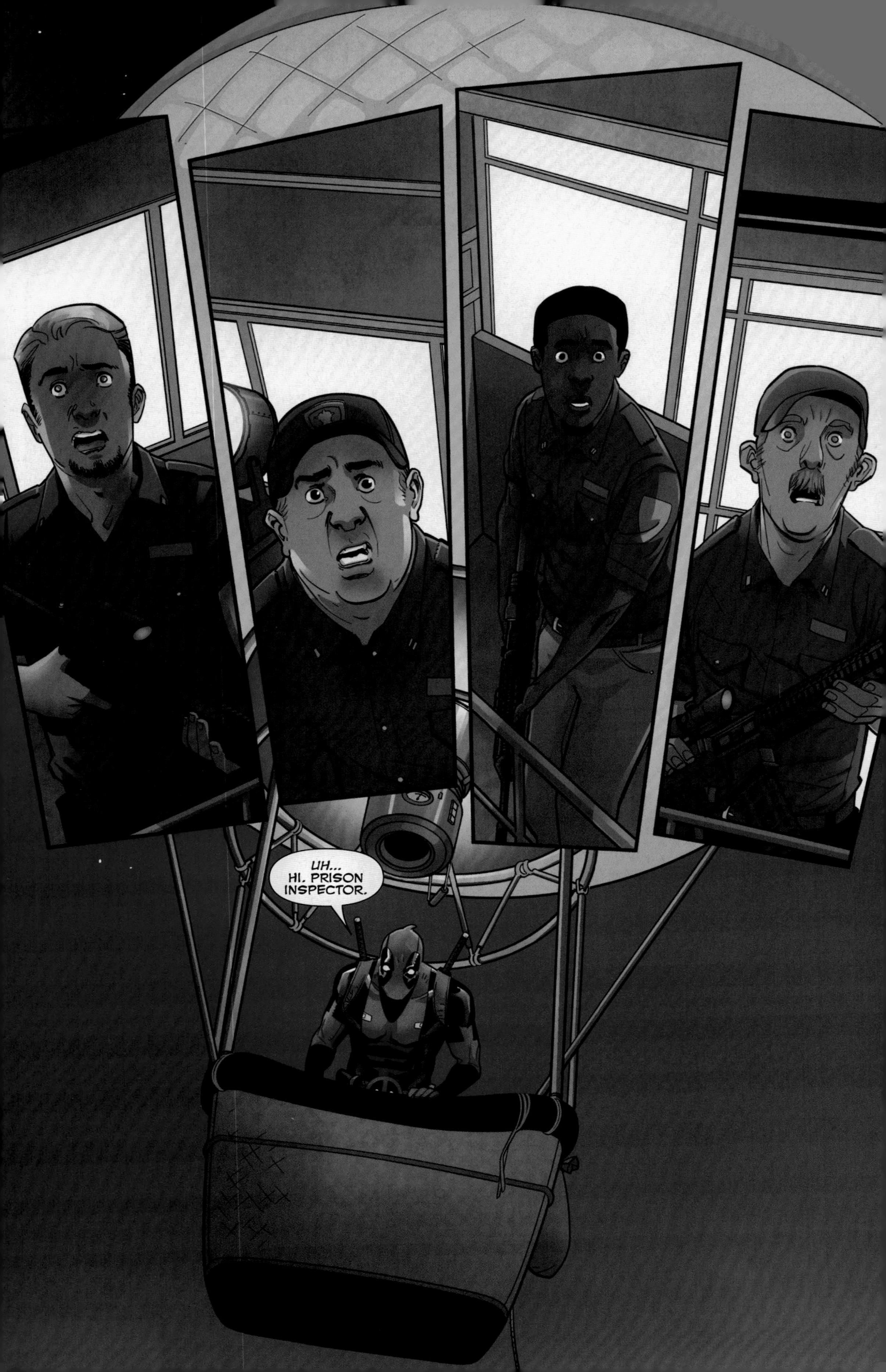
UH... HI. PRISON INSPECTOR.

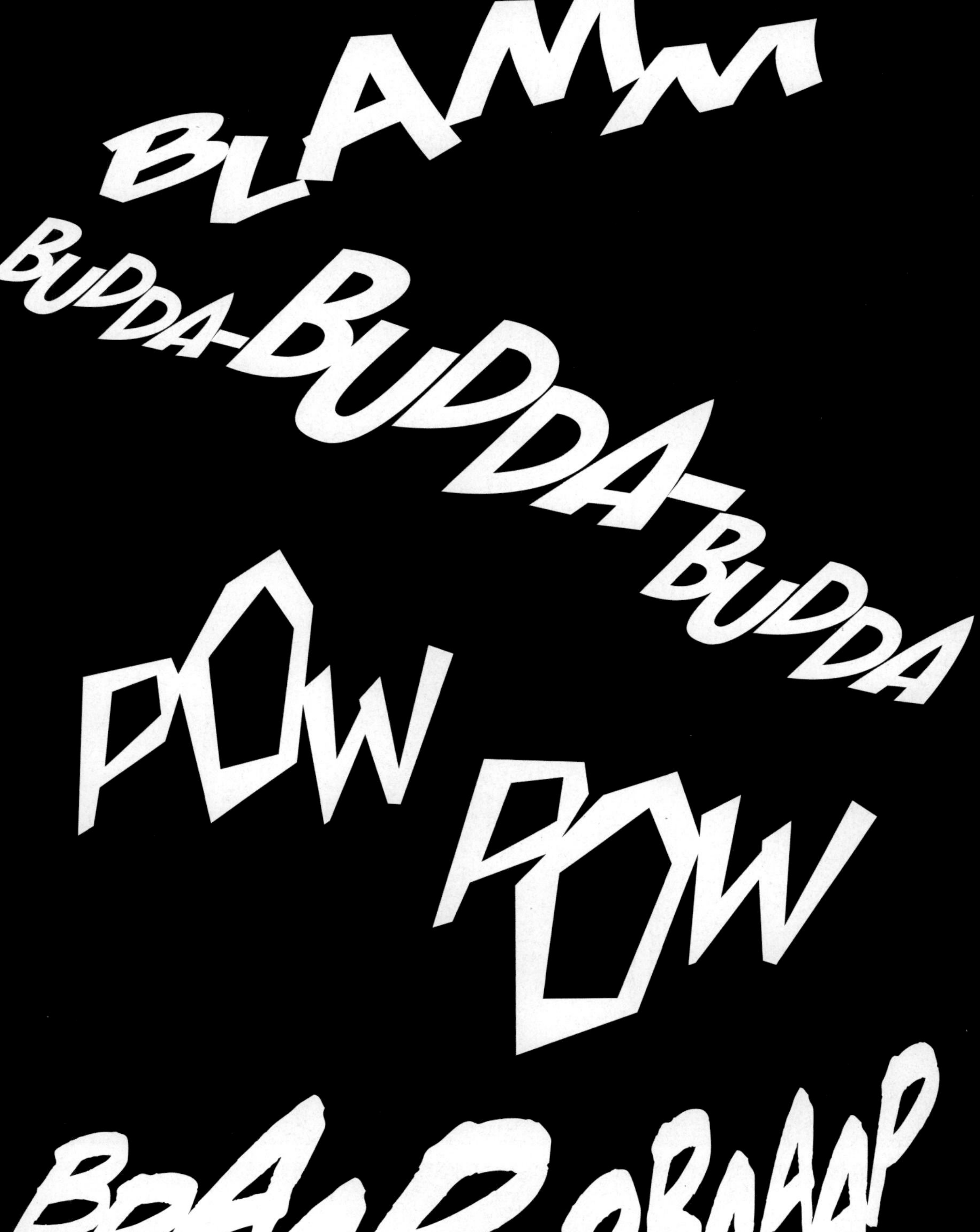
BLAMM
BUDDA-BUDDA-BUDDA
POW POW
BRAAAP BRAAAP

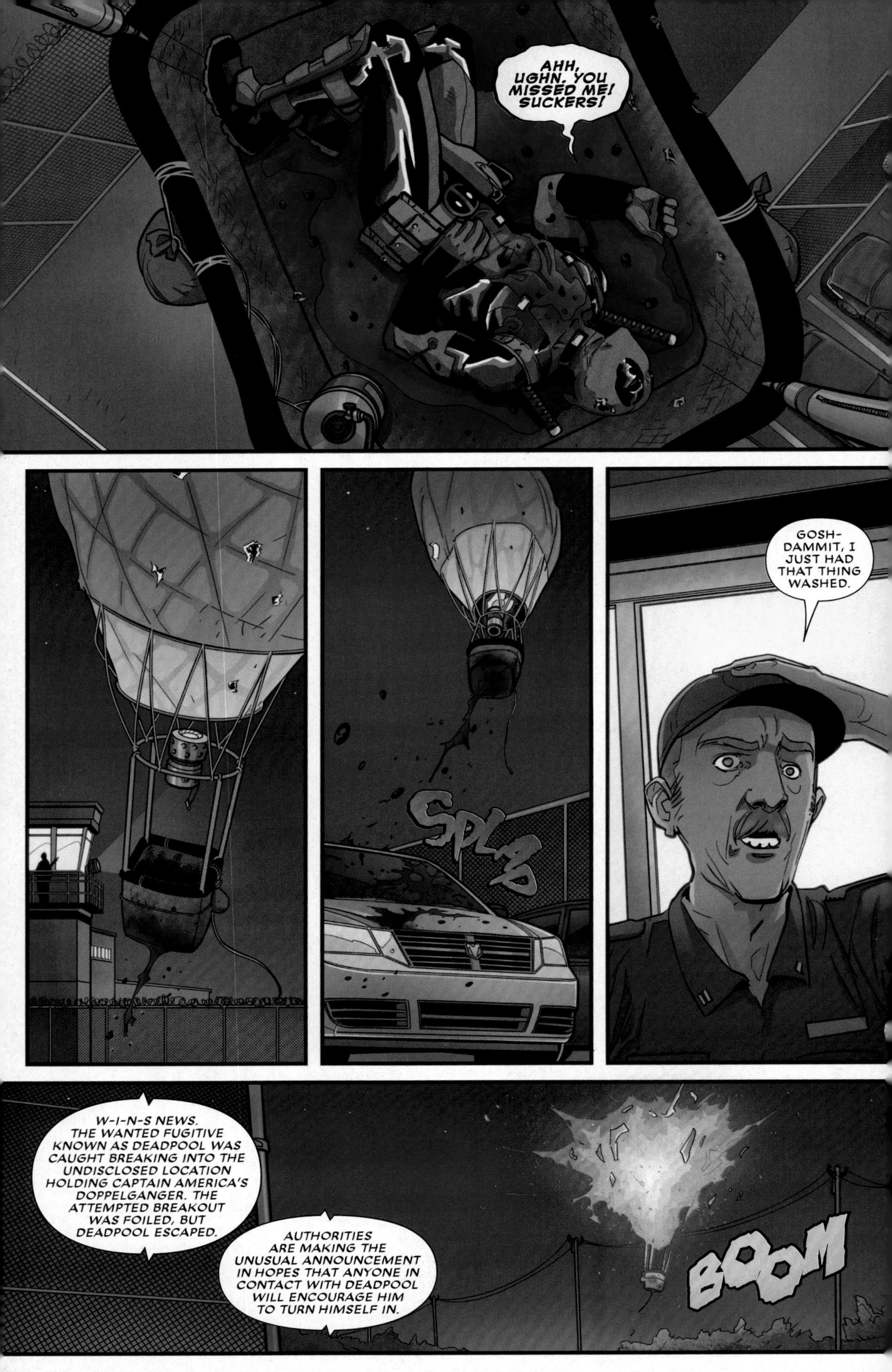
AHH, UGHN. YOU MISSED ME! SUCKERS!
SPLAT
GOSH-DAMMIT, I JUST HAD THAT THING WASHED.
W-I-N-S NEWS. THE WANTED FUGITIVE KNOWN AS DEADPOOL WAS CAUGHT BREAKING INTO THE UNDISCLOSED LOCATION HOLDING CAPTAIN AMERICA'S DOPPELGANGER. THE ATTEMPTED BREAKOUT WAS FOILED, BUT DEADPOOL ESCAPED.
AUTHORITIES ARE MAKING THE UNUSUAL ANNOUNCEMENT IN HOPES THAT ANYONE IN CONTACT WITH DEADPOOL WILL ENCOURAGE HIM TO TURN HIMSELF IN.
BOOM

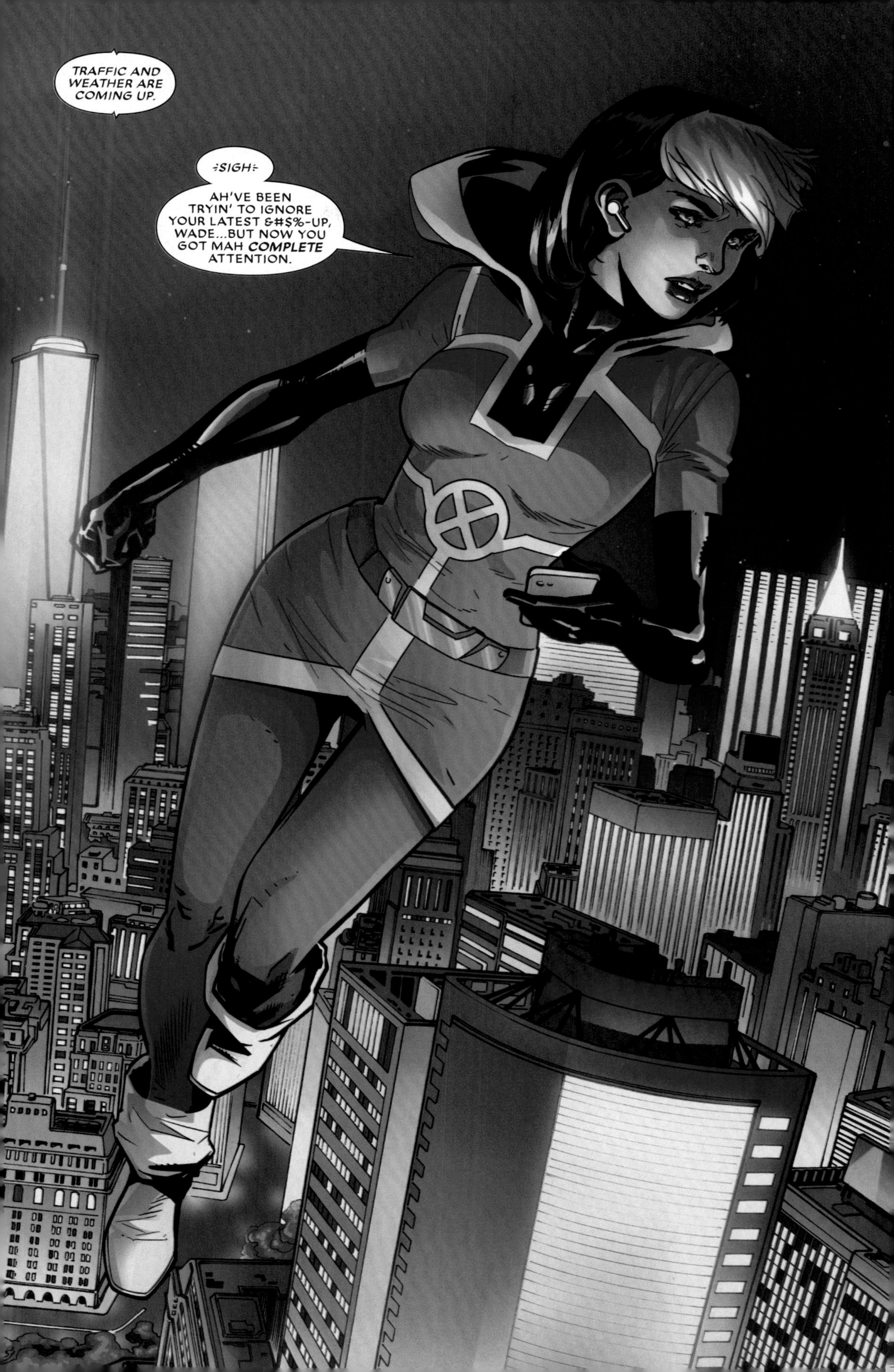
TRAFFIC AND WEATHER ARE COMING UP.
=SIGH=
AH'VE BEEN TRYIN' TO IGNORE YOUR LATEST &#$%-UP, WADE...BUT NOW YOU GOT MAH *COMPLETE* ATTENTION.

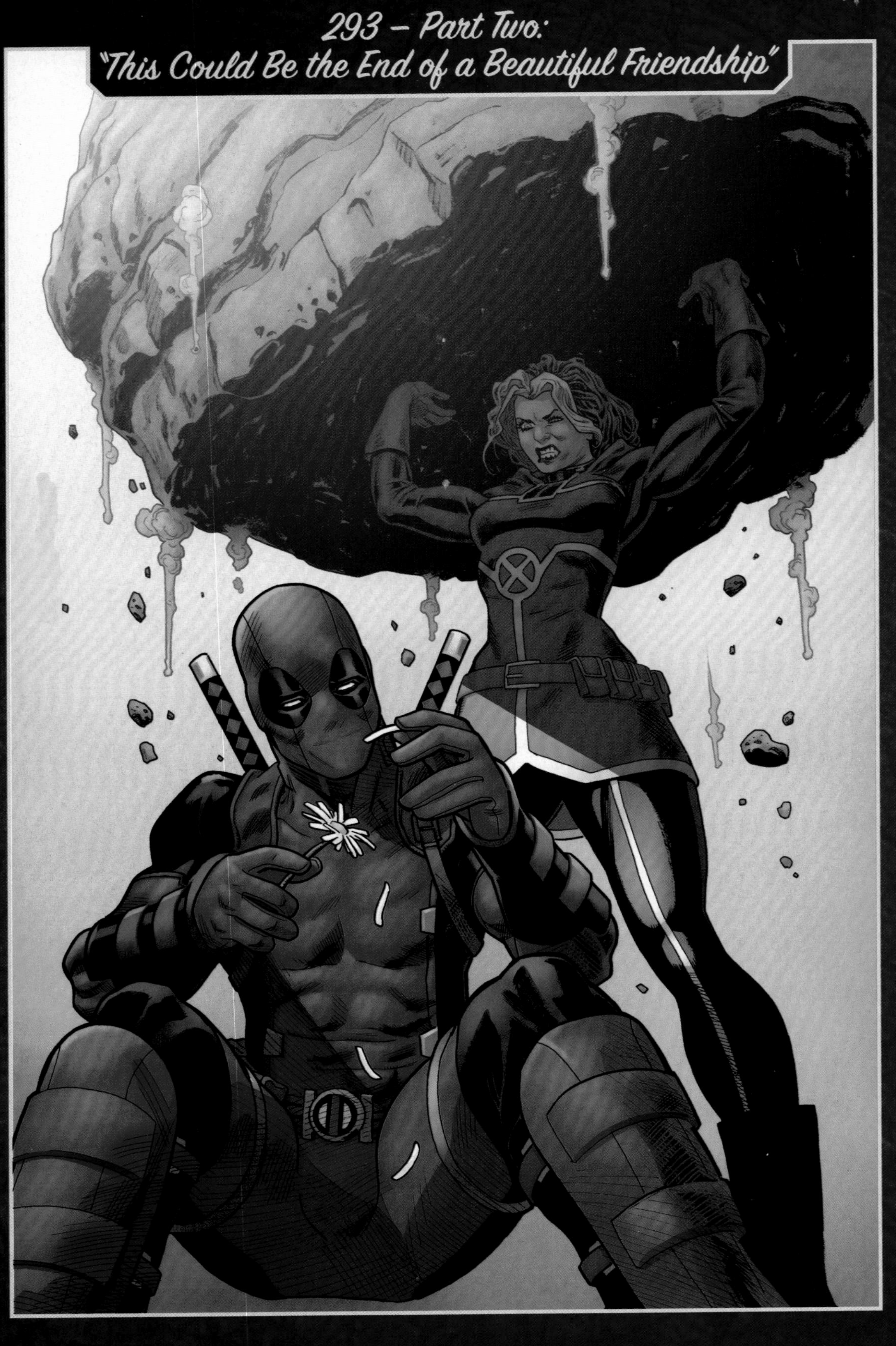
293 – Part Two:
"This Could Be the End of a Beautiful Friendship"

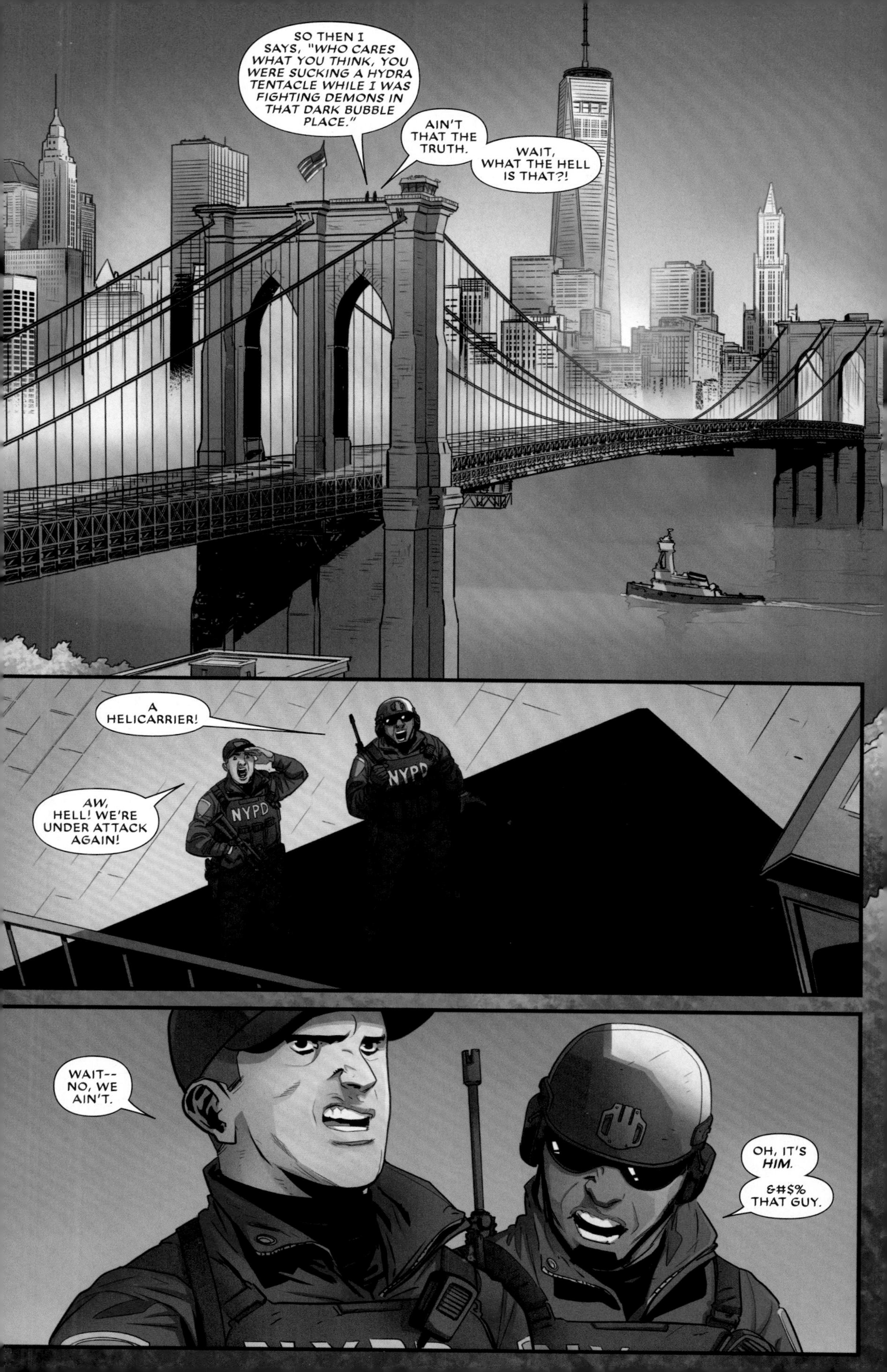

SO THEN I SAYS, "WHO CARES WHAT YOU THINK, YOU WERE SUCKING A HYDRA TENTACLE WHILE I WAS FIGHTING DEMONS IN THAT DARK BUBBLE PLACE."
AIN'T THAT THE TRUTH.
WAIT, WHAT THE HELL IS THAT?!
A HELICARRIER!
AW, HELL! WE'RE UNDER ATTACK AGAIN!
WAIT-- NO, WE AIN'T.
OH, IT'S *HIM*.
&#$% THAT GUY.
NYPD
NYPD

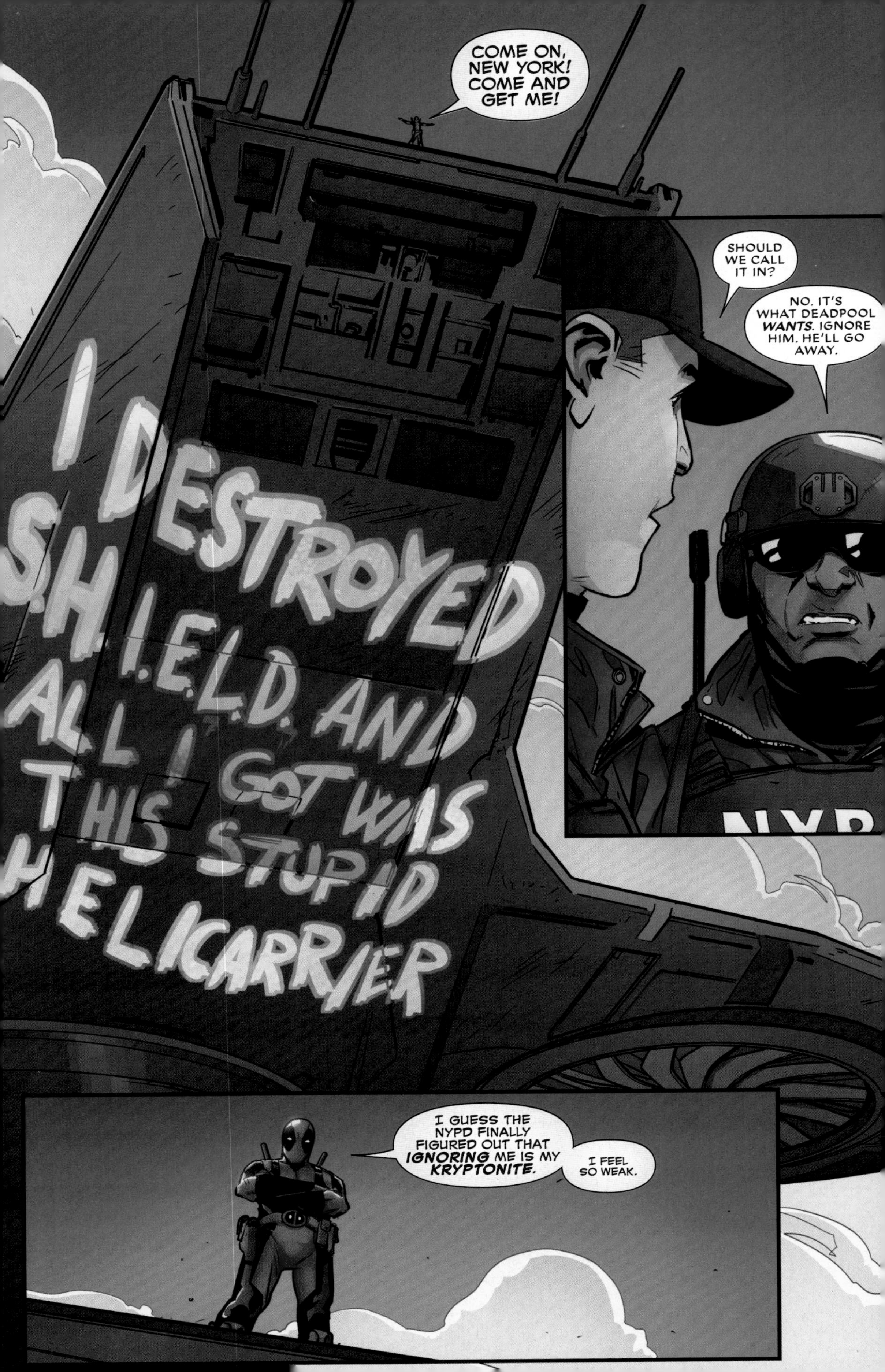
COME ON, NEW YORK! COME AND GET ME!
I DESTROYED S.H.I.E.L.D. AND ALL I GOT WAS THIS STUPID HELICARRIER
SHOULD WE CALL IT IN?
NO. IT'S WHAT DEADPOOL WANTS. IGNORE HIM. HE'LL GO AWAY.
NYPD
I GUESS THE NYPD FINALLY FIGURED OUT THAT IGNORING ME IS MY KRYPTONITE.
I FEEL SO WEAK.

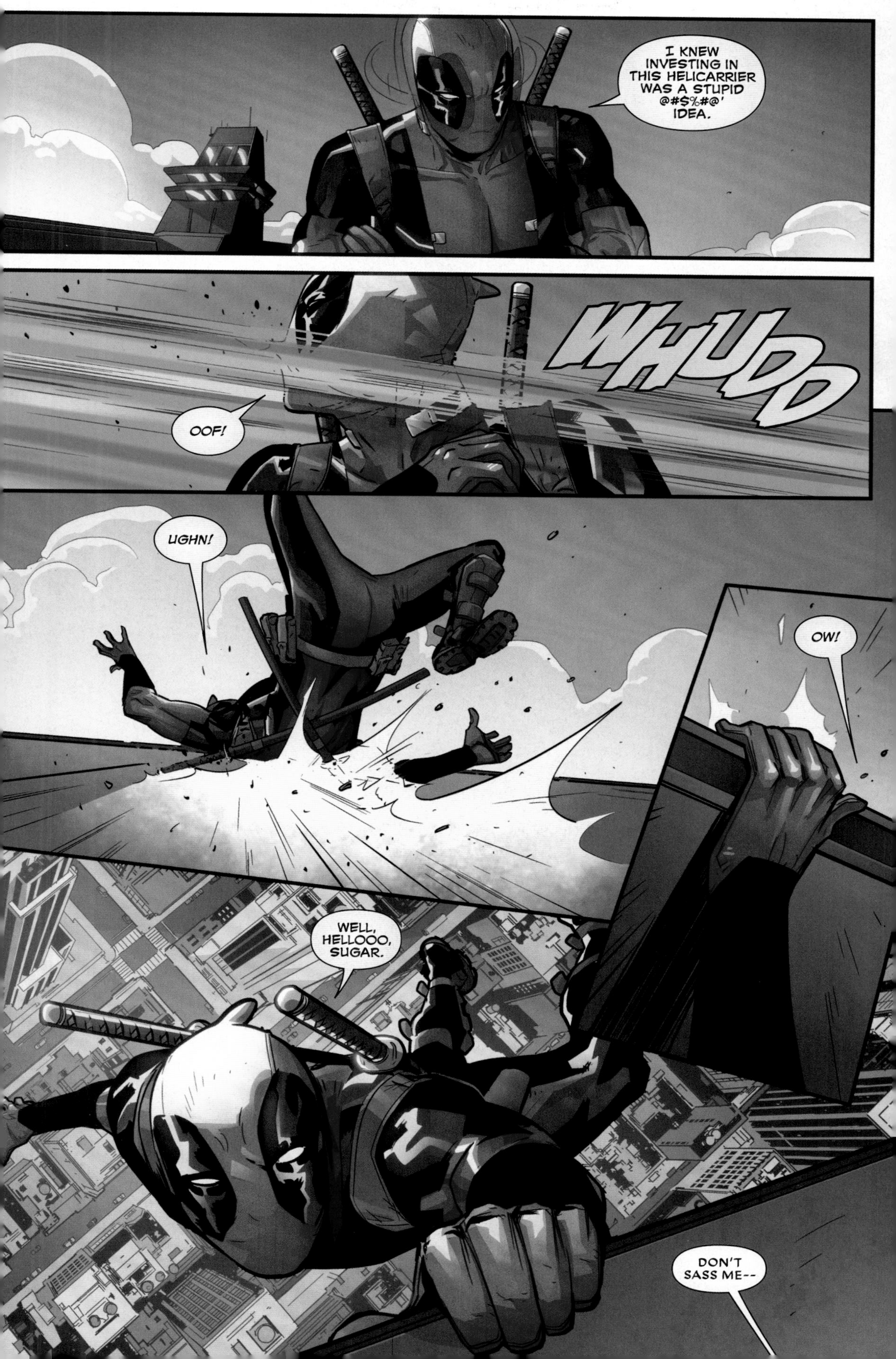
I KNEW INVESTING IN THIS HELICARRIER WAS A STUPID @#$%#@' IDEA.
WHUDD
OOF!
UGHN!
OW!
WELL, HELLOOO, SUGAR.
DON'T SASS ME--

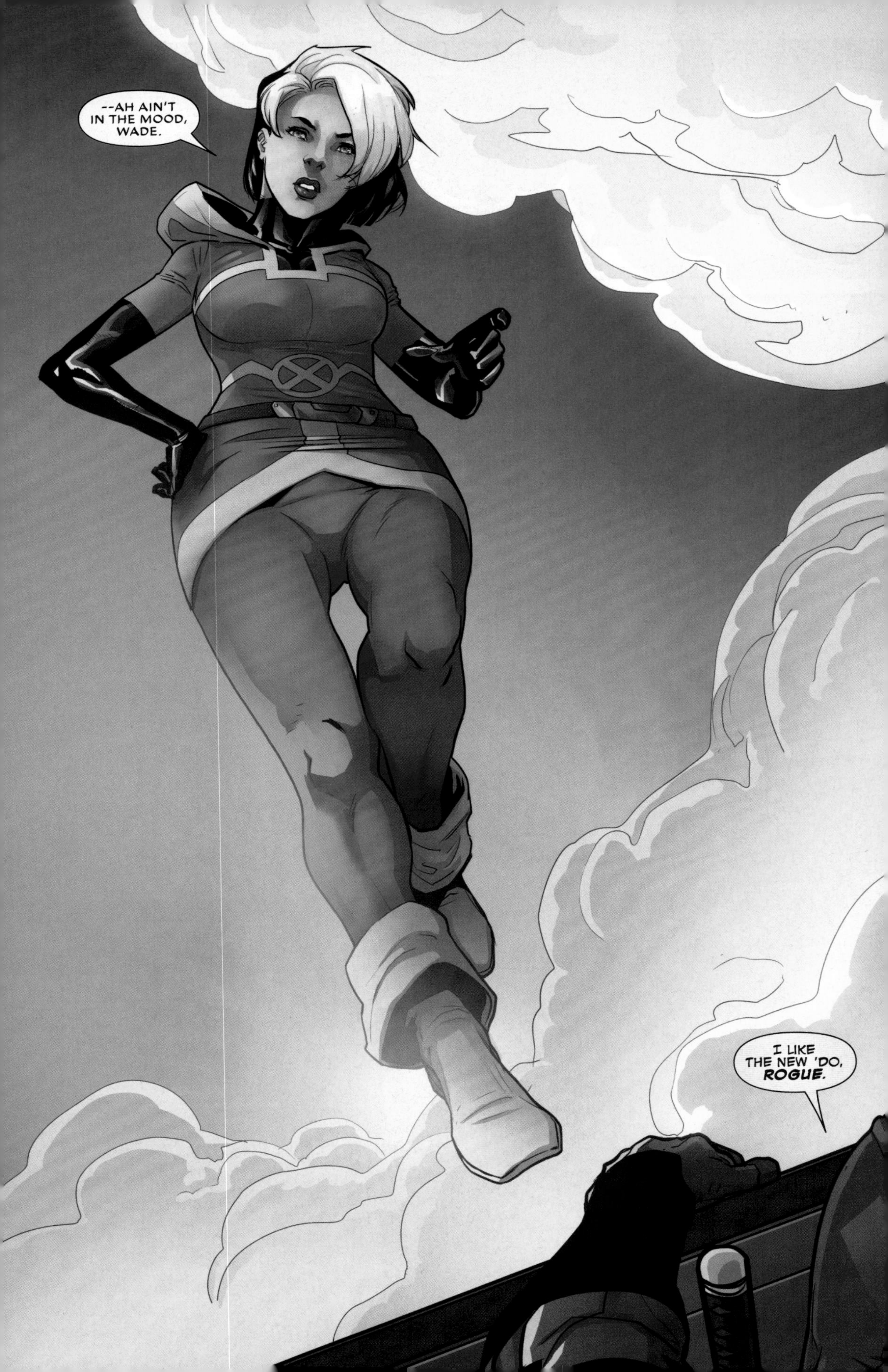
--AH AIN'T IN THE MOOD, WADE.
I LIKE THE NEW 'DO, ROGUE.

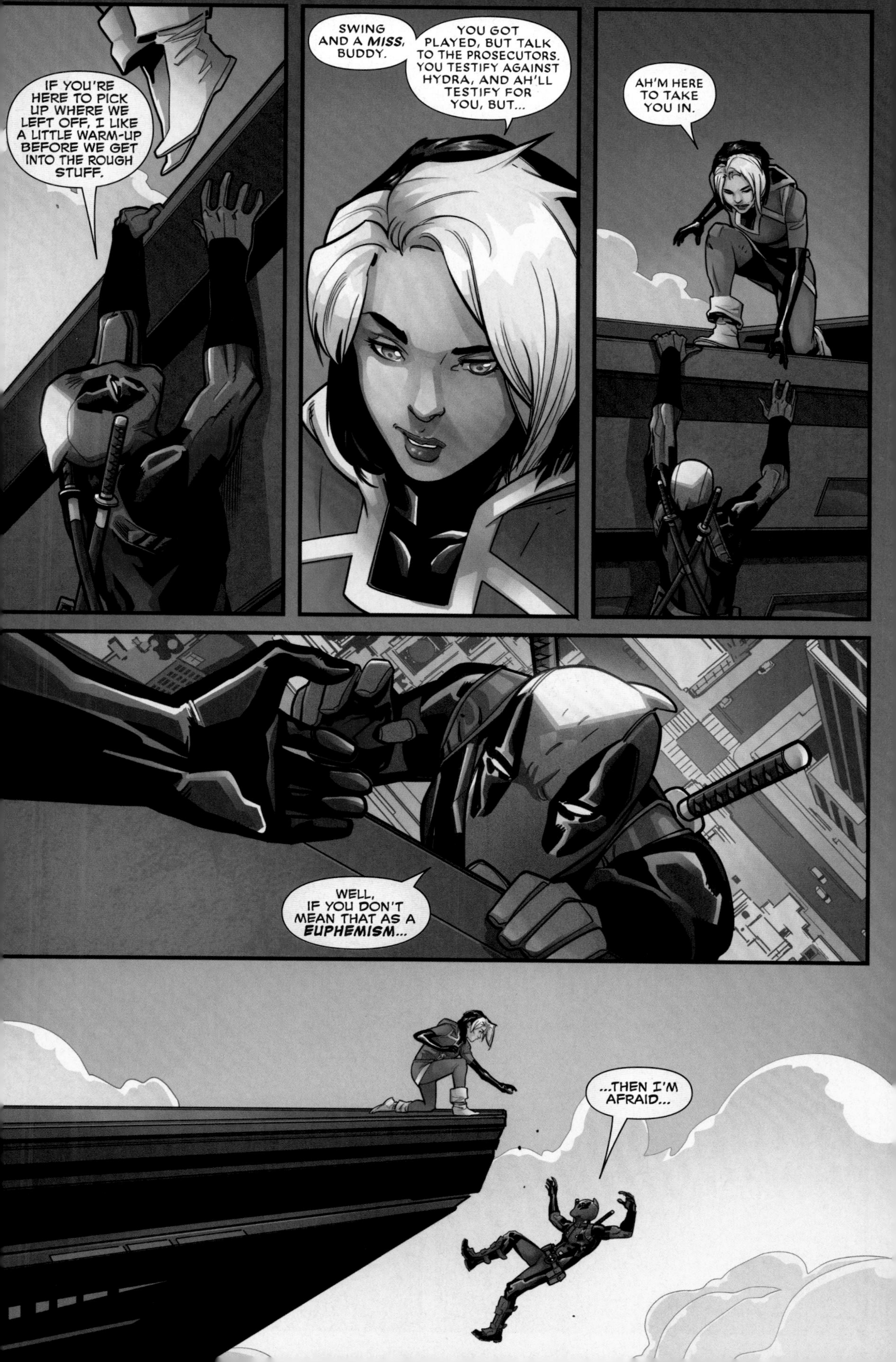
IF YOU'RE HERE TO PICK UP WHERE WE LEFT OFF, I LIKE A LITTLE WARM-UP BEFORE WE GET INTO THE ROUGH STUFF.
SWING AND A MISS, BUDDY.
YOU GOT PLAYED, BUT TALK TO THE PROSECUTORS. YOU TESTIFY AGAINST HYDRA, AND AH'LL TESTIFY FOR YOU, BUT...
AH'M HERE TO TAKE YOU IN.
WELL, IF YOU DON'T MEAN THAT AS A EUPHEMISM...
...THEN I'M AFRAID...

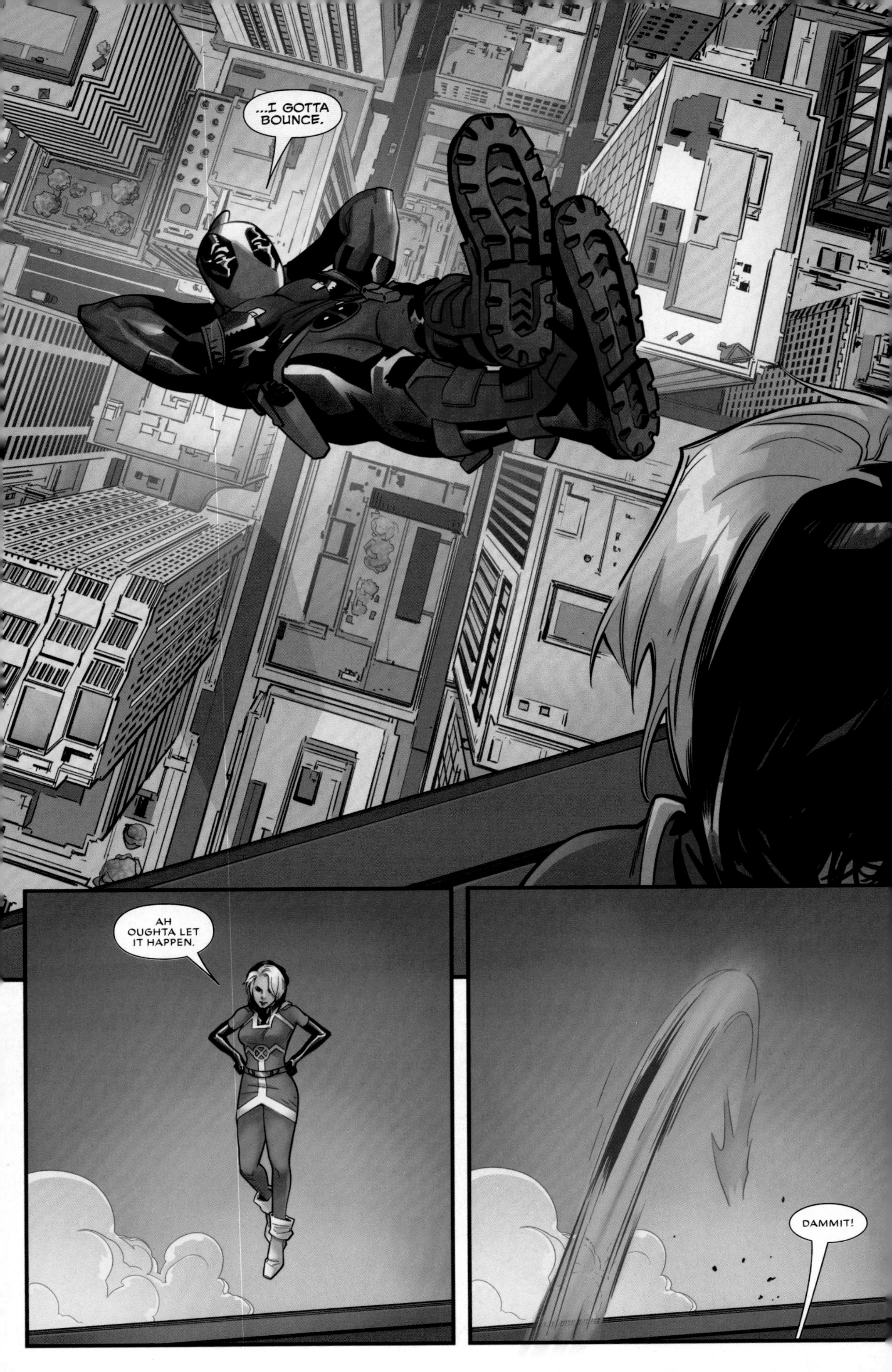
...I GOTTA BOUNCE.
AH OUGHTA LET IT HAPPEN.
DAMMIT!

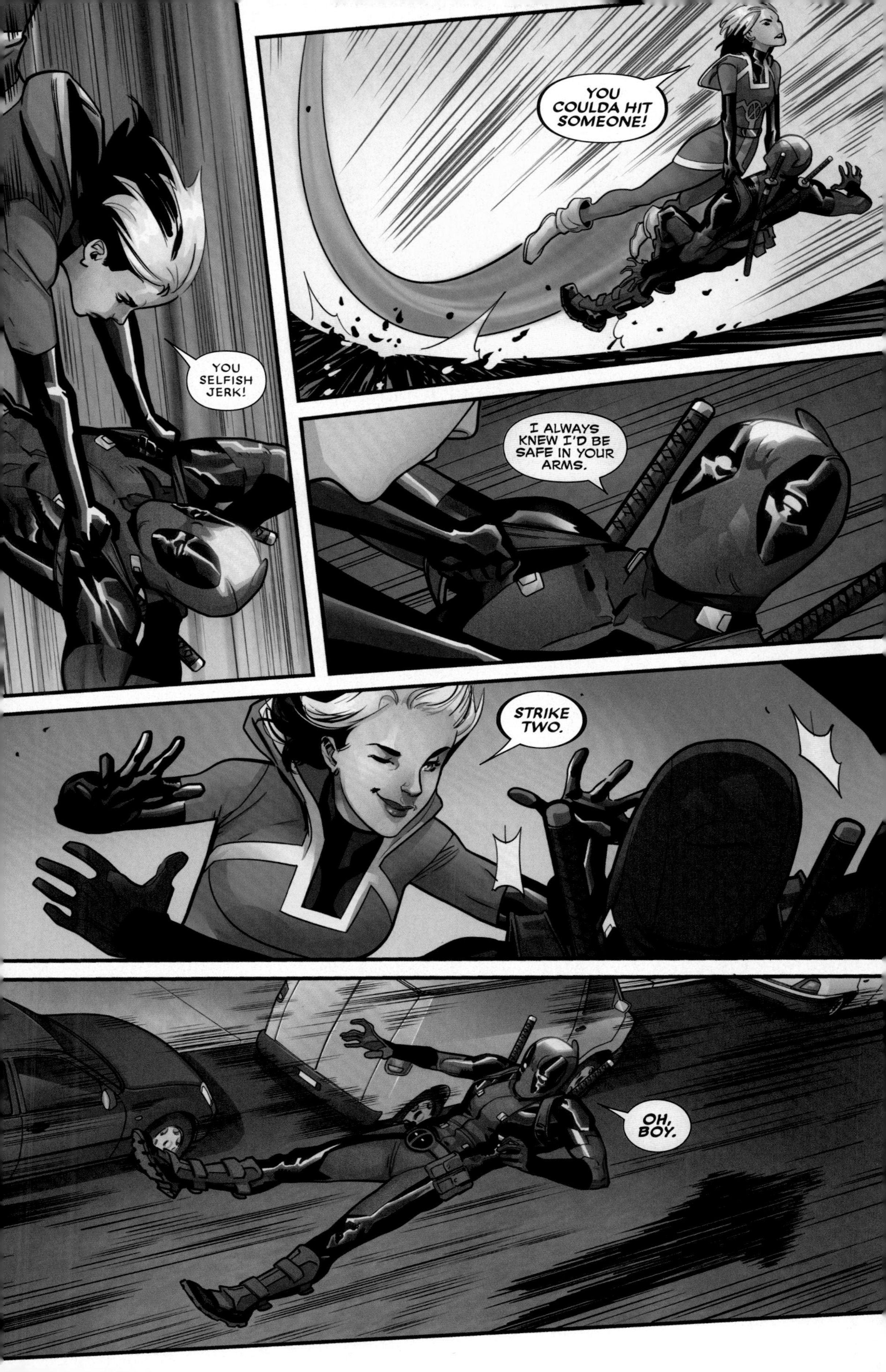
YOU COULDA HIT SOMEONE!
YOU SELFISH JERK!
I ALWAYS KNEW I'D BE SAFE IN YOUR ARMS.
STRIKE TWO.
OH, BOY.

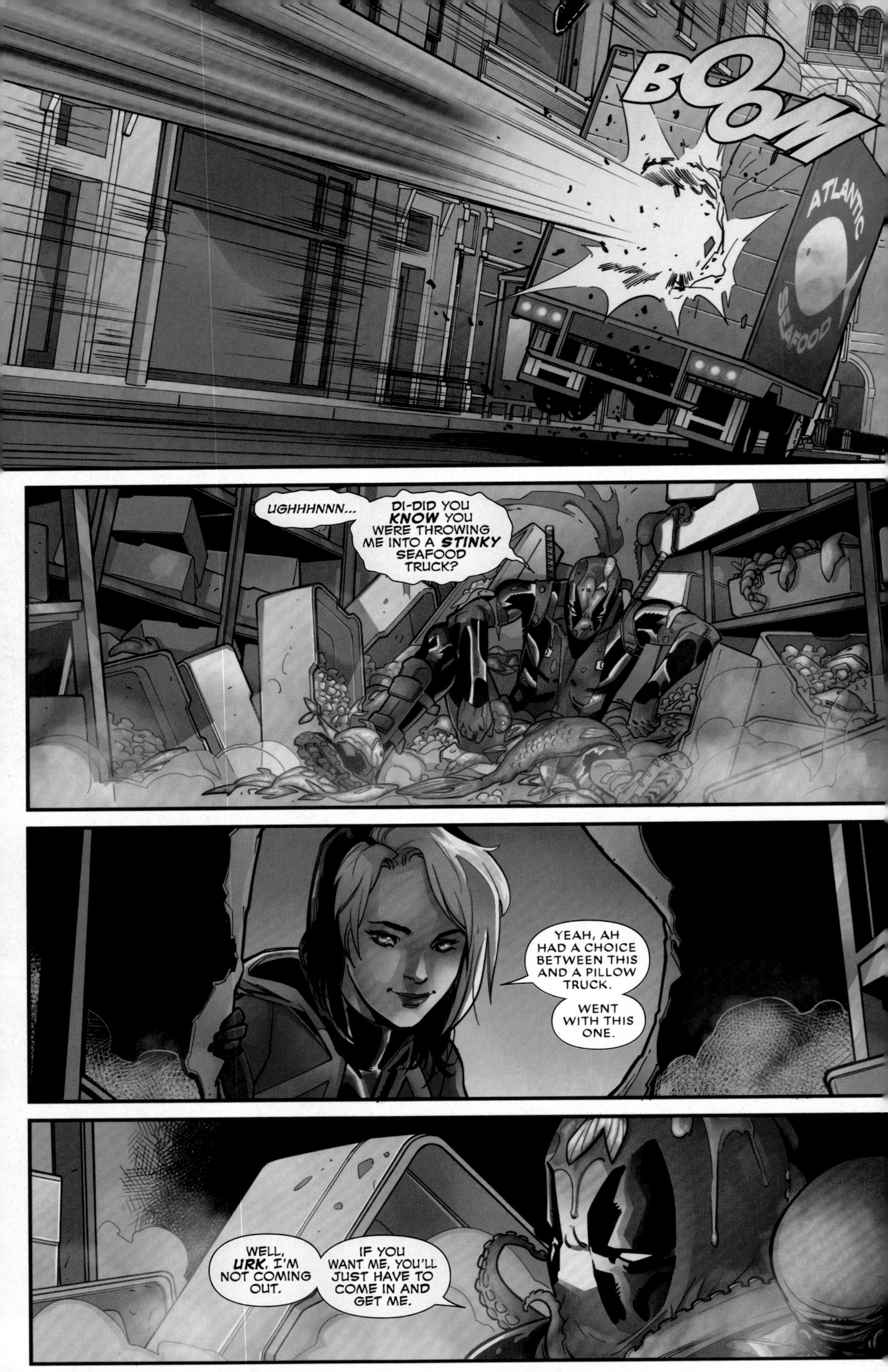
BOOOM
ATLANTIC SEAFOOD
UGHHHNNN...
DI-DID YOU KNOW YOU WERE THROWING ME INTO A STINKY SEAFOOD TRUCK?
YEAH, AH HAD A CHOICE BETWEEN THIS AND A PILLOW TRUCK.
WENT WITH THIS ONE.
WELL, URK, I'M NOT COMING OUT.
IF YOU WANT ME, YOU'LL JUST HAVE TO COME IN AND GET ME.

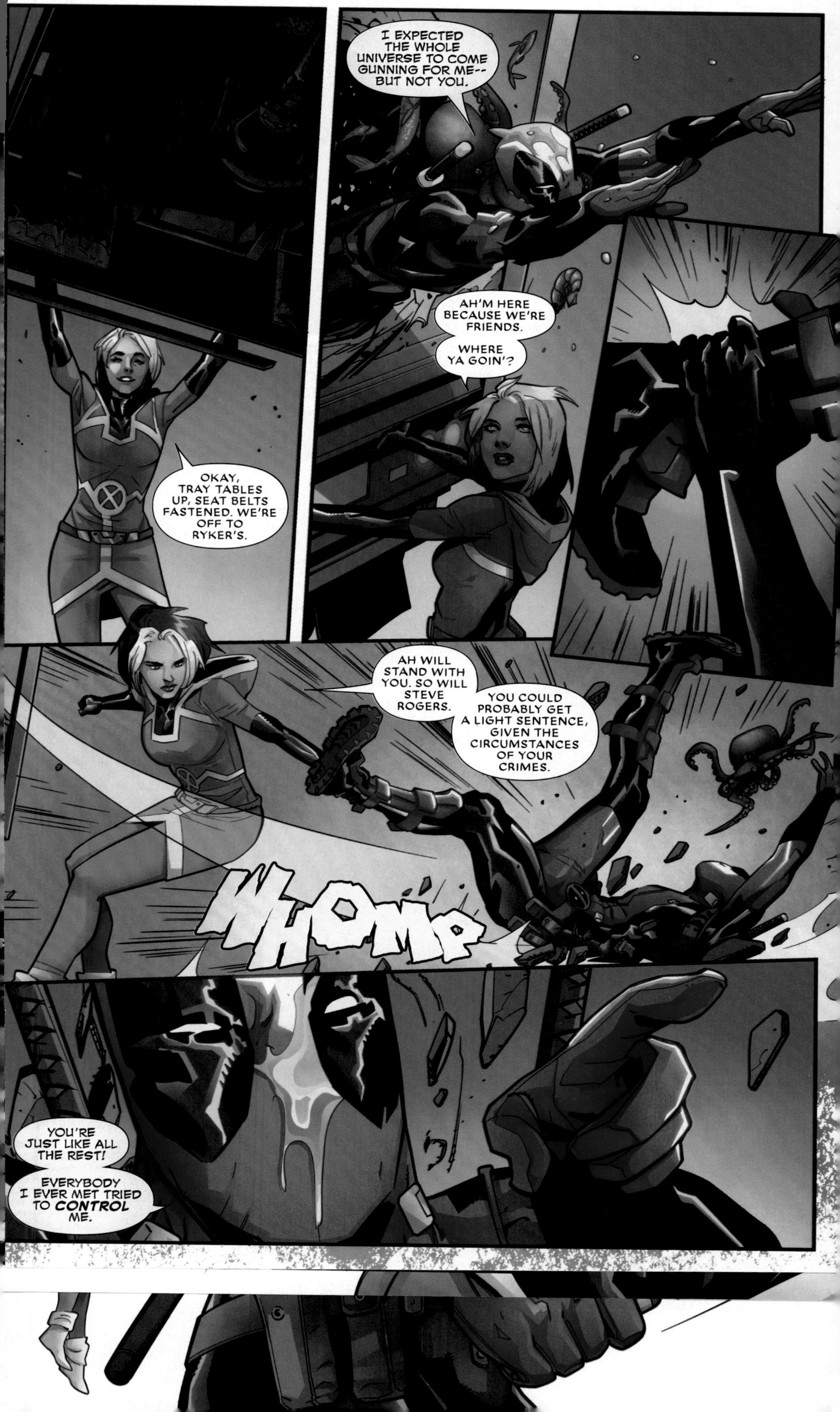

I EXPECTED THE WHOLE UNIVERSE TO COME GUNNING FOR ME-- BUT NOT YOU.
AH'M HERE BECAUSE WE'RE FRIENDS.
WHERE YA GOIN'?
OKAY, TRAY TABLES UP, SEAT BELTS FASTENED. WE'RE OFF TO RYKER'S.
AH WILL STAND WITH YOU. SO WILL STEVE ROGERS.
YOU COULD PROBABLY GET A LIGHT SENTENCE, GIVEN THE CIRCUMSTANCES OF YOUR CRIMES.
WHOMP
YOU'RE JUST LIKE ALL THE REST!
EVERYBODY I EVER MET TRIED TO **CONTROL** ME.

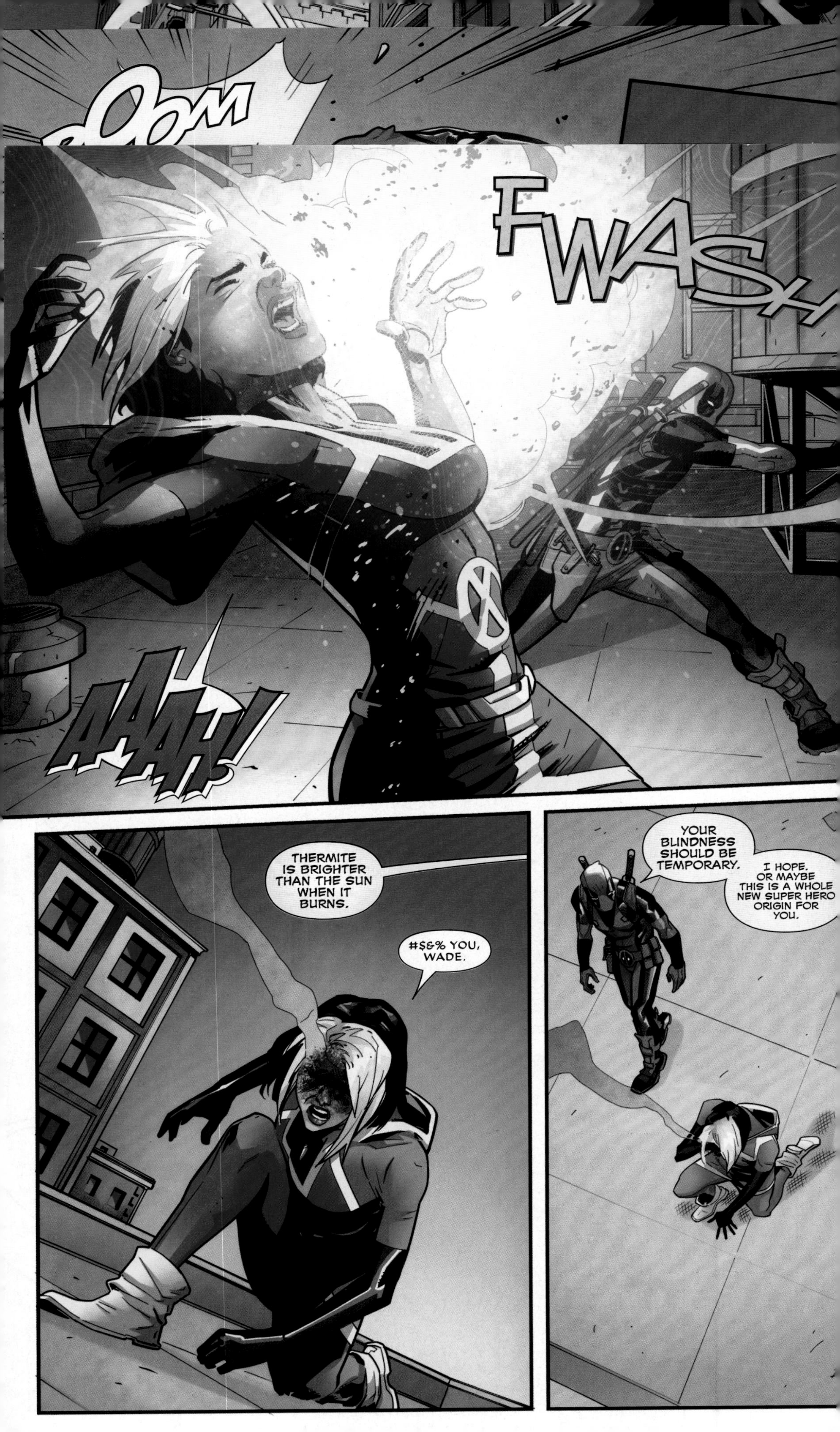
FOOM
FWASH
AAAH!
THERMITE IS BRIGHTER THAN THE SUN WHEN IT BURNS.
#$&% YOU, WADE.
YOUR BLINDNESS SHOULD BE TEMPORARY.
I HOPE. OR MAYBE THIS IS A WHOLE NEW SUPER HERO ORIGIN FOR YOU.

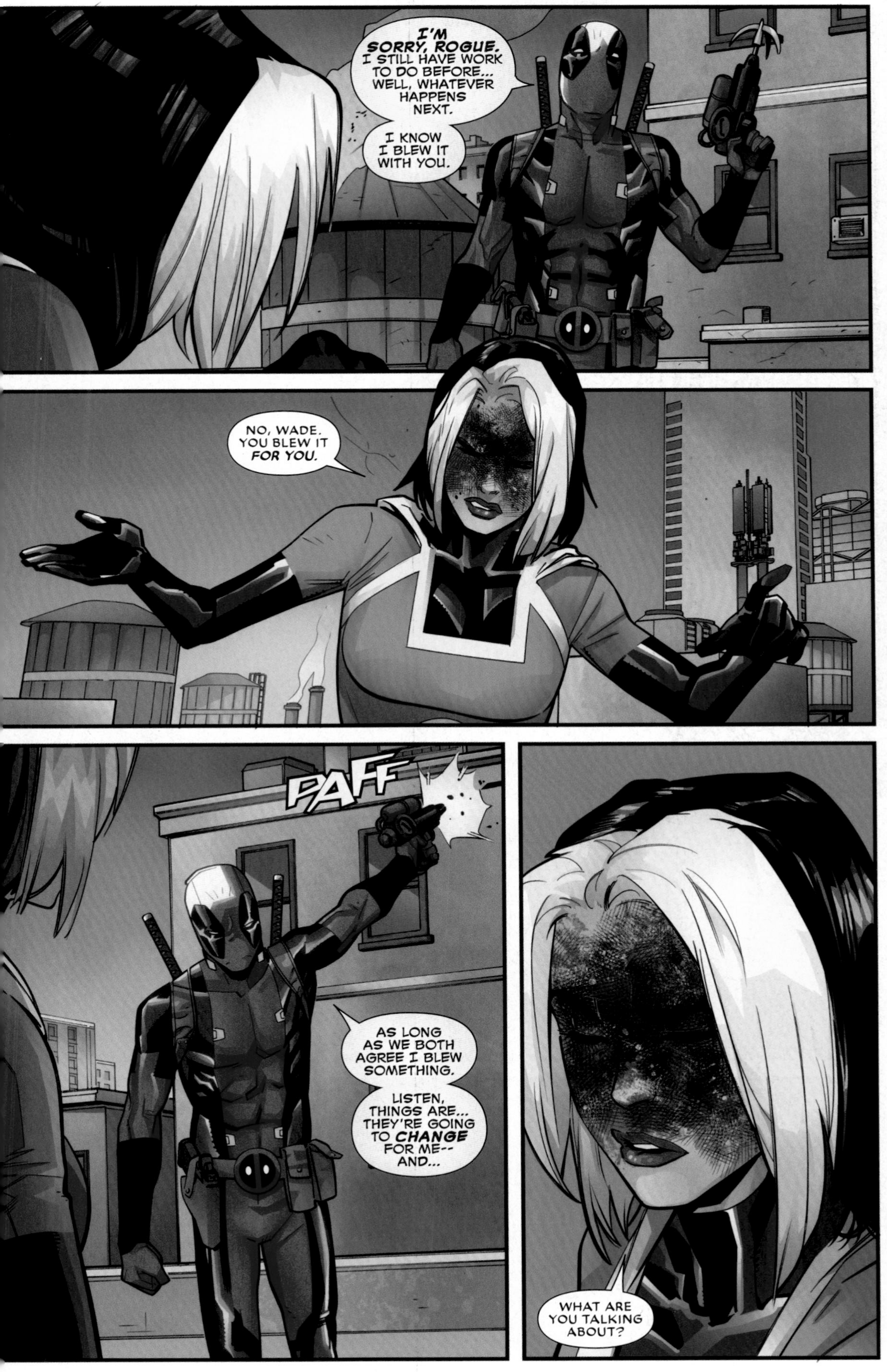
I'M SORRY, ROGUE. I STILL HAVE WORK TO DO BEFORE... WELL, WHATEVER HAPPENS NEXT.
I KNOW I BLEW IT WITH YOU.
NO, WADE. YOU BLEW IT FOR YOU.
PAFF
AS LONG AS WE BOTH AGREE I BLEW SOMETHING.
LISTEN, THINGS ARE... THEY'RE GOING TO CHANGE FOR ME-- AND...
WHAT ARE YOU TALKING ABOUT?

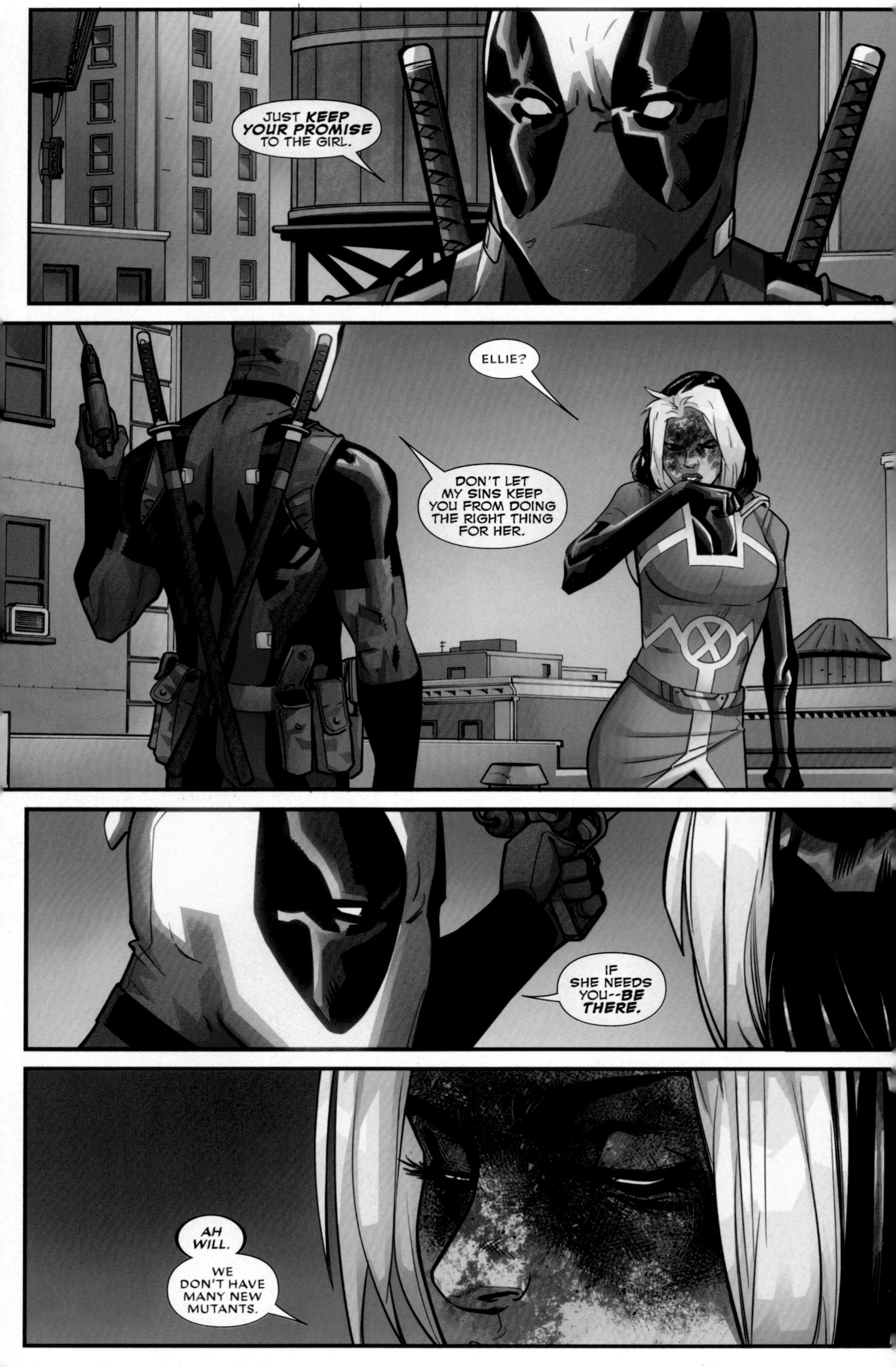
JUST **KEEP YOUR PROMISE** TO THE GIRL.
ELLIE?
DON'T LET MY **SINS** KEEP YOU FROM **DOING** THE RIGHT THING FOR HER.
IF SHE NEEDS YOU--**BE THERE.**
AH WILL.
WE DON'T HAVE MANY NEW MUTANTS.

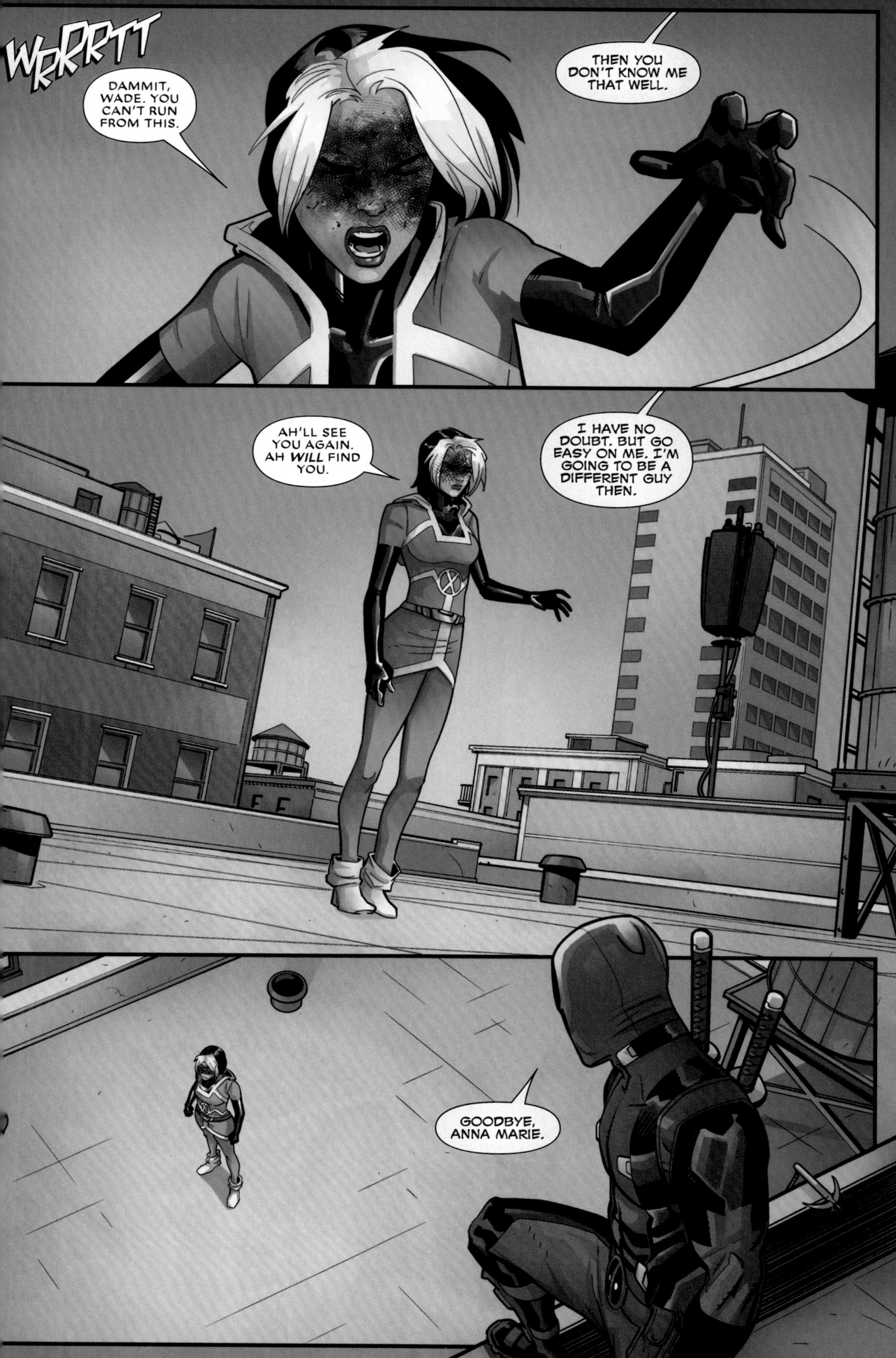
WRRRTT
DAMMIT, WADE. YOU CAN'T RUN FROM THIS.
THEN YOU DON'T KNOW ME THAT WELL.
AH'LL SEE YOU AGAIN. AH WILL FIND YOU.
I HAVE NO DOUBT. BUT GO EASY ON ME. I'M GOING TO BE A DIFFERENT GUY THEN.
GOODBYE, ANNA MARIE.

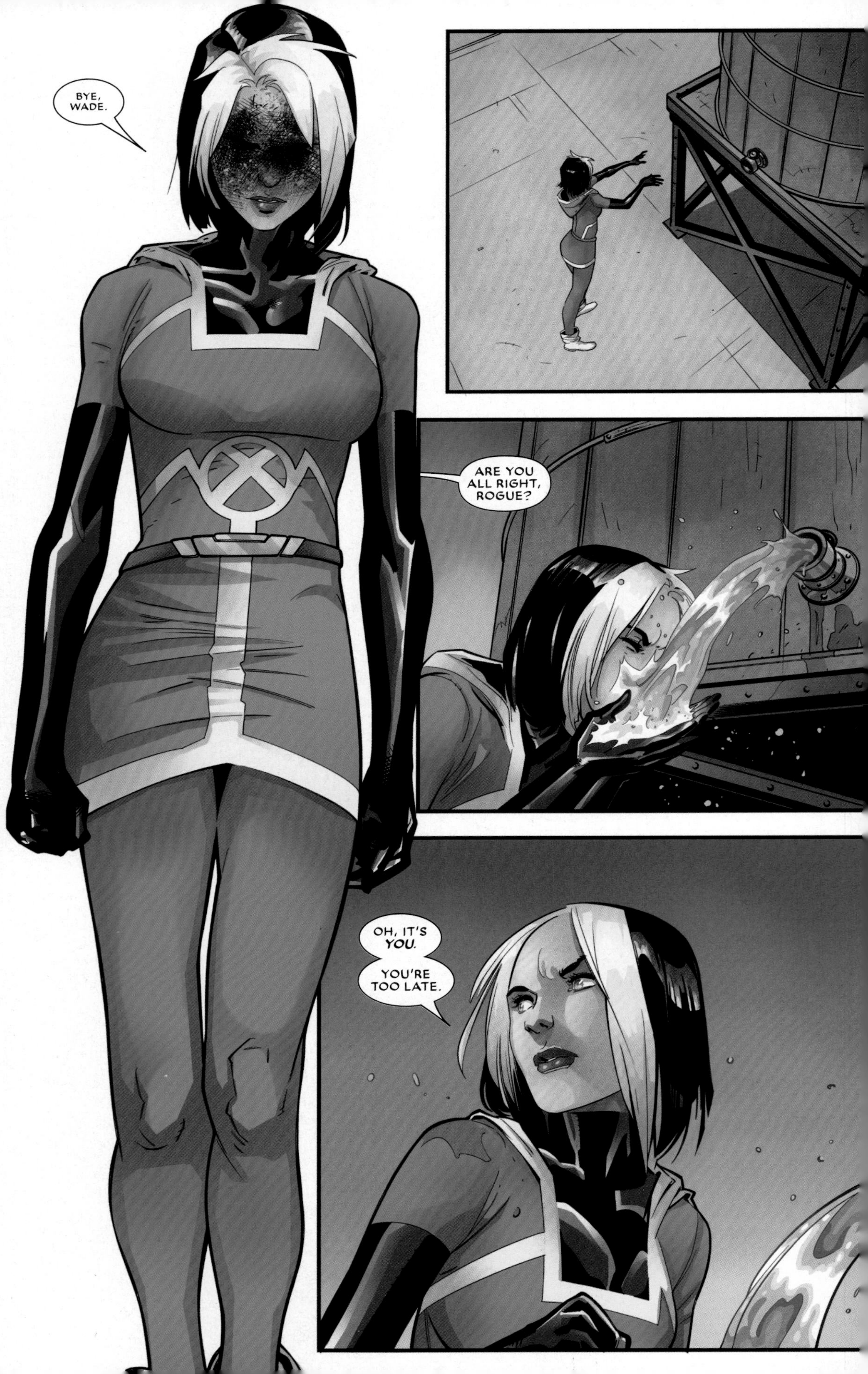
BYE, WADE.
ARE YOU ALL RIGHT, ROGUE?
OH, IT'S *YOU*.
YOU'RE TOO LATE.

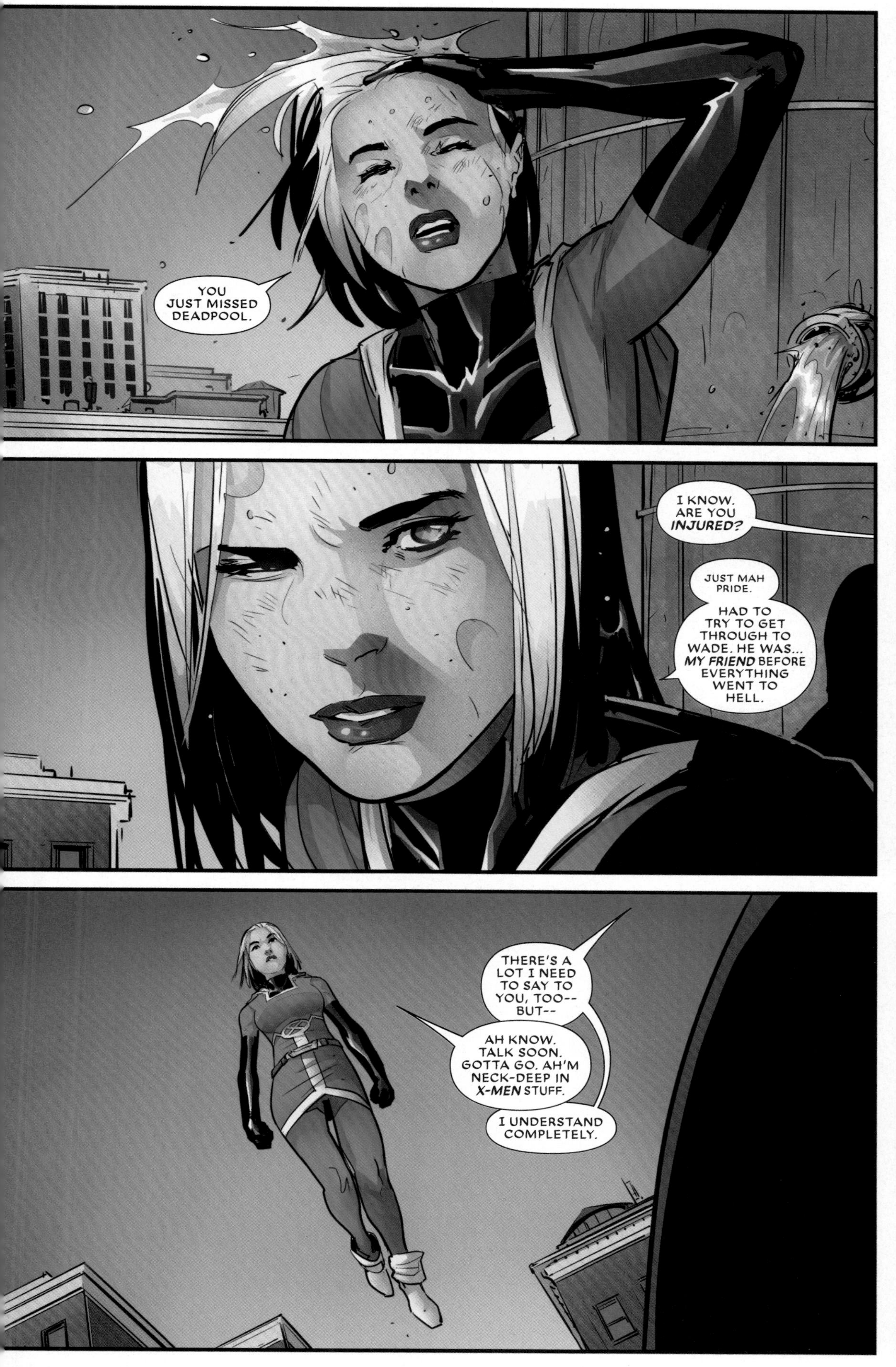
YOU JUST MISSED DEADPOOL.
I KNOW. ARE YOU *INJURED?*
JUST MAH PRIDE.
HAD TO TRY TO GET THROUGH TO WADE. HE WAS... *MY FRIEND* BEFORE EVERYTHING WENT TO HELL.
THERE'S A LOT I NEED TO SAY TO YOU, TOO-- BUT--
AH KNOW. TALK SOON. GOTTA GO. AH'M NECK-DEEP IN *X-MEN* STUFF.
I UNDERSTAND COMPLETELY.

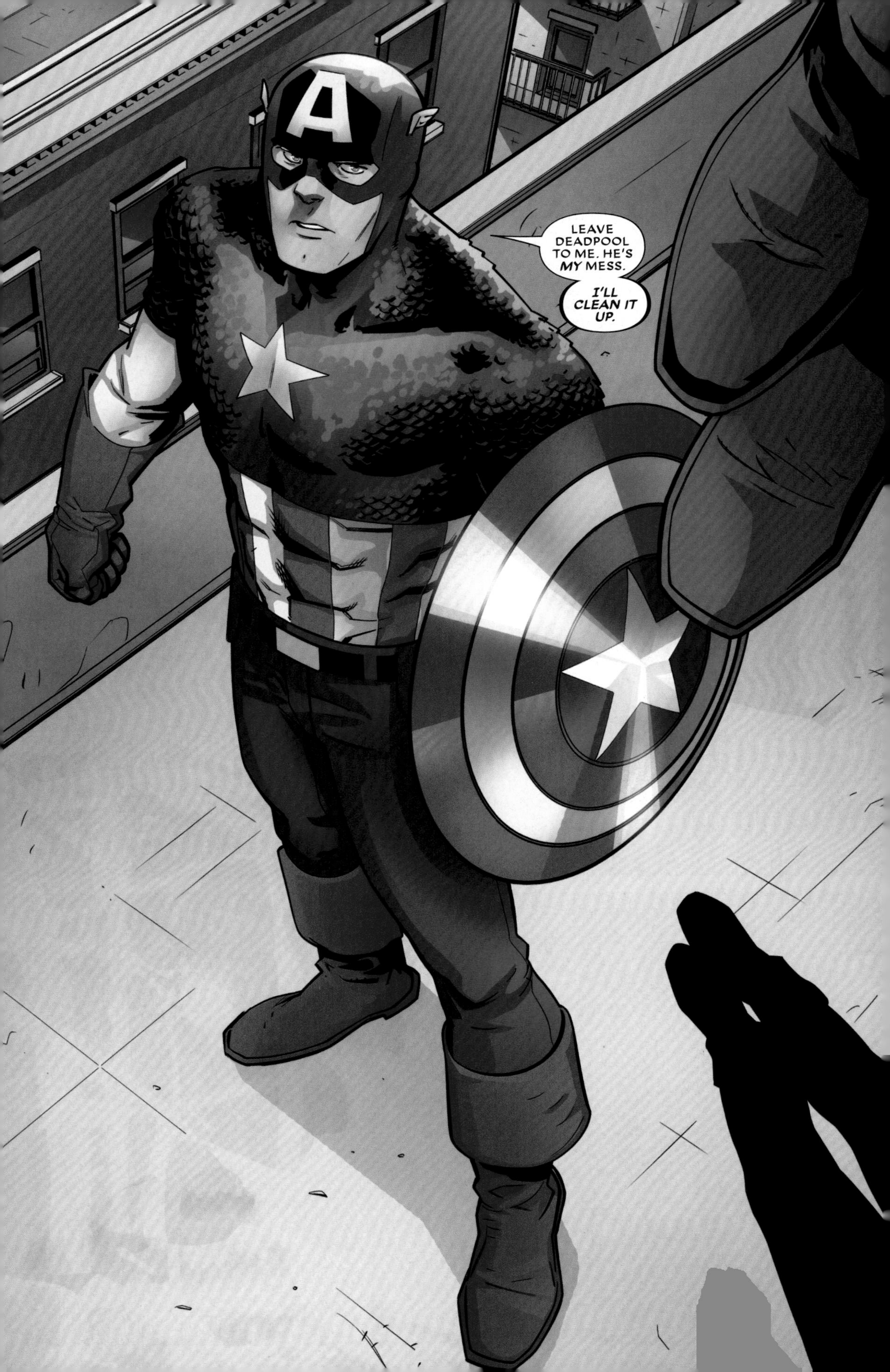

LEAVE DEADPOOL TO ME. HE'S *MY* MESS.
I'LL CLEAN IT UP.

294 – Part Three: "Beat It"

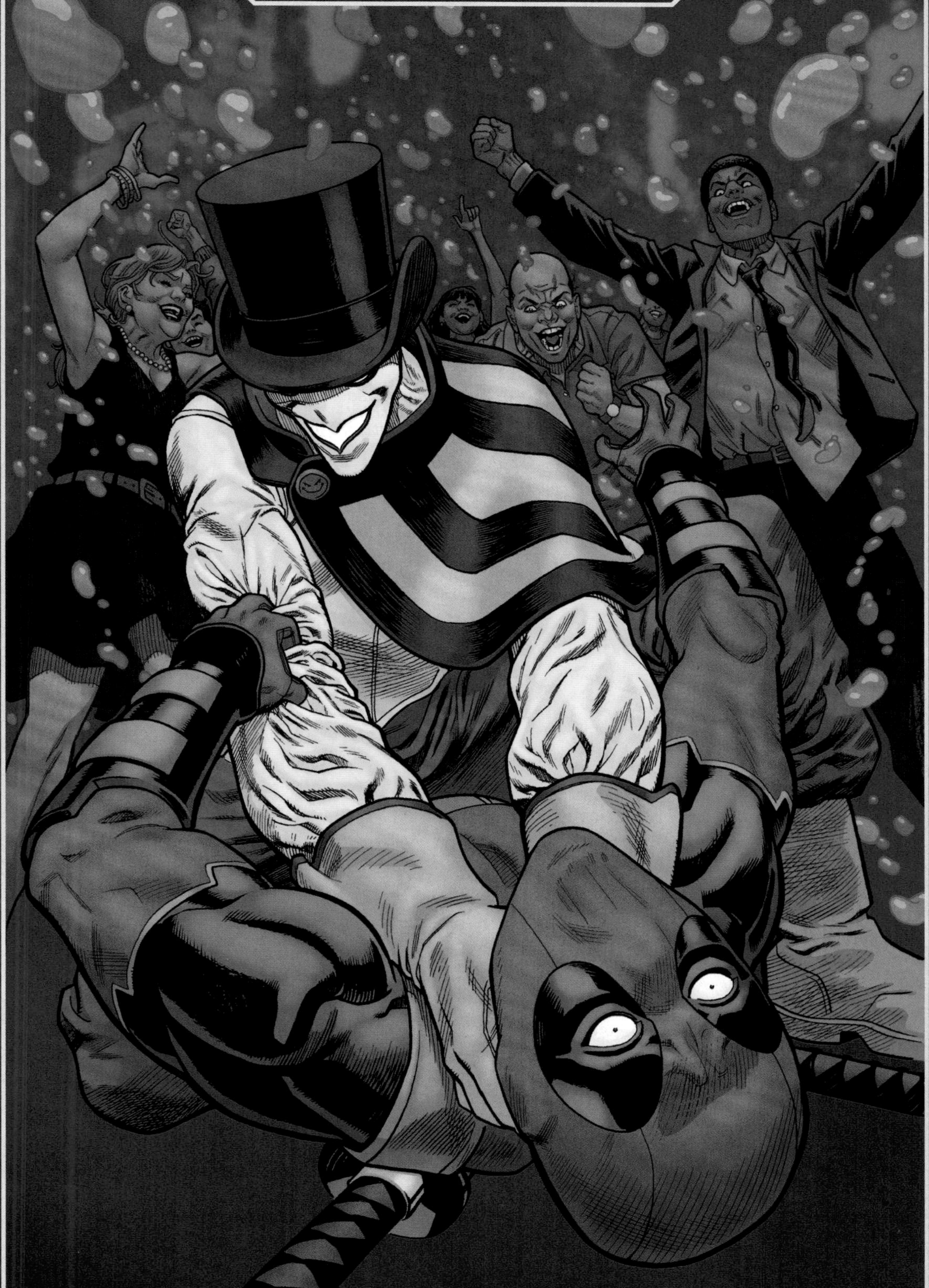

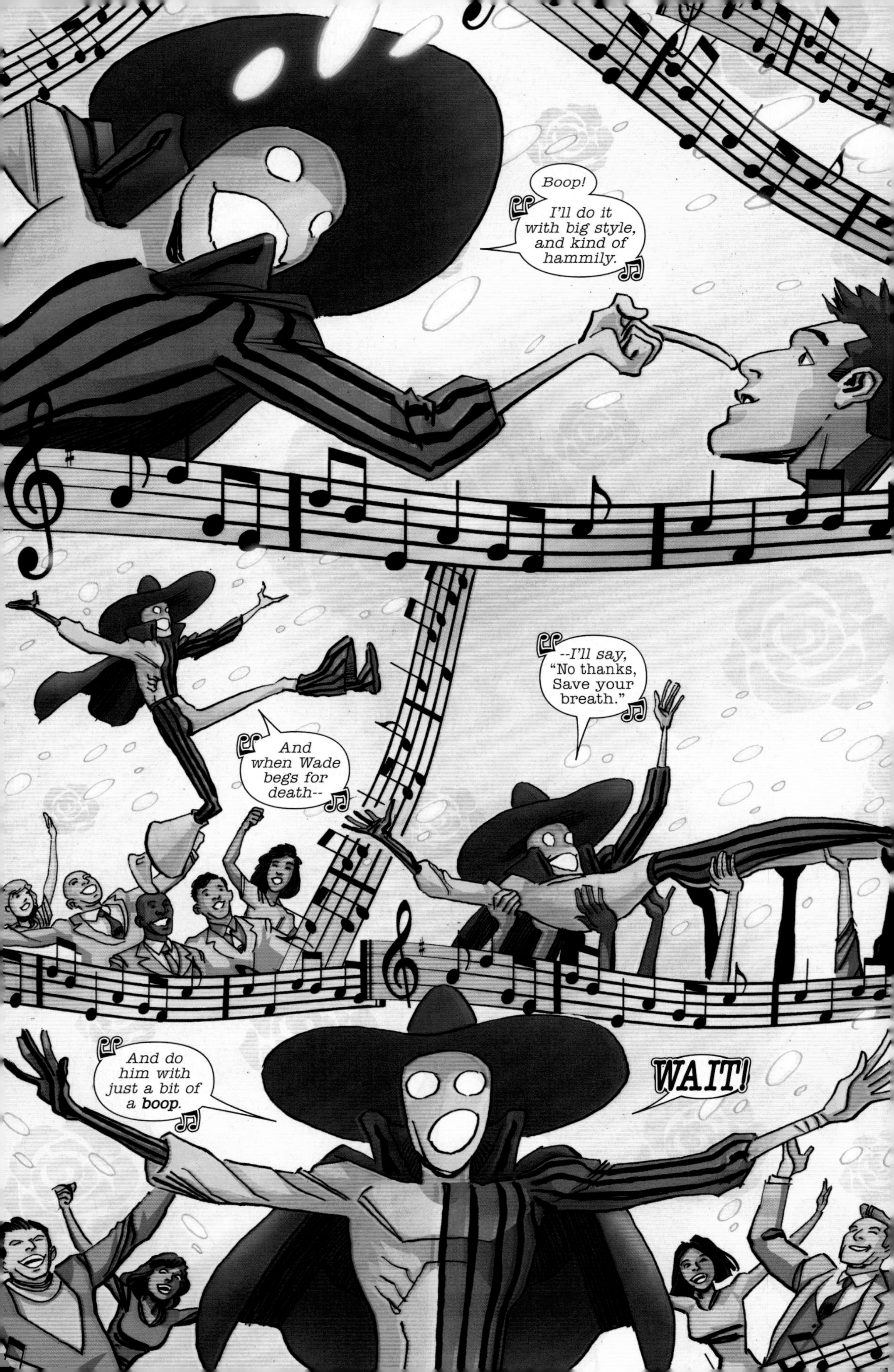
Boop!
I'll do it with big style, and kind of hammily.
And when Wade begs for death--
--I'll say, "No thanks, Save your breath."
And do him with just a bit of a **boop**.
WAIT!

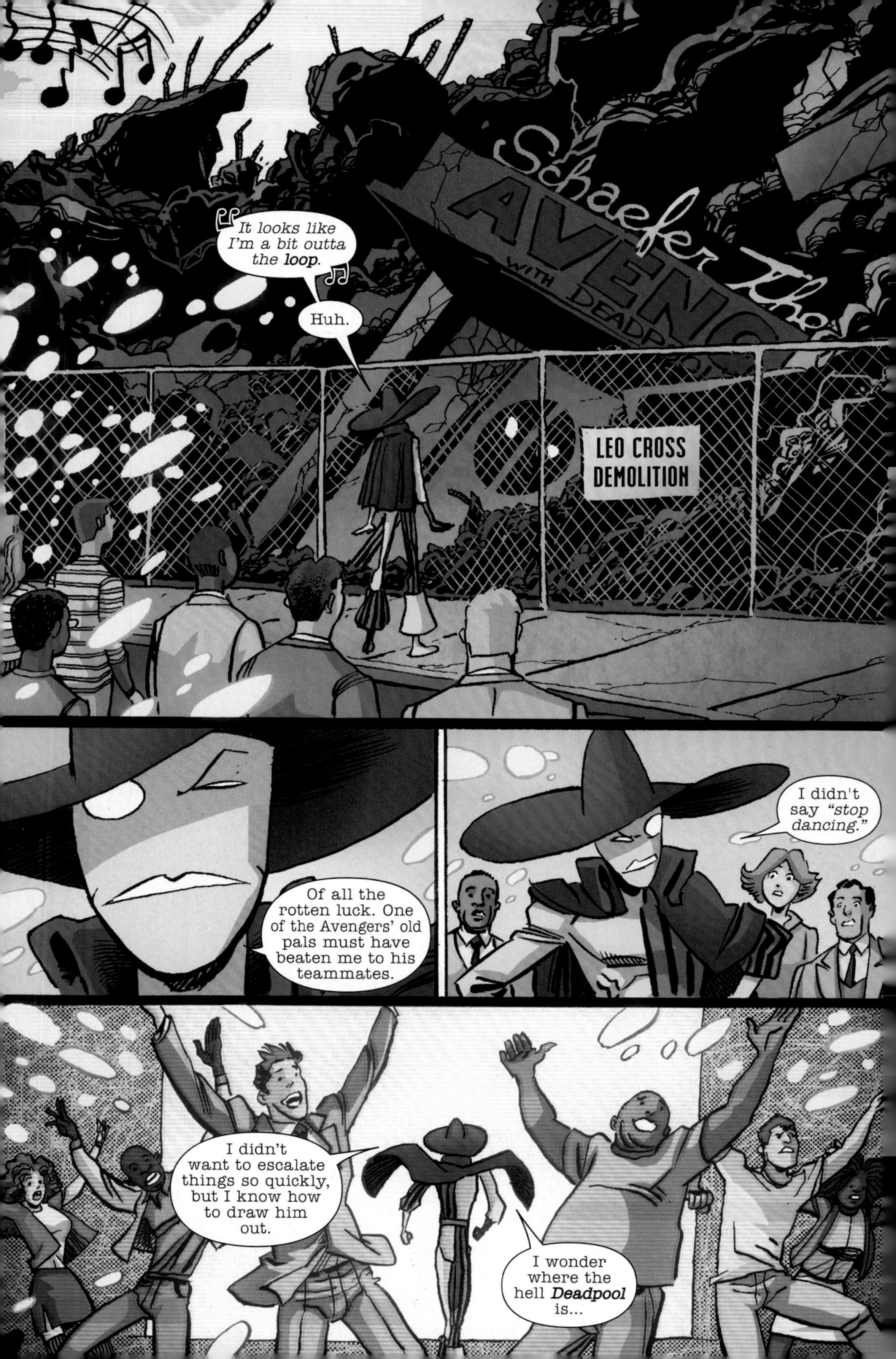

Schaefer The
AVENG
WITH DEADP
It looks like I'm a bit outta the **loop**.
Huh.
LEO CROSS DEMOLITION
Of all the rotten luck. One of the Avengers' old pals must have beaten me to his teammates.
I didn't say *"stop dancing."*
I didn't want to escalate things so quickly, but I know how to draw him out.
I wonder where the hell ***Deadpool*** is...

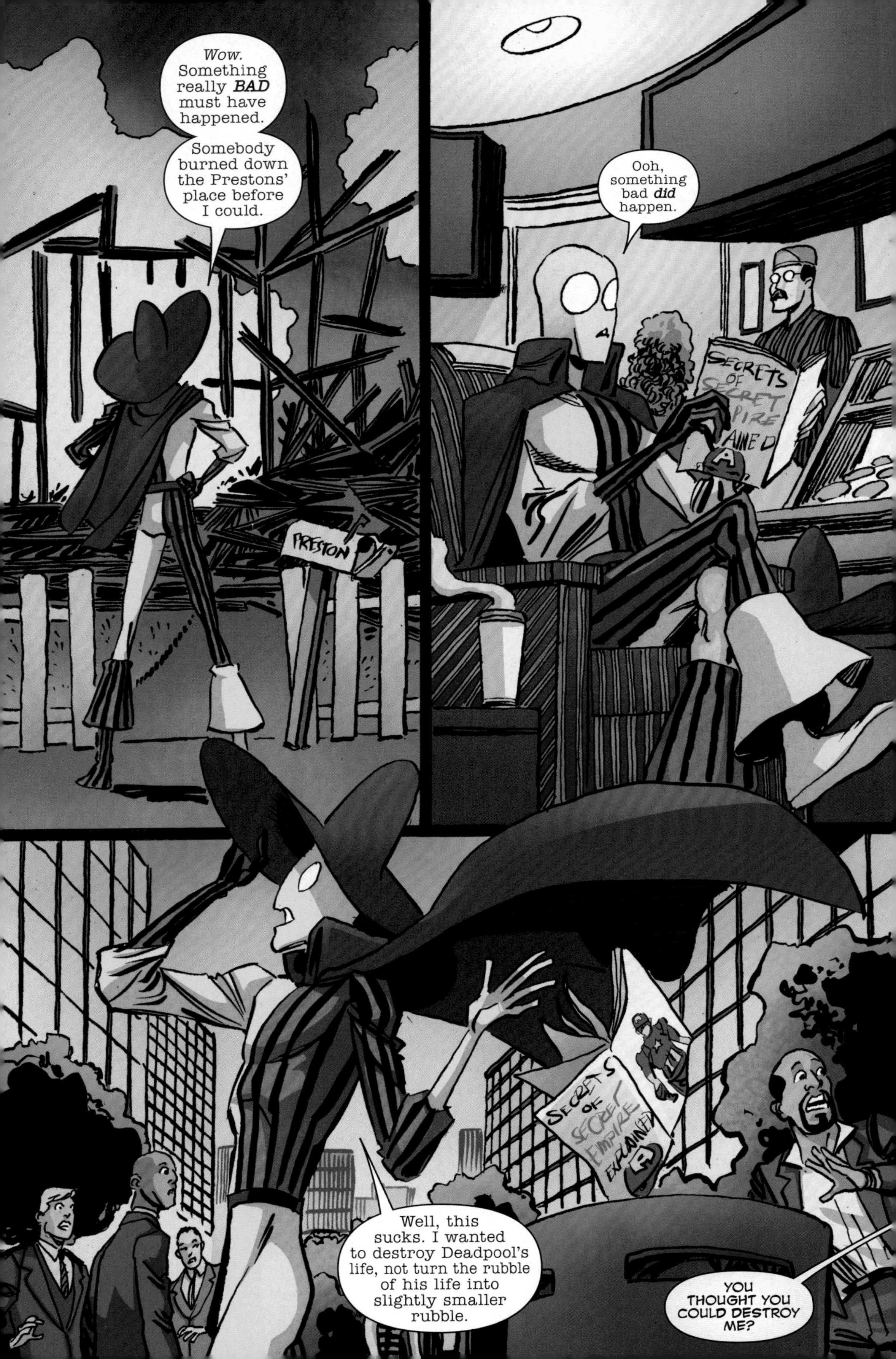
Wow. Something really BAD must have happened.
Somebody burned down the Prestons' place before I could.
PRESTON
Ooh, something bad did happen.
SECRETS OF SECRET EMPIRE EXPLAINED
Well, this sucks. I wanted to destroy Deadpool's life, not turn the rubble of his life into slightly smaller rubble.
YOU THOUGHT YOU COULD DESTROY ME?

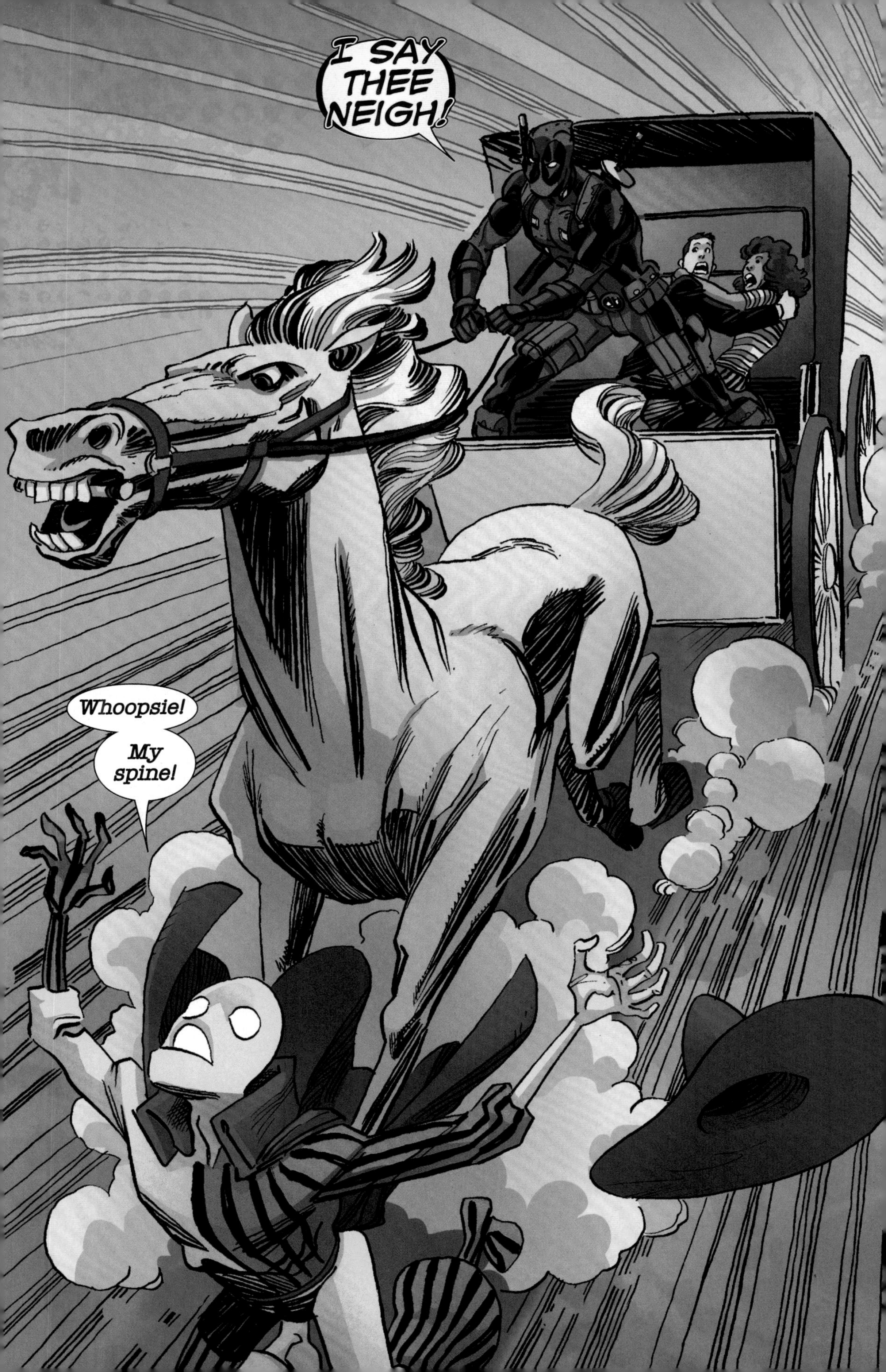
I SAY THEE NEIGH!
Whoopsie!
My spine!

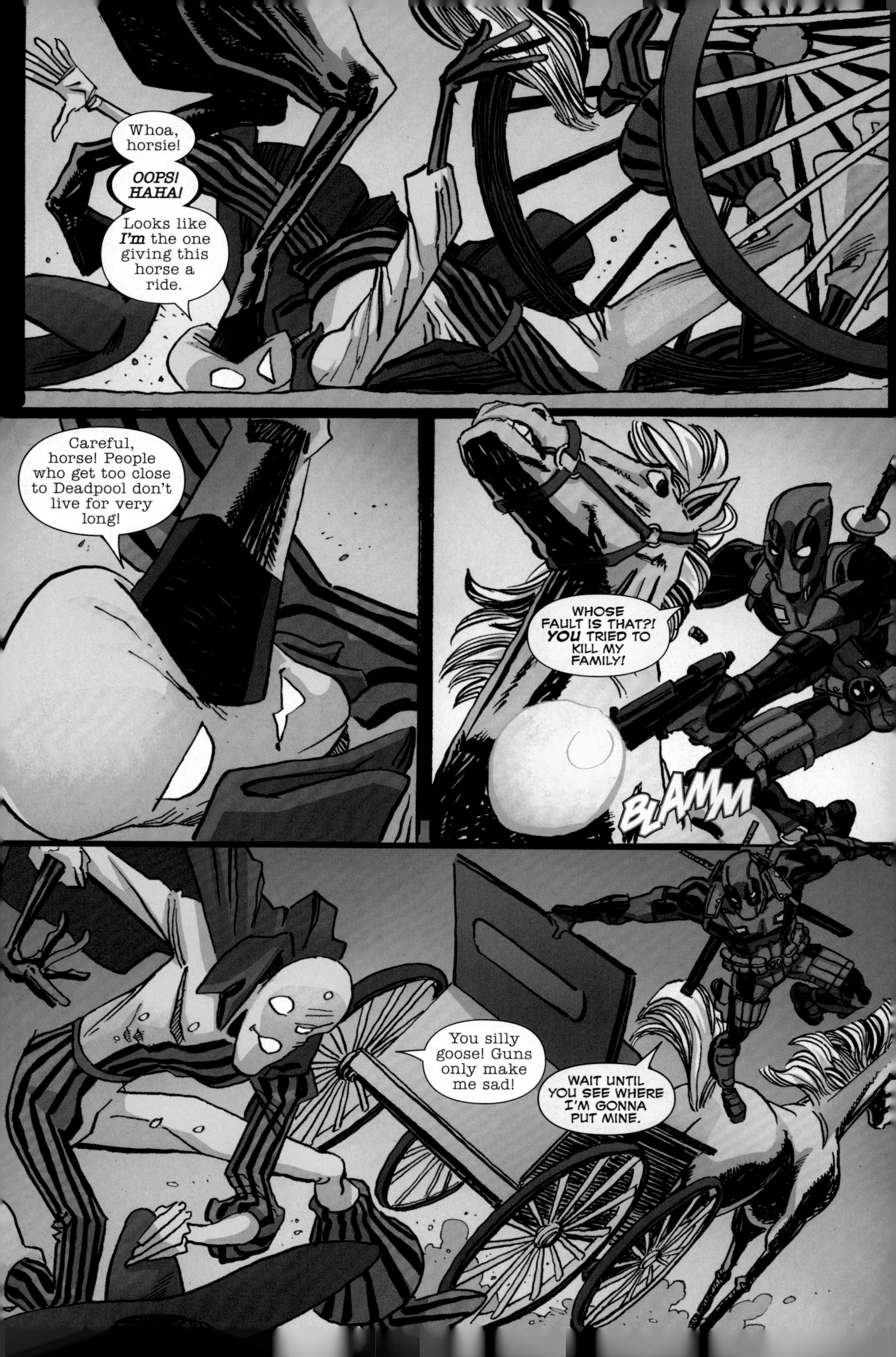

Whoa, horsie!
OOPS! HAHA!
Looks like I'm the one giving this horse a ride.
Careful, horse! People who get too close to Deadpool don't live for very long!
WHOSE FAULT IS THAT?! YOU TRIED TO KILL MY FAMILY!
BLAMM
You silly goose! Guns only make me sad!
WAIT UNTIL YOU SEE WHERE I'M GONNA PUT MINE.

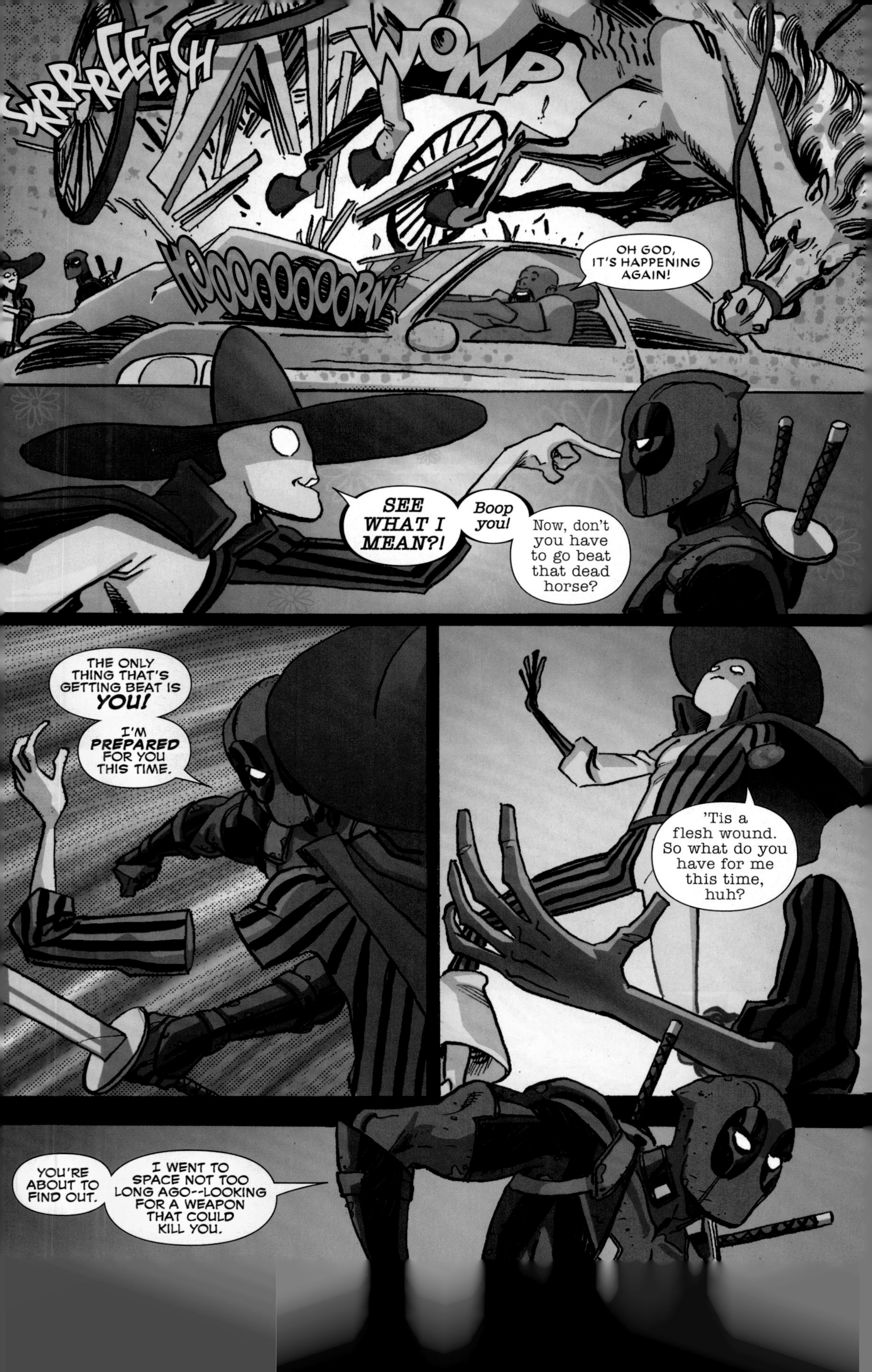
SKRREEECH
WOMP
HOOOOOOOORN
OH GOD, IT'S HAPPENING AGAIN!
SEE WHAT I MEAN?!
Boop you!
Now, don't you have to go beat that dead horse?
THE ONLY THING THAT'S GETTING BEAT IS YOU!
I'M PREPARED FOR YOU THIS TIME.
'Tis a flesh wound. So what do you have for me this time, huh?
YOU'RE ABOUT TO FIND OUT.
I WENT TO SPACE NOT TOO LONG AGO--LOOKING FOR A WEAPON THAT COULD KILL YOU.

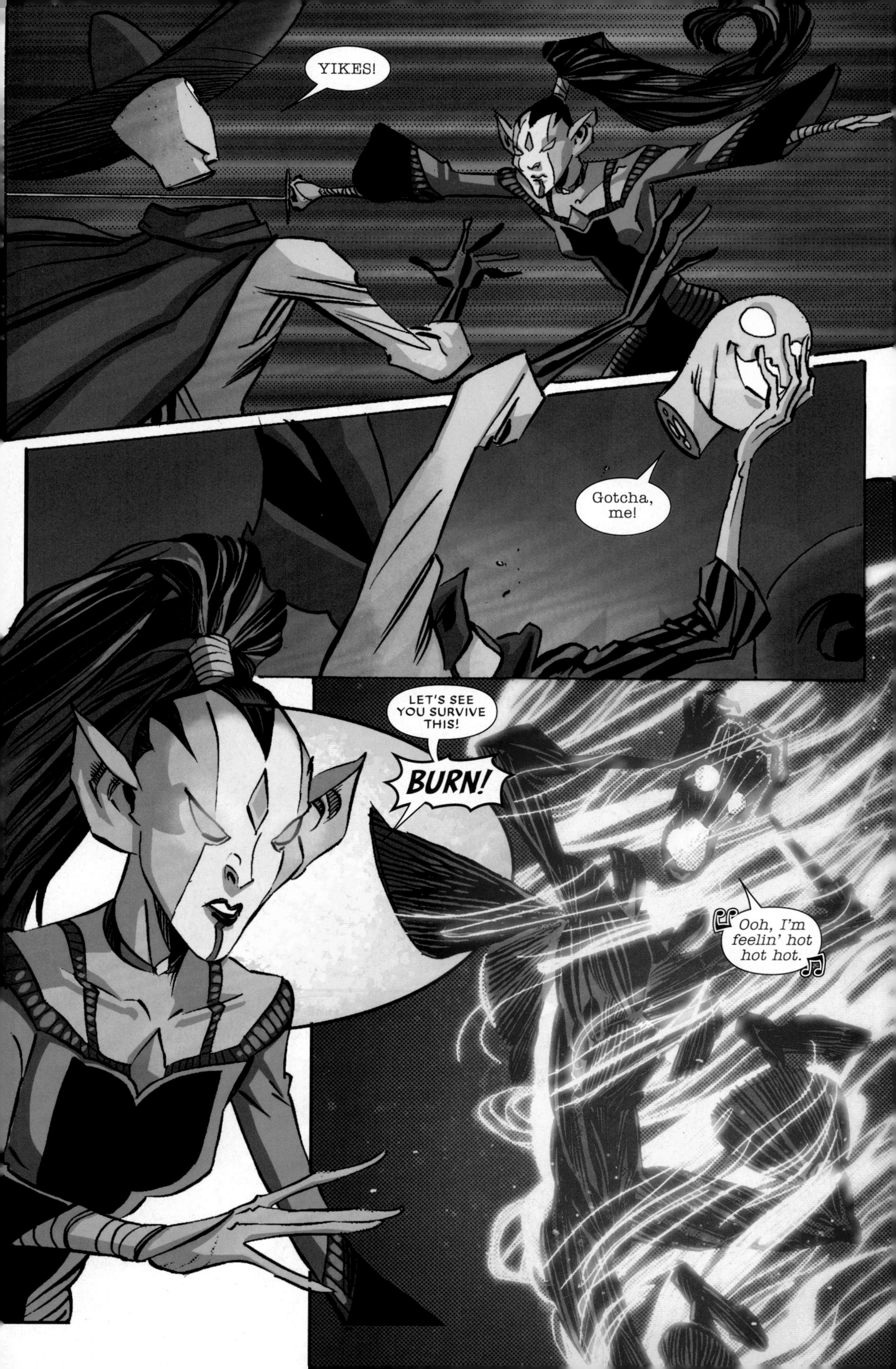
YIKES!
Gotcha, me!
LET'S SEE YOU SURVIVE THIS!
BURN!
Ooh, I'm feelin' hot hot hot.

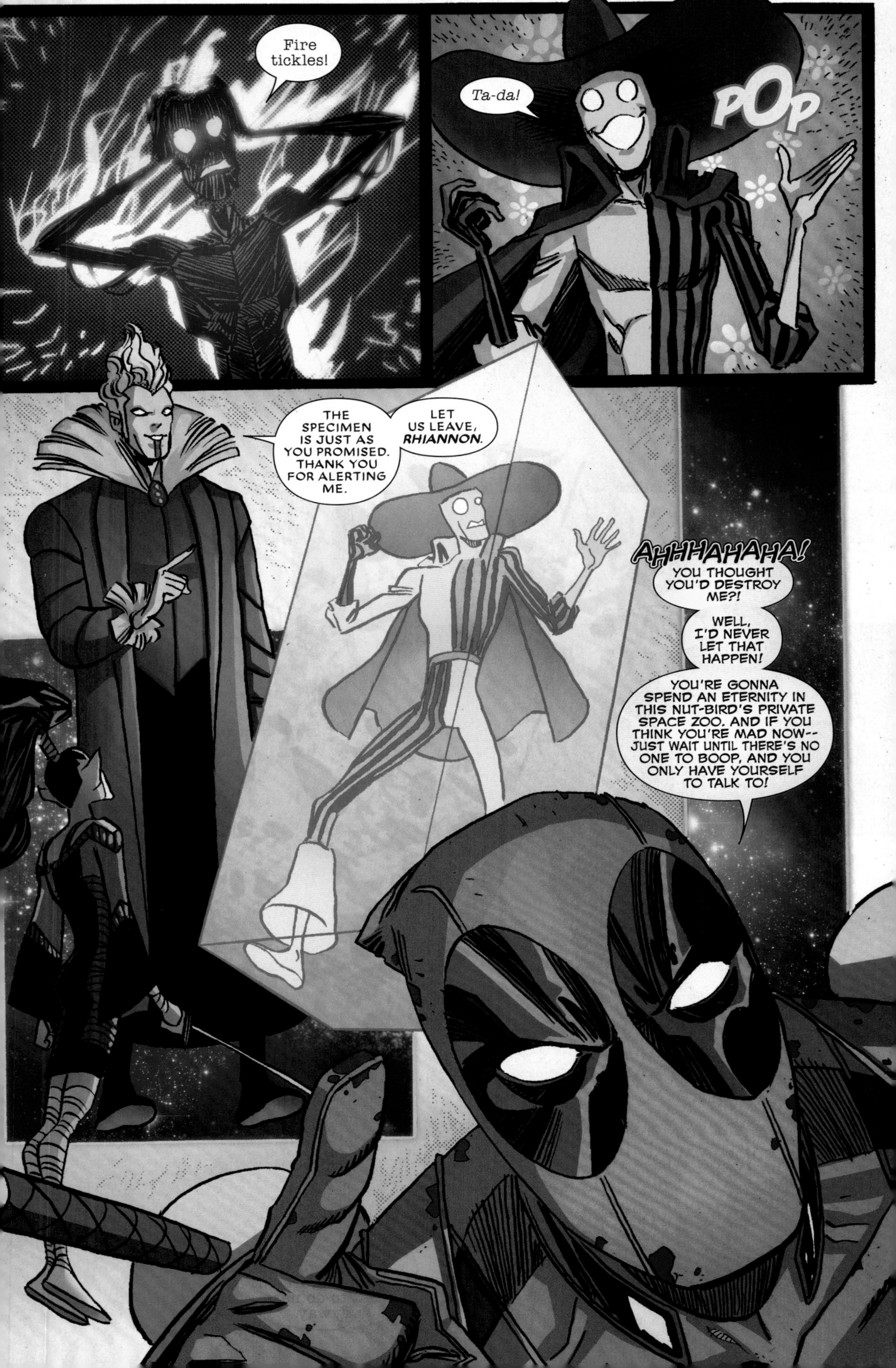
Fire tickles!
Ta-da!
POP
THE SPECIMEN IS JUST AS YOU PROMISED. THANK YOU FOR ALERTING ME.
LET US LEAVE, RHIANNON.
AHHHAHAHA!
YOU THOUGHT YOU'D DESTROY ME?!
WELL, I'D NEVER LET THAT HAPPEN!
YOU'RE GONNA SPEND AN ETERNITY IN THIS NUT-BIRD'S PRIVATE SPACE ZOO. AND IF YOU THINK YOU'RE MAD NOW-- JUST WAIT UNTIL THERE'S NO ONE TO BOOP, AND YOU ONLY HAVE YOURSELF TO TALK TO!

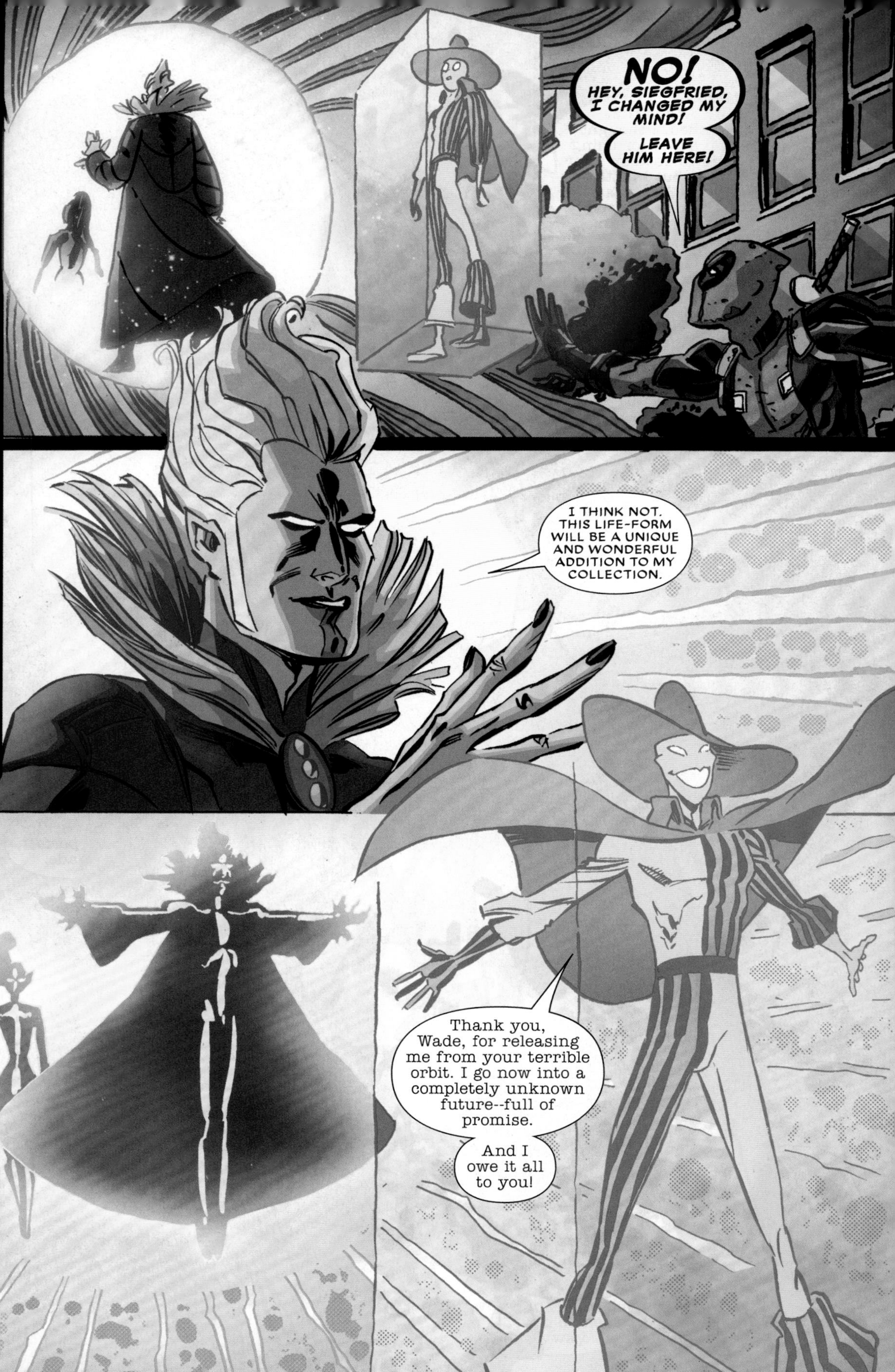
NO! HEY, SIEGFRIED, I CHANGED MY MIND!
LEAVE HIM HERE!
I THINK NOT. THIS LIFE-FORM WILL BE A UNIQUE AND WONDERFUL ADDITION TO MY COLLECTION.
Thank you, Wade, for releasing me from your terrible orbit. I go now into a completely unknown future--full of promise.
And I owe it all to you!

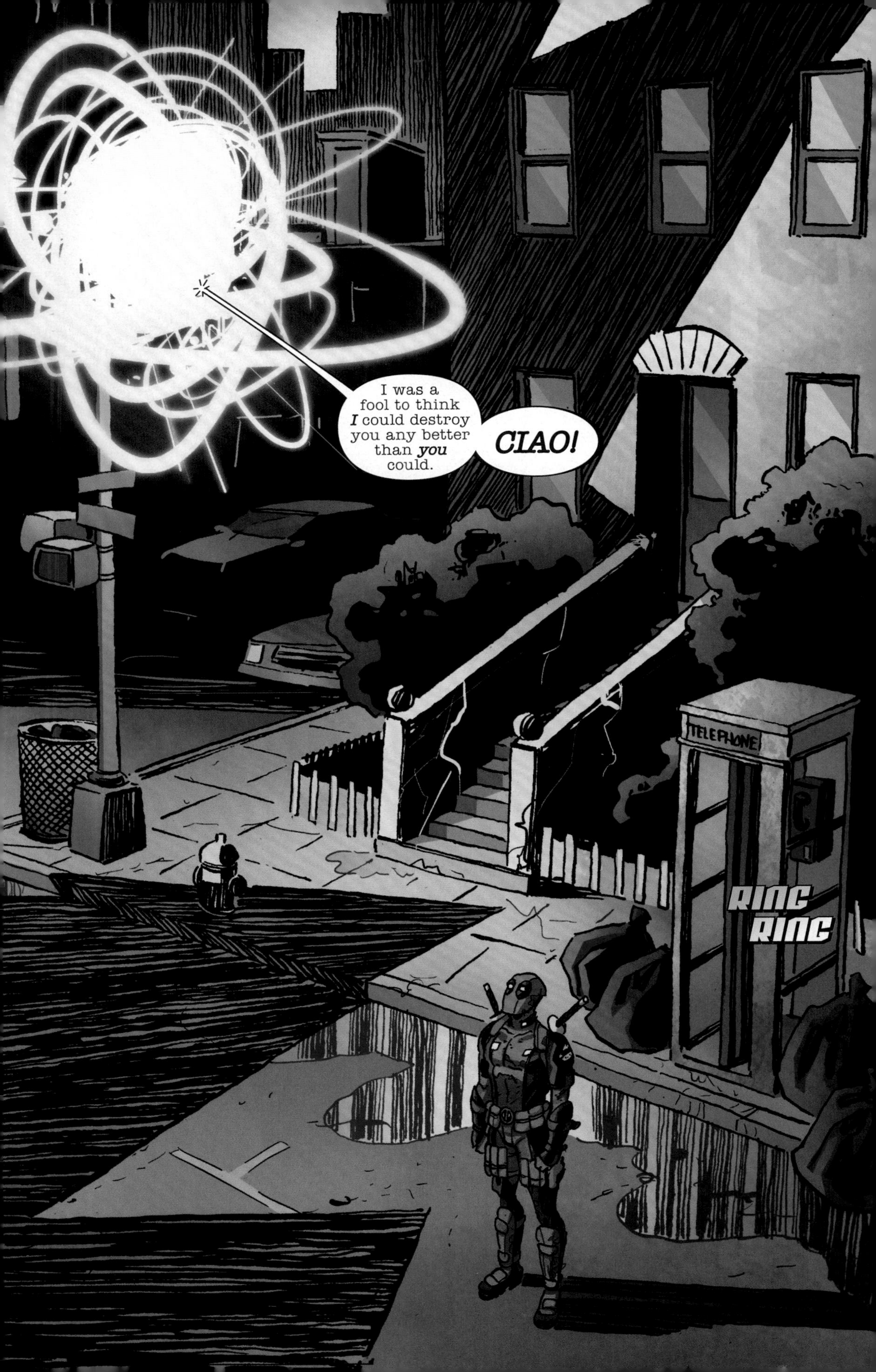
I was a fool to think *I* could destroy you any better than ***you*** could.
CIAO!
TELEPHONE
RING RING

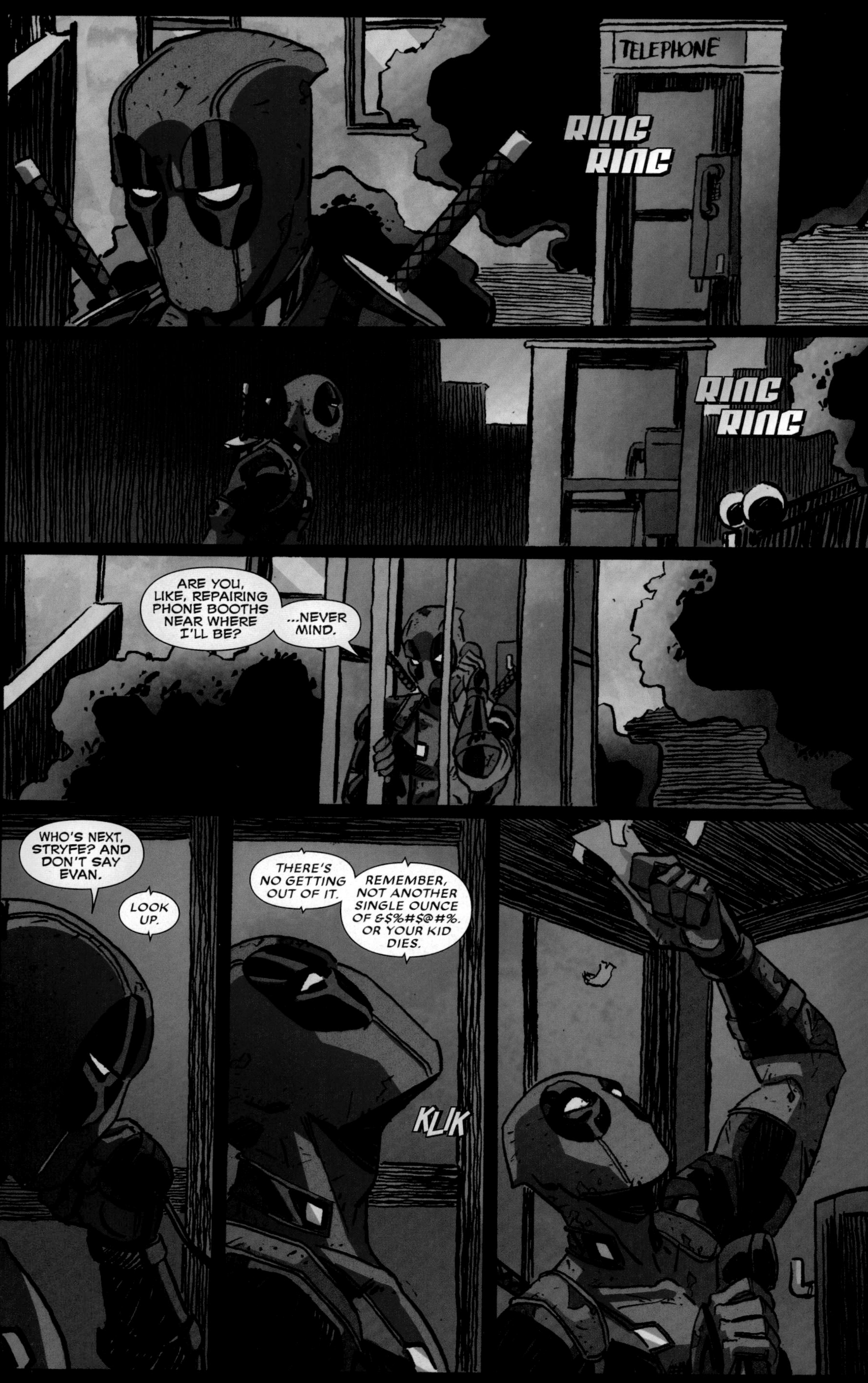
TELEPHONE
RING RING
RING RING
ARE YOU, LIKE, REPAIRING PHONE BOOTHS NEAR WHERE I'LL BE?
...NEVER MIND.
WHO'S NEXT, STRYFE? AND DON'T SAY EVAN.
LOOK UP.
THERE'S NO GETTING OUT OF IT.
REMEMBER, NOT ANOTHER SINGLE OUNCE OF &$%#$@#%. OR YOUR KID DIES.
KLIK

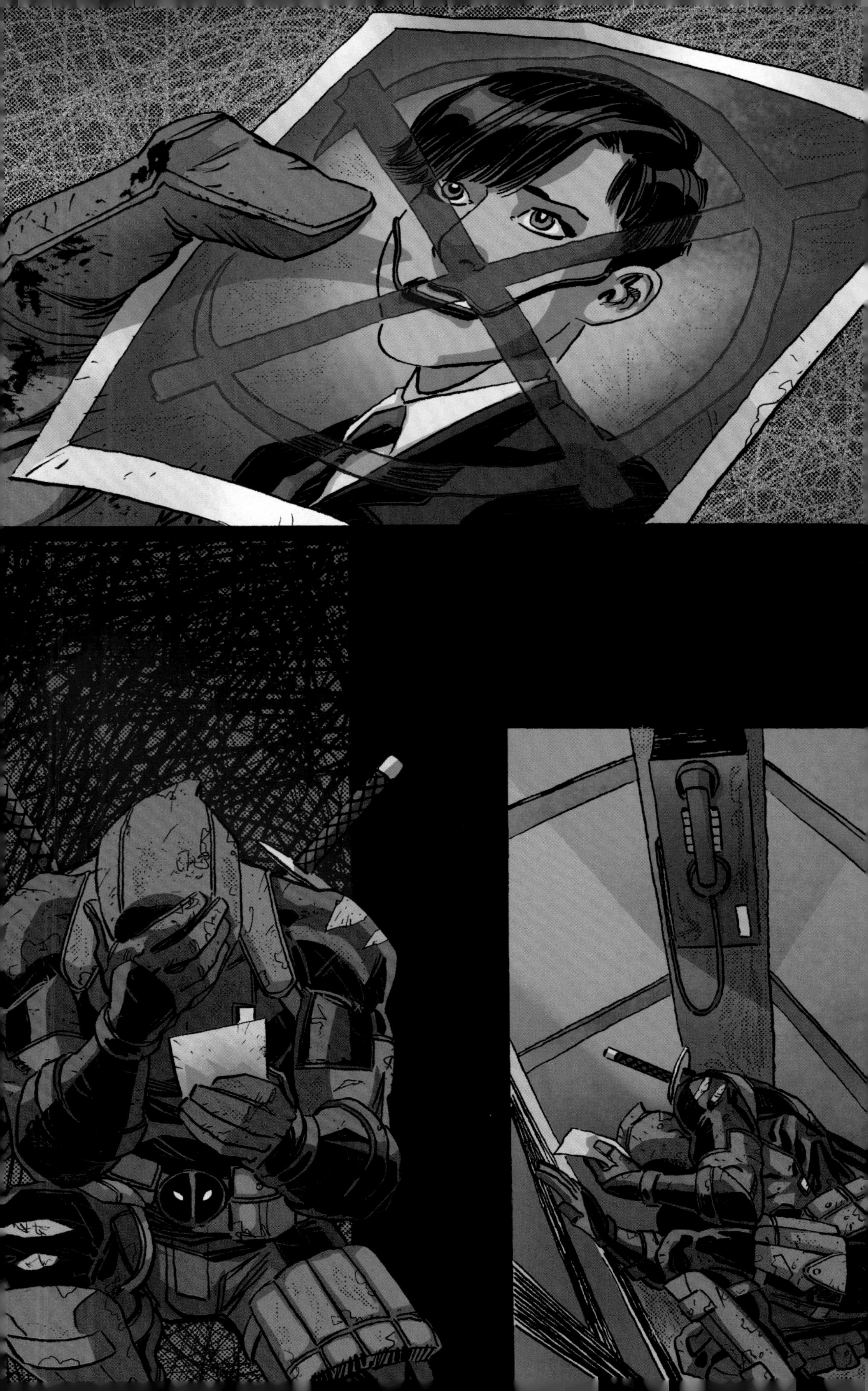

295 – Part Four: "The Uncanny Ex-Man"

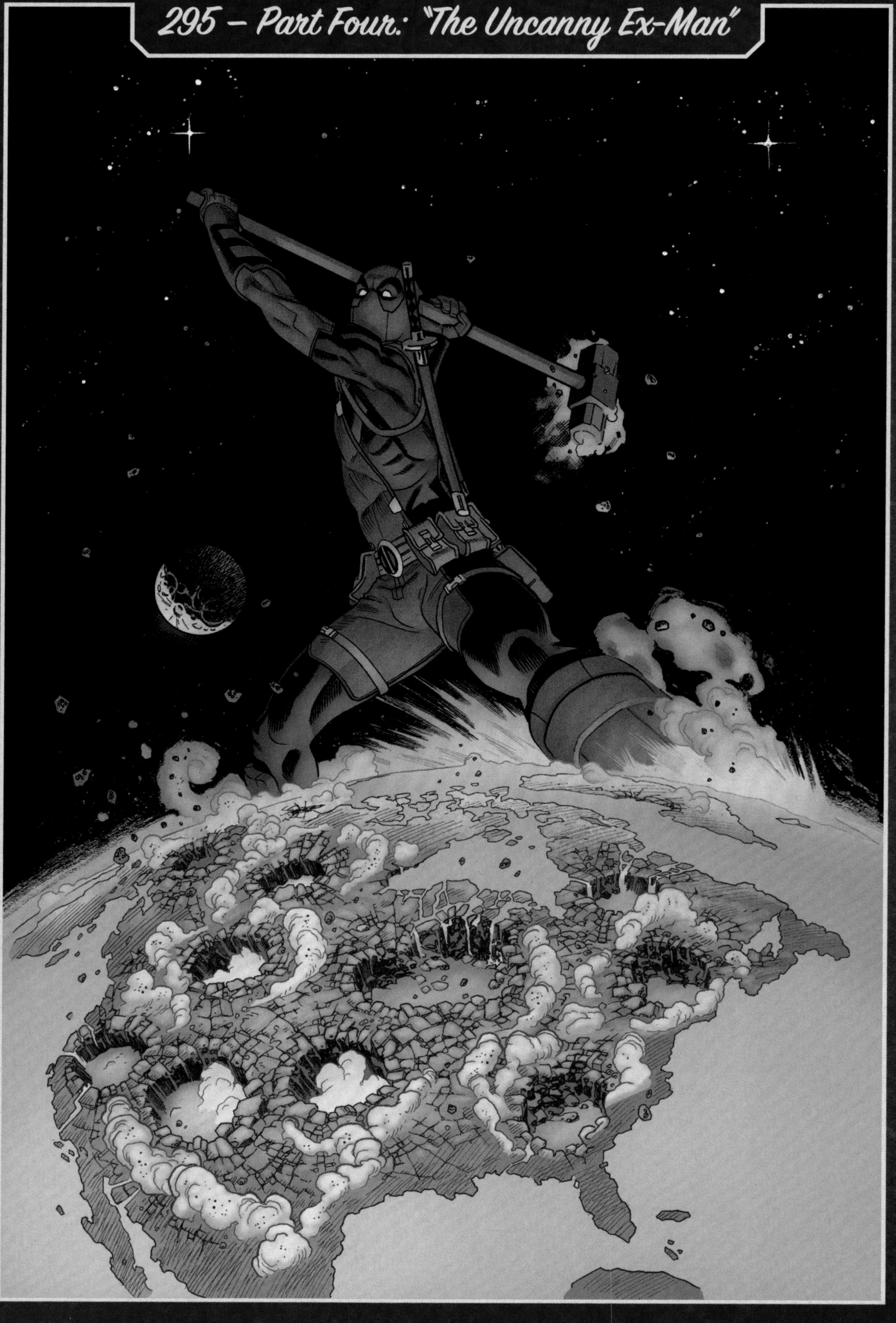

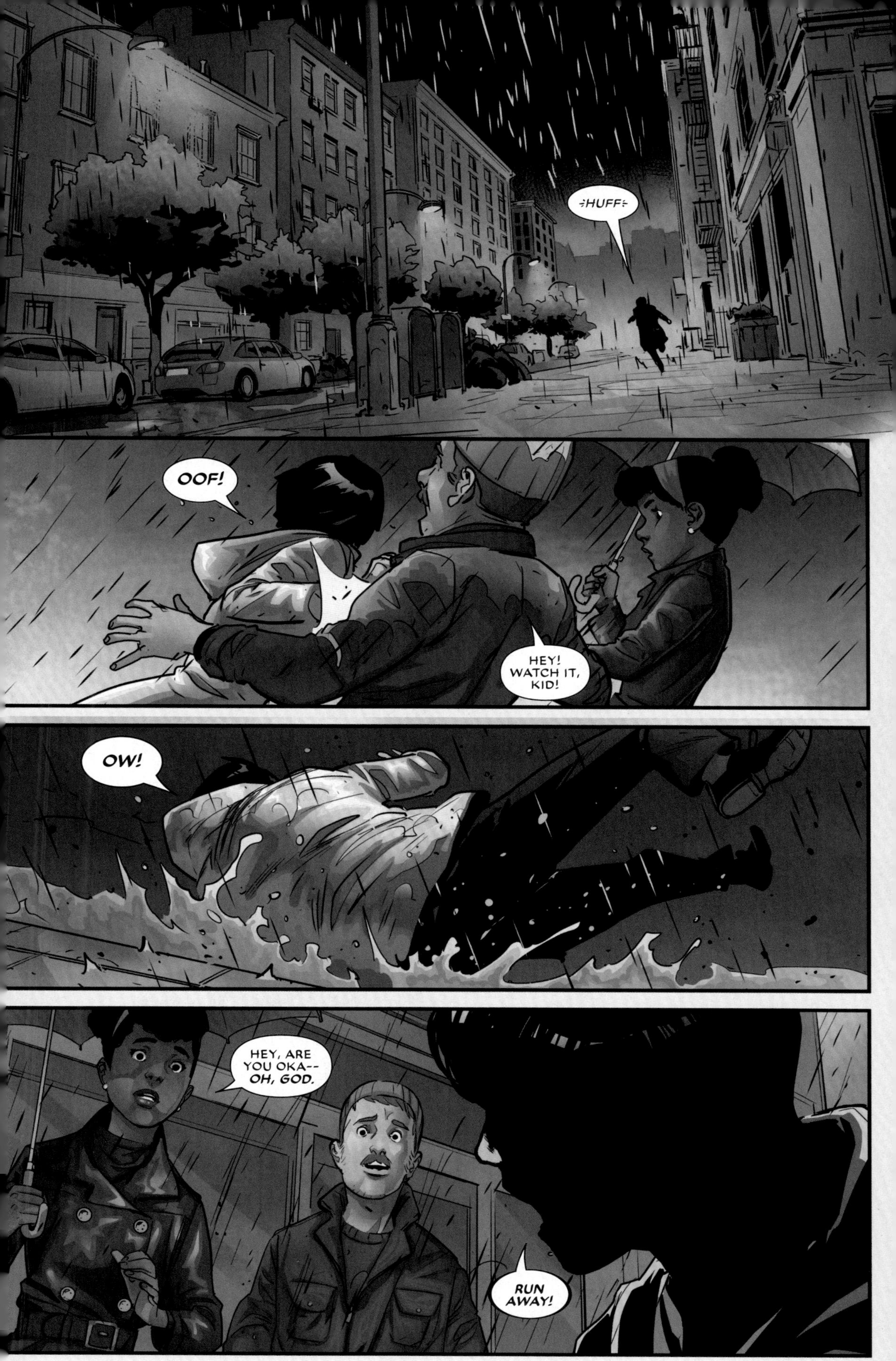
=HUFF=
OOF!
HEY! WATCH IT, KID!
OW!
HEY, ARE YOU OKA-- OH, GOD.
RUN AWAY!

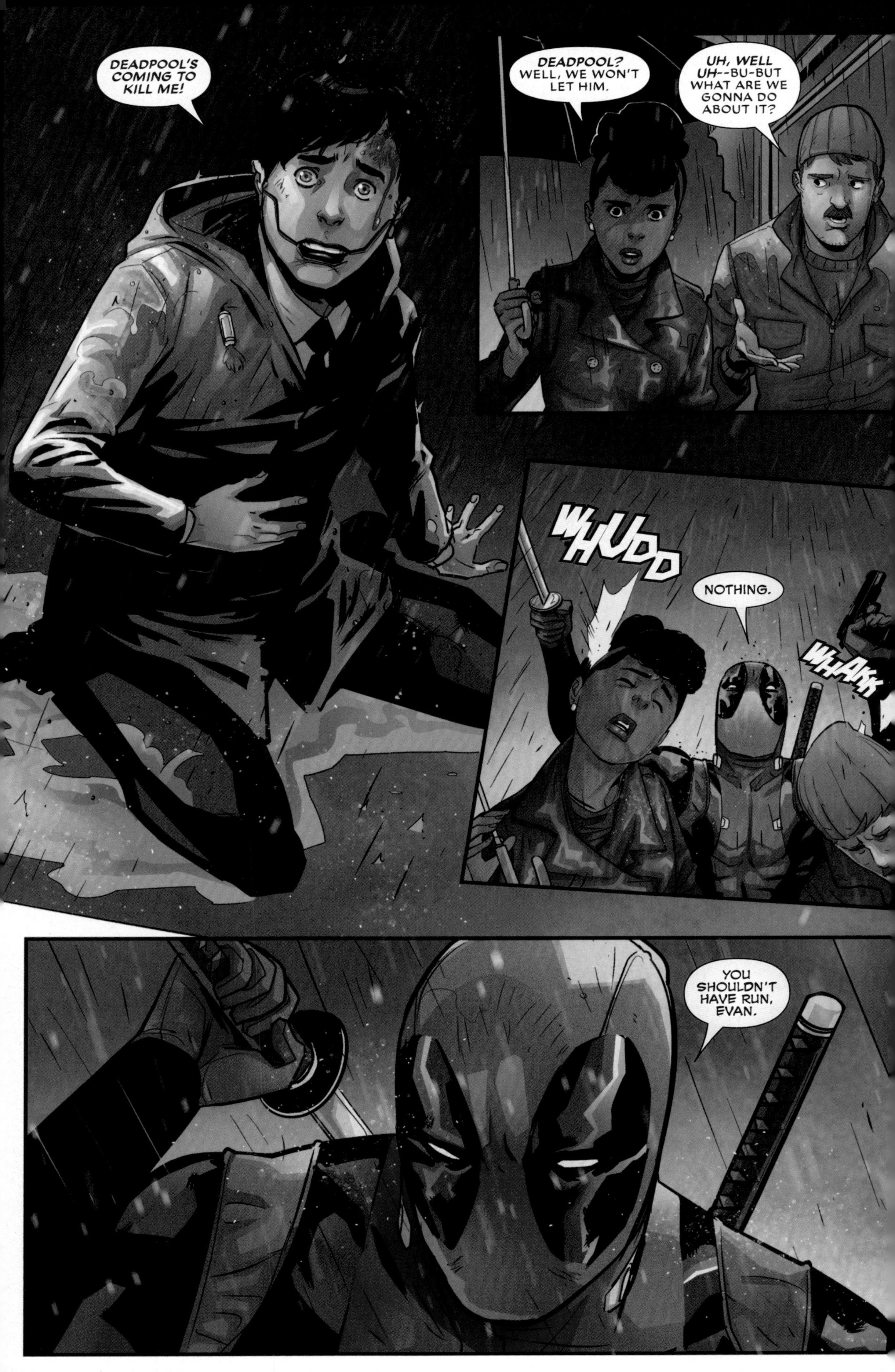
DEADPOOL'S COMING TO KILL ME!
DEADPOOL? WELL, WE WON'T LET HIM.
UH, WELL UH--BU-BUT WHAT ARE WE GONNA DO ABOUT IT?
WHUDD
NOTHING.
WHAKK
YOU SHOULDN'T HAVE RUN, EVAN.

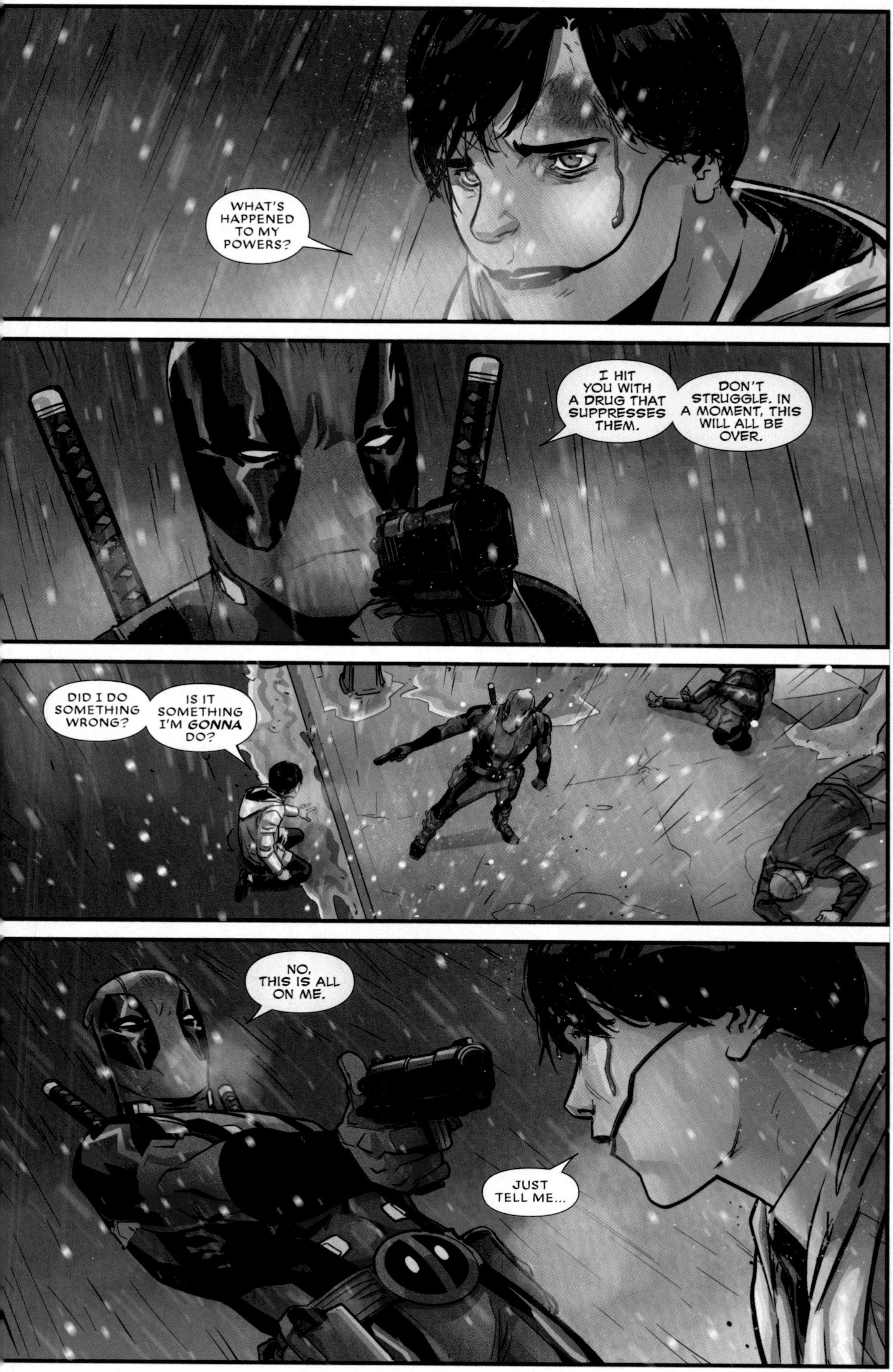
WHAT'S HAPPENED TO MY POWERS?
I HIT YOU WITH A DRUG THAT SUPPRESSES THEM.
DON'T STRUGGLE. IN A MOMENT, THIS WILL ALL BE OVER.
DID I DO SOMETHING WRONG?
IS IT SOMETHING I'M GONNA DO?
NO, THIS IS ALL ON ME.
JUST TELL ME...

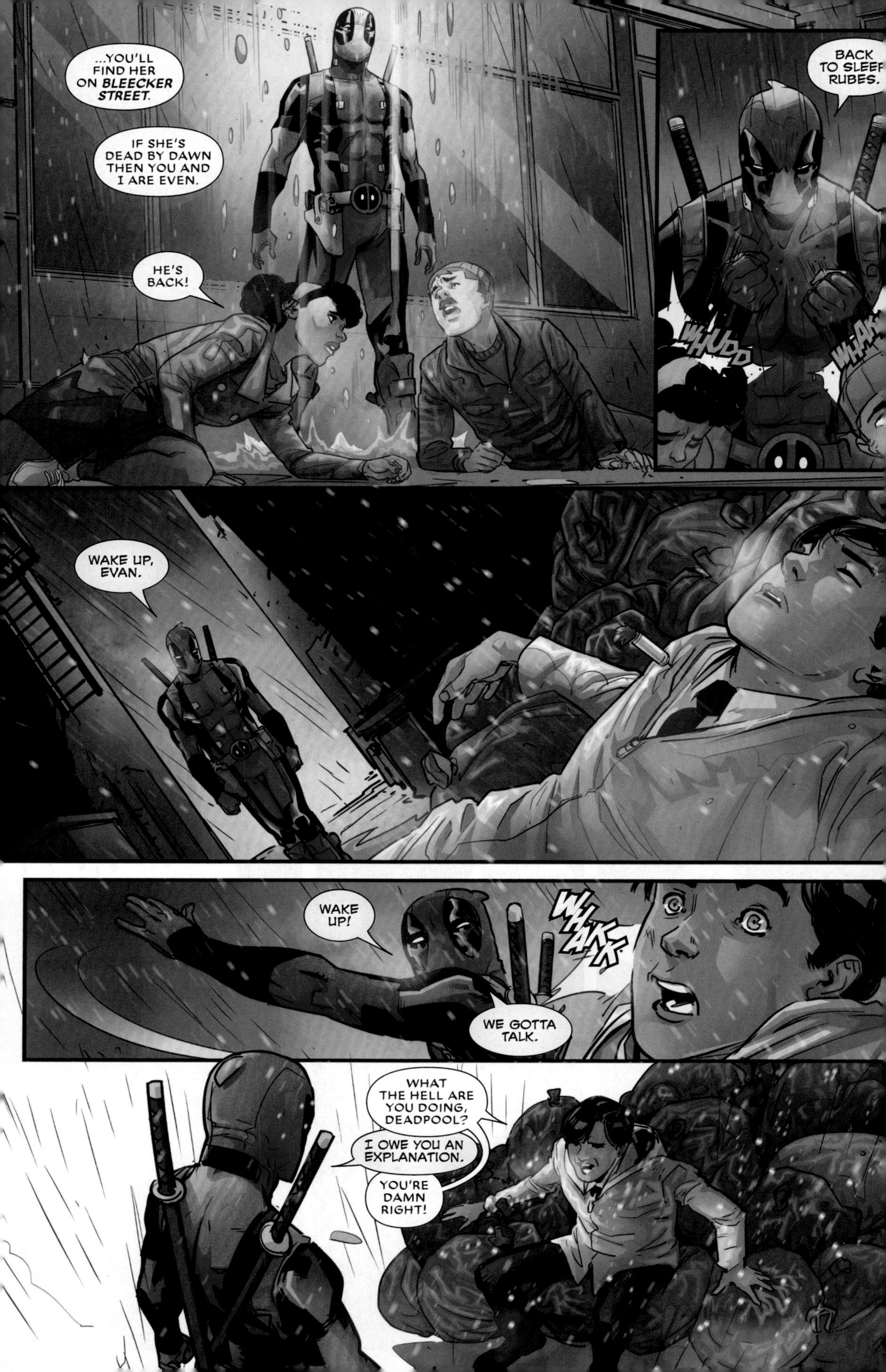

...YOU'LL FIND HER ON BLEECKER STREET.
IF SHE'S DEAD BY DAWN THEN YOU AND I ARE EVEN.
HE'S BACK!
BACK TO SLEEP RUBES.
WHUDD
WAKE UP, EVAN.
WAKE UP!
WHAKK
WE GOTTA TALK.
WHAT THE HELL ARE YOU DOING, DEADPOOL?
I OWE YOU AN EXPLANATION.
YOU'RE DAMN RIGHT!

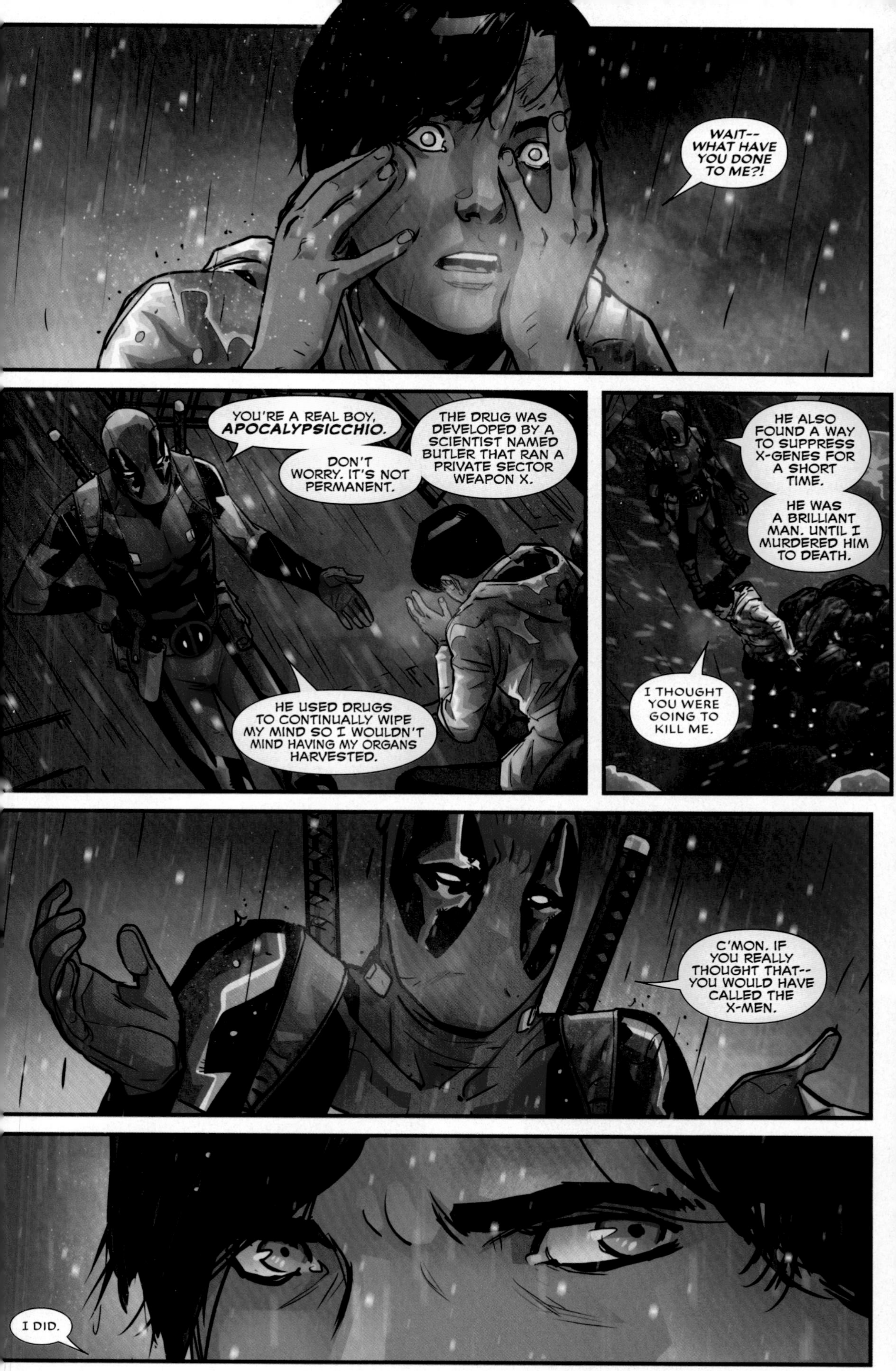

WAIT-- WHAT HAVE YOU DONE TO ME?!
YOU'RE A REAL BOY, APOCALYPSICCHIO.
DON'T WORRY. IT'S NOT PERMANENT.
THE DRUG WAS DEVELOPED BY A SCIENTIST NAMED BUTLER THAT RAN A PRIVATE SECTOR WEAPON X.
HE USED DRUGS TO CONTINUALLY WIPE MY MIND SO I WOULDN'T MIND HAVING MY ORGANS HARVESTED.
HE ALSO FOUND A WAY TO SUPPRESS X-GENES FOR A SHORT TIME.
HE WAS A BRILLIANT MAN. UNTIL I MURDERED HIM TO DEATH.
I THOUGHT YOU WERE GOING TO KILL ME.
C'MON. IF YOU REALLY THOUGHT THAT-- YOU WOULD HAVE CALLED THE X-MEN.
I DID.

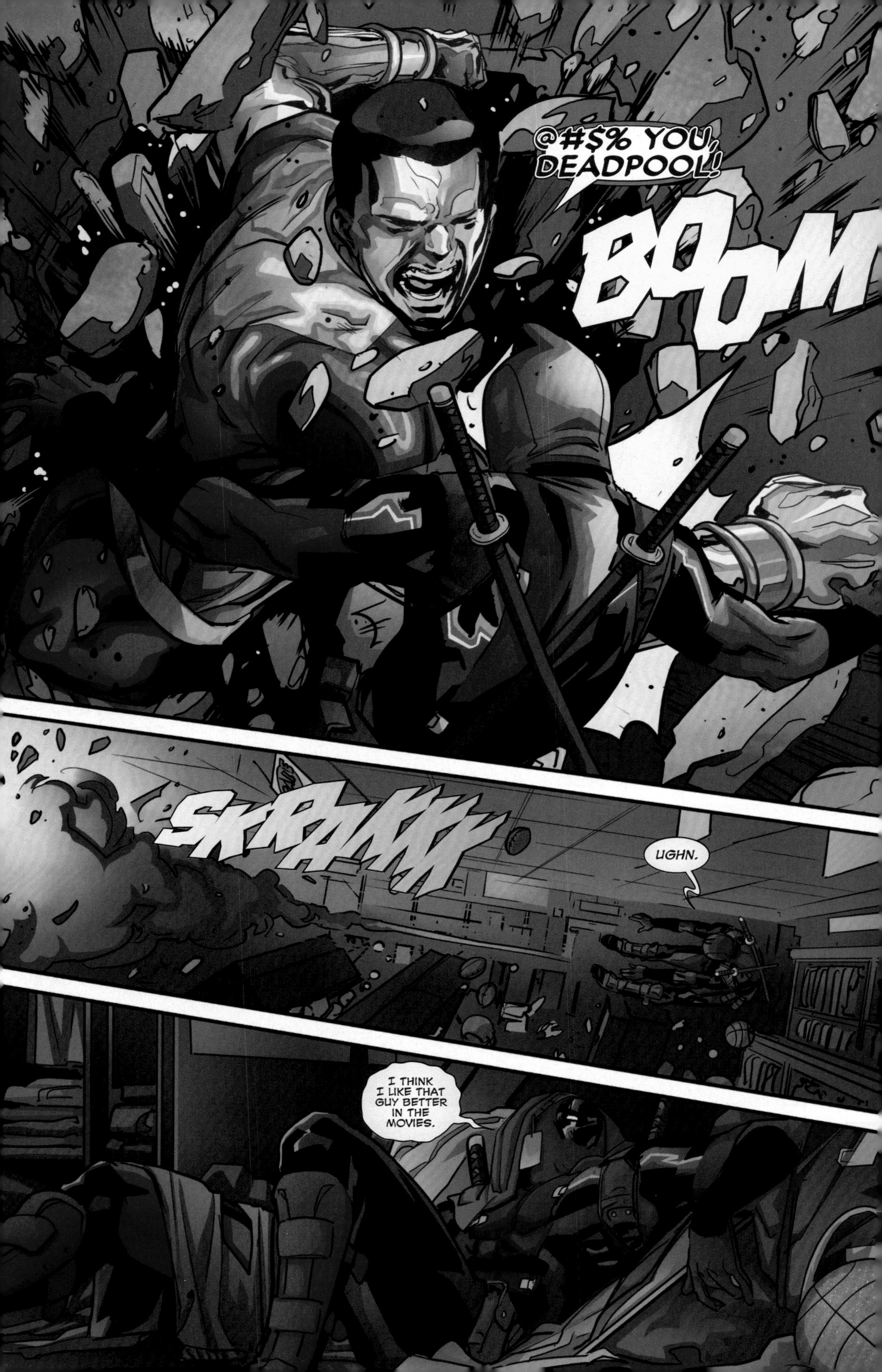

@#$% YOU, DEADPOOL!
BOOM
SKRAKKK
UGHN.
I THINK I LIKE THAT GUY BETTER IN THE MOVIES.

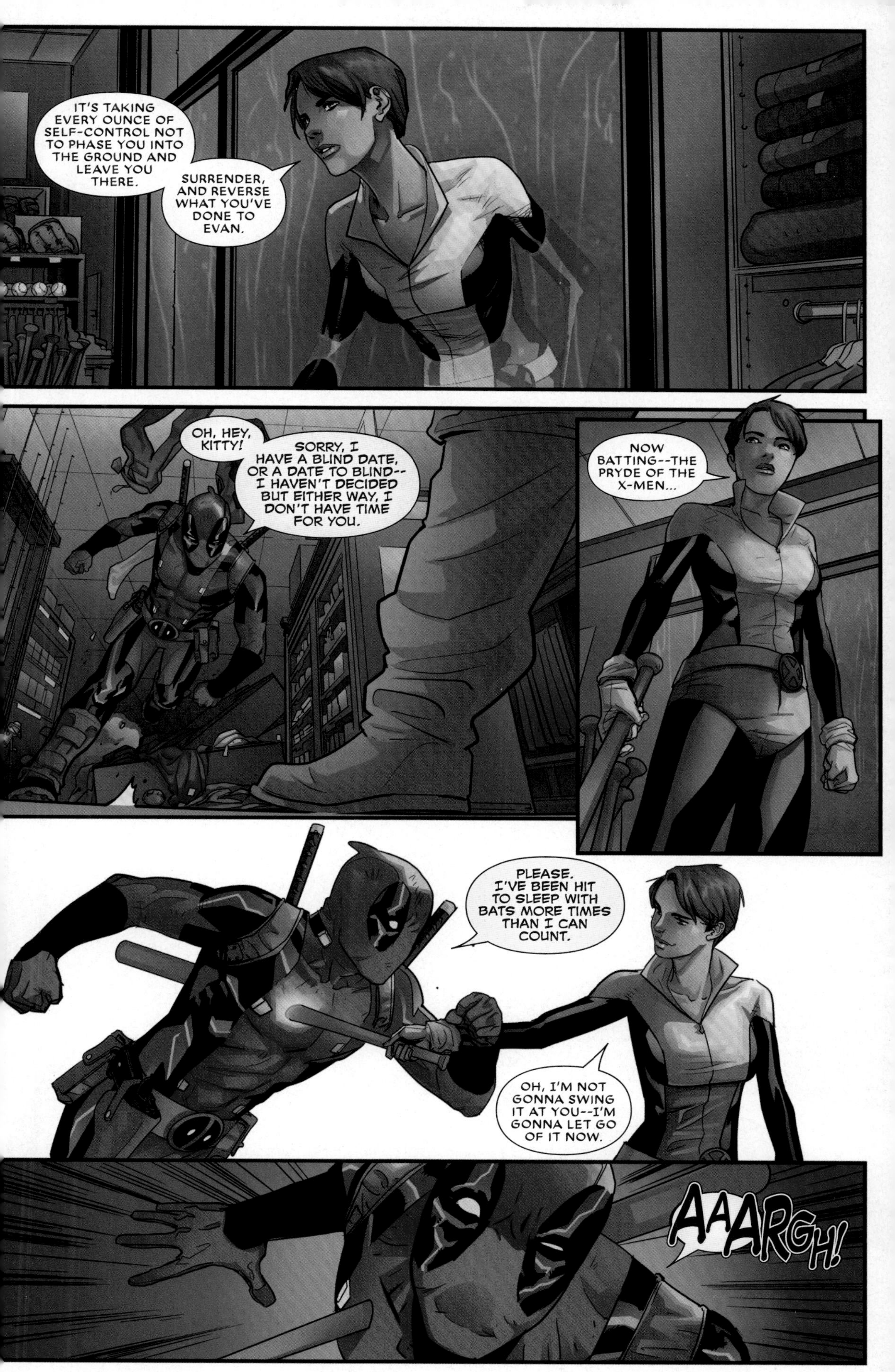
IT'S TAKING EVERY OUNCE OF SELF-CONTROL NOT TO PHASE YOU INTO THE GROUND AND LEAVE YOU THERE.
SURRENDER, AND REVERSE WHAT YOU'VE DONE TO EVAN.
OH, HEY, KITTY!
SORRY, I HAVE A BLIND DATE, OR A DATE TO BLIND-- I HAVEN'T DECIDED BUT EITHER WAY, I DON'T HAVE TIME FOR YOU.
NOW BATTING--THE PRYDE OF THE X-MEN...
PLEASE. I'VE BEEN HIT TO SLEEP WITH BATS MORE TIMES THAN I CAN COUNT.
OH, I'M NOT GONNA SWING IT AT YOU--I'M GONNA LET GO OF IT NOW.
AAARGH!

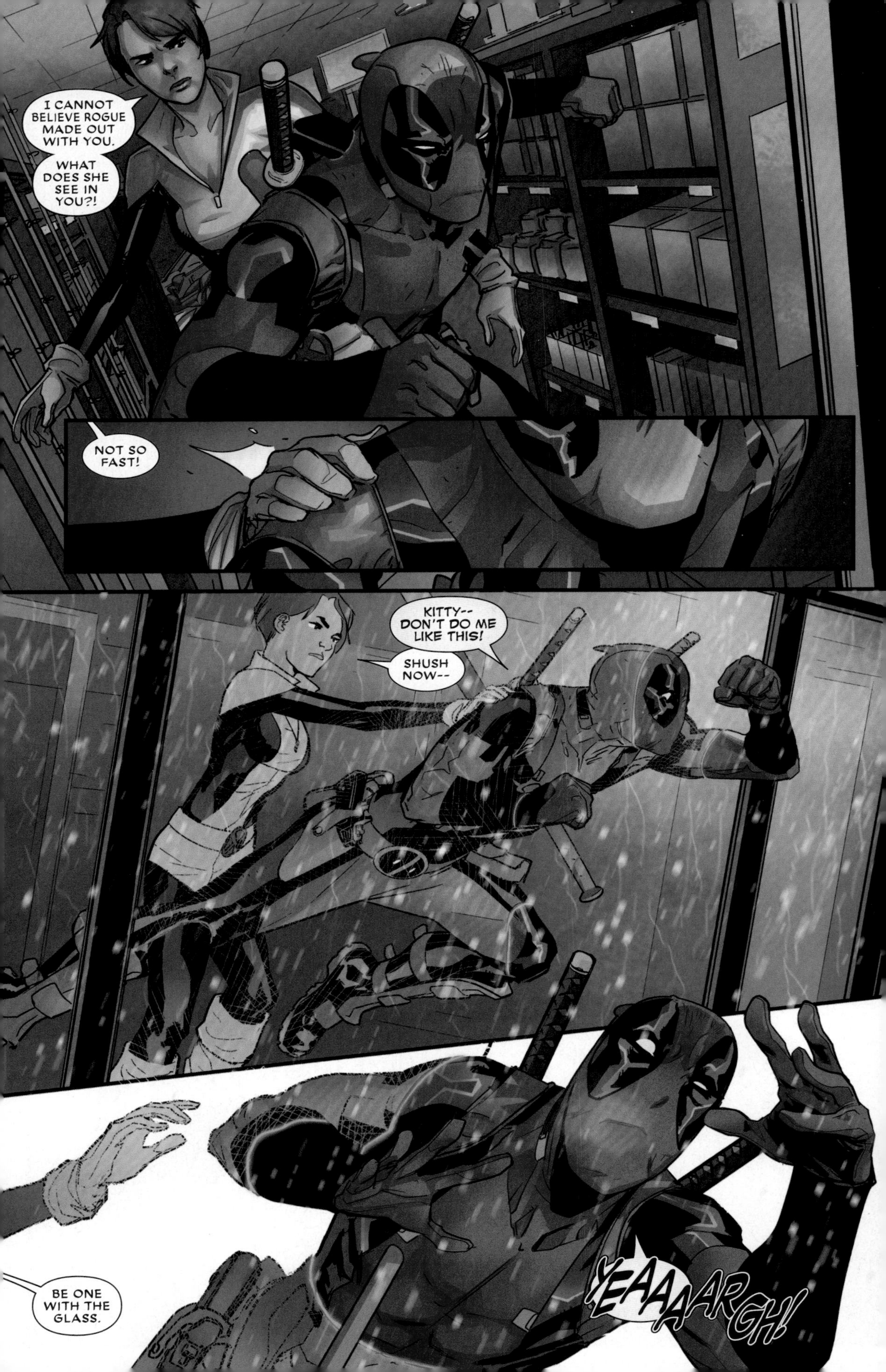
I CANNOT BELIEVE ROGUE MADE OUT WITH YOU.
WHAT DOES SHE SEE IN YOU?!
NOT SO FAST!
KITTY-- DON'T DO ME LIKE THIS!
SHUSH NOW--
BE ONE WITH THE GLASS.
YEAAAARGH!

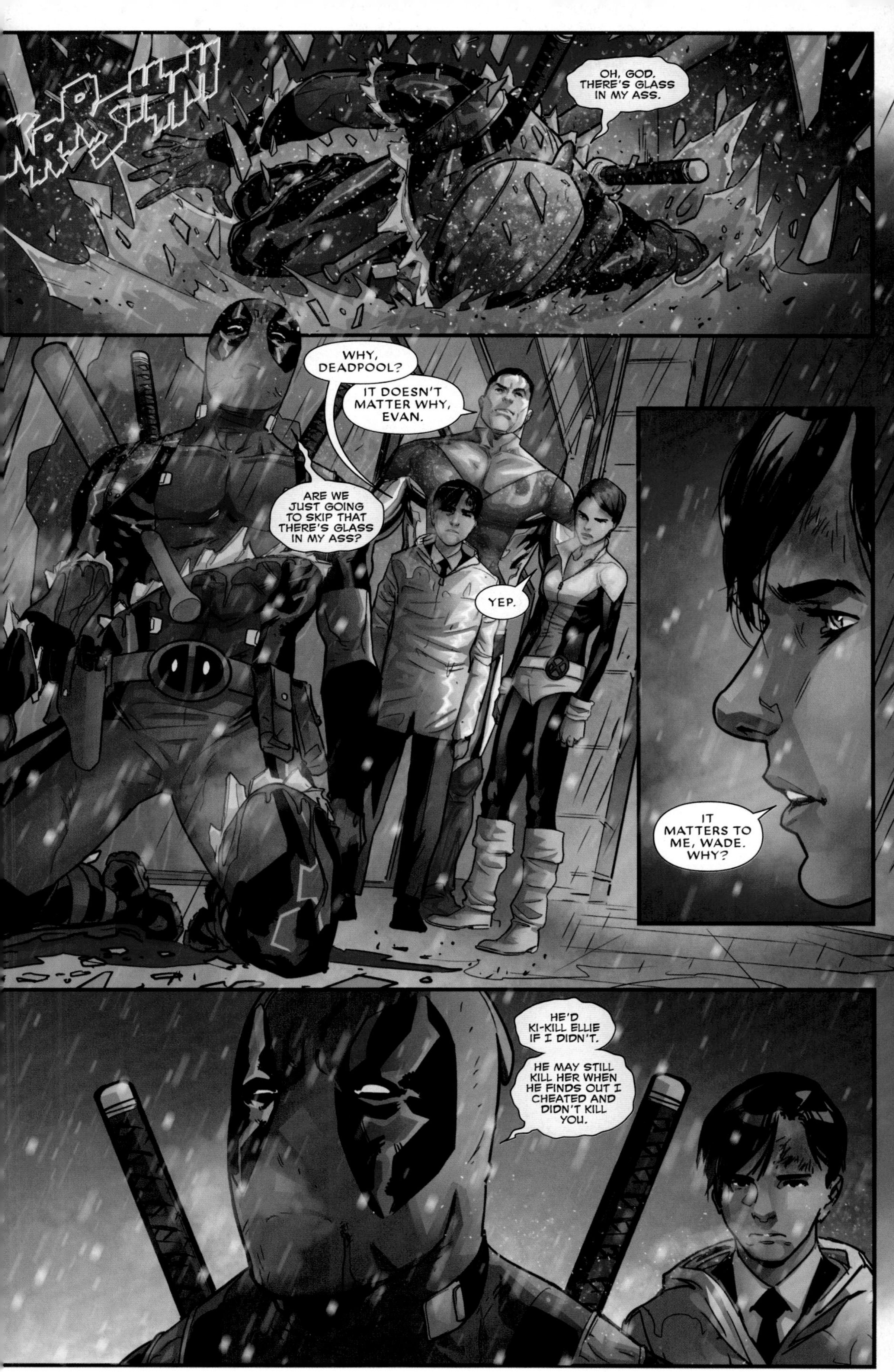

OH, GOD. THERE'S GLASS IN MY ASS.
WHY, DEADPOOL?
IT DOESN'T MATTER WHY, EVAN.
ARE WE JUST GOING TO SKIP THAT THERE'S GLASS IN MY ASS?
YEP.
IT MATTERS TO ME, WADE. WHY?
HE'D KI-KILL ELLIE IF I DIDN'T.
HE MAY STILL KILL HER WHEN HE FINDS OUT I CHEATED AND DIDN'T KILL YOU.

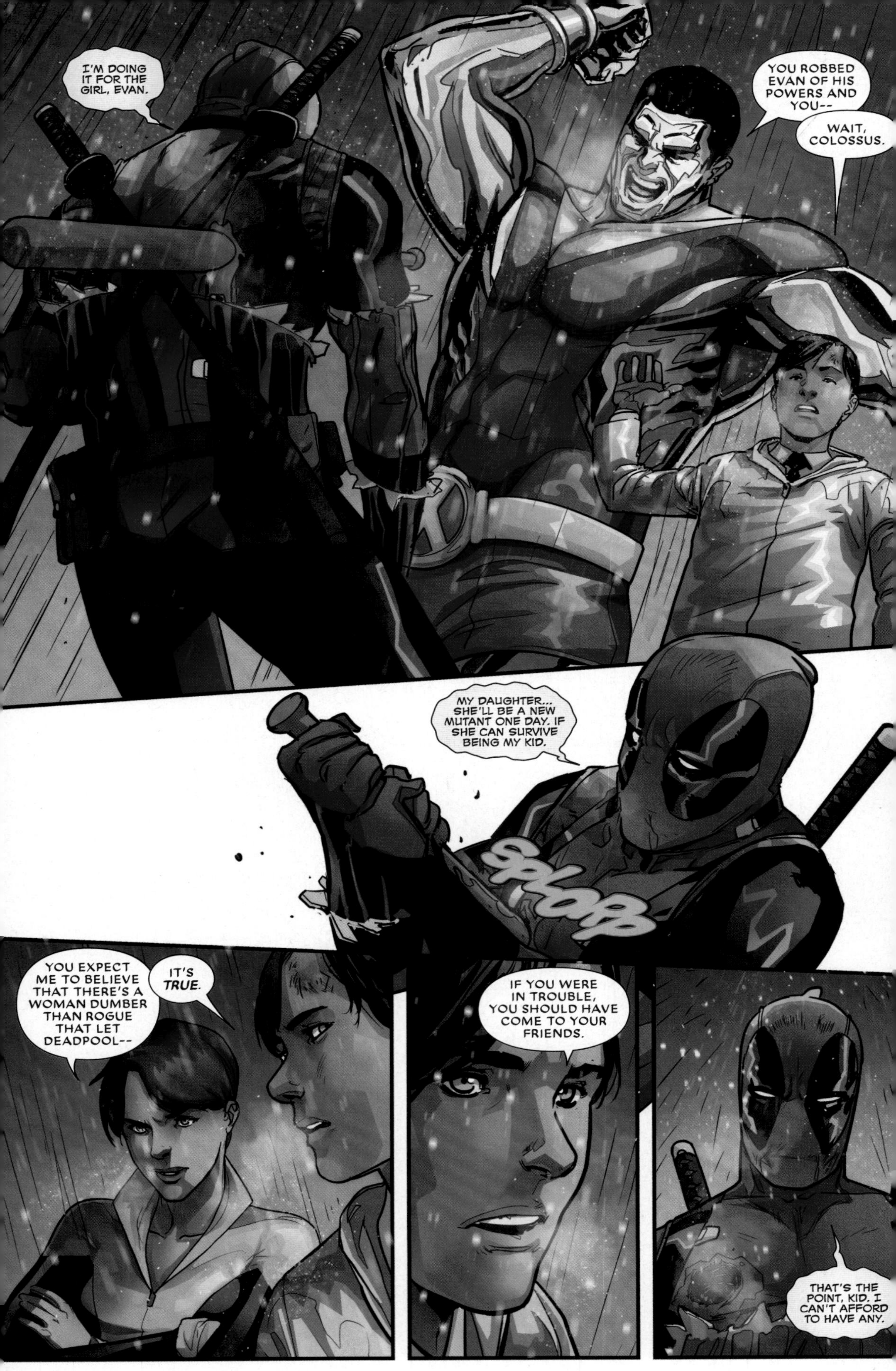
I'M DOING IT FOR THE GIRL, EVAN.
YOU ROBBED EVAN OF HIS POWERS AND YOU--
WAIT, COLOSSUS.
MY DAUGHTER... SHE'LL BE A NEW MUTANT ONE DAY. IF SHE CAN SURVIVE BEING MY KID.
SPLOP
YOU EXPECT ME TO BELIEVE THAT THERE'S A WOMAN DUMBER THAN ROGUE THAT LET DEADPOOL--
IT'S *TRUE*.
IF YOU WERE IN TROUBLE, YOU SHOULD HAVE COME TO YOUR FRIENDS.
THAT'S THE POINT, KID. I CAN'T AFFORD TO HAVE ANY.

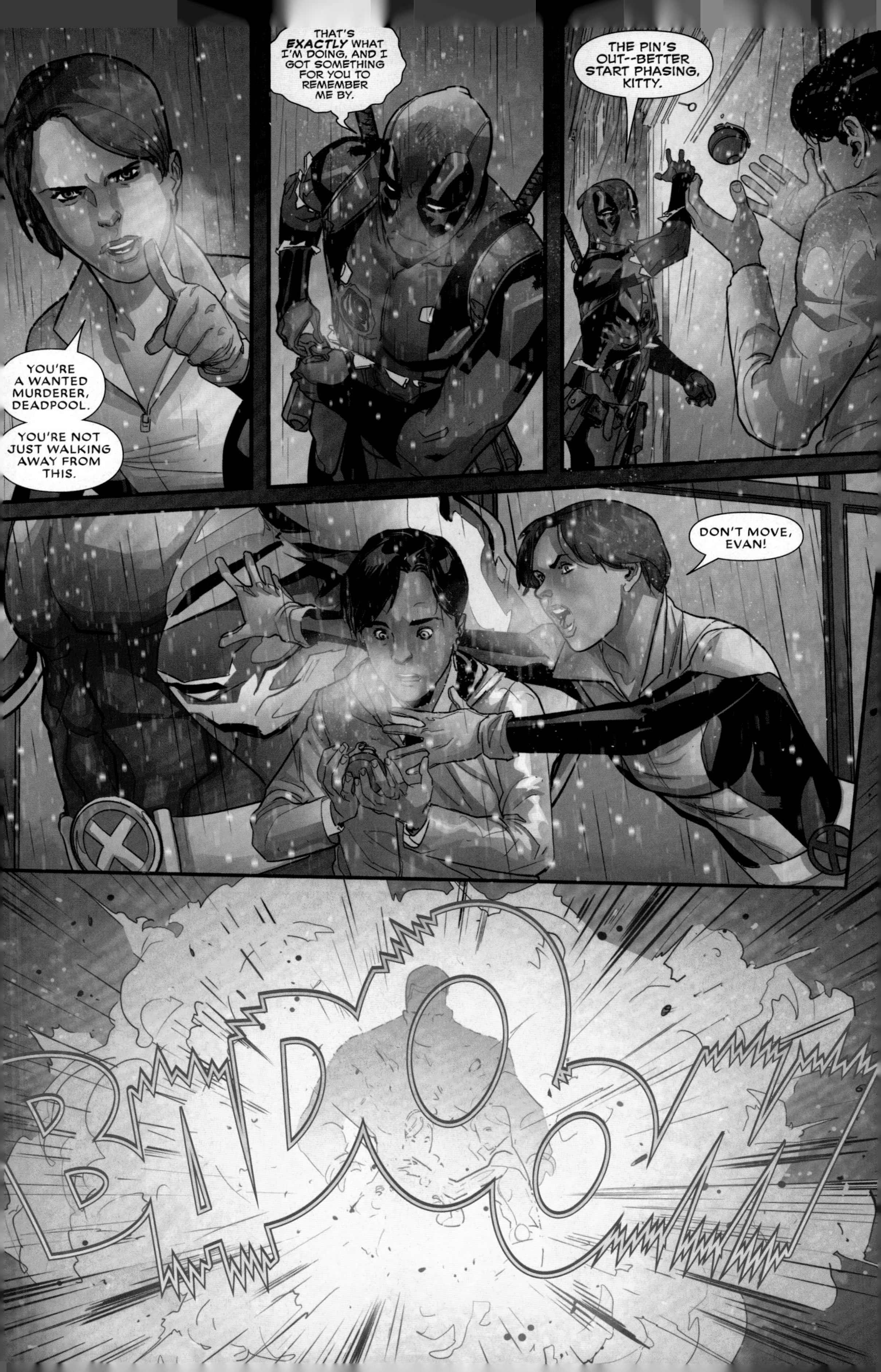
YOU'RE A WANTED MURDERER, DEADPOOL.
YOU'RE NOT JUST WALKING AWAY FROM THIS.
THAT'S EXACTLY WHAT I'M DOING, AND I GOT SOMETHING FOR YOU TO REMEMBER ME BY.
THE PIN'S OUT--BETTER START PHASING, KITTY.
DON'T MOVE, EVAN!
BBDOOM!

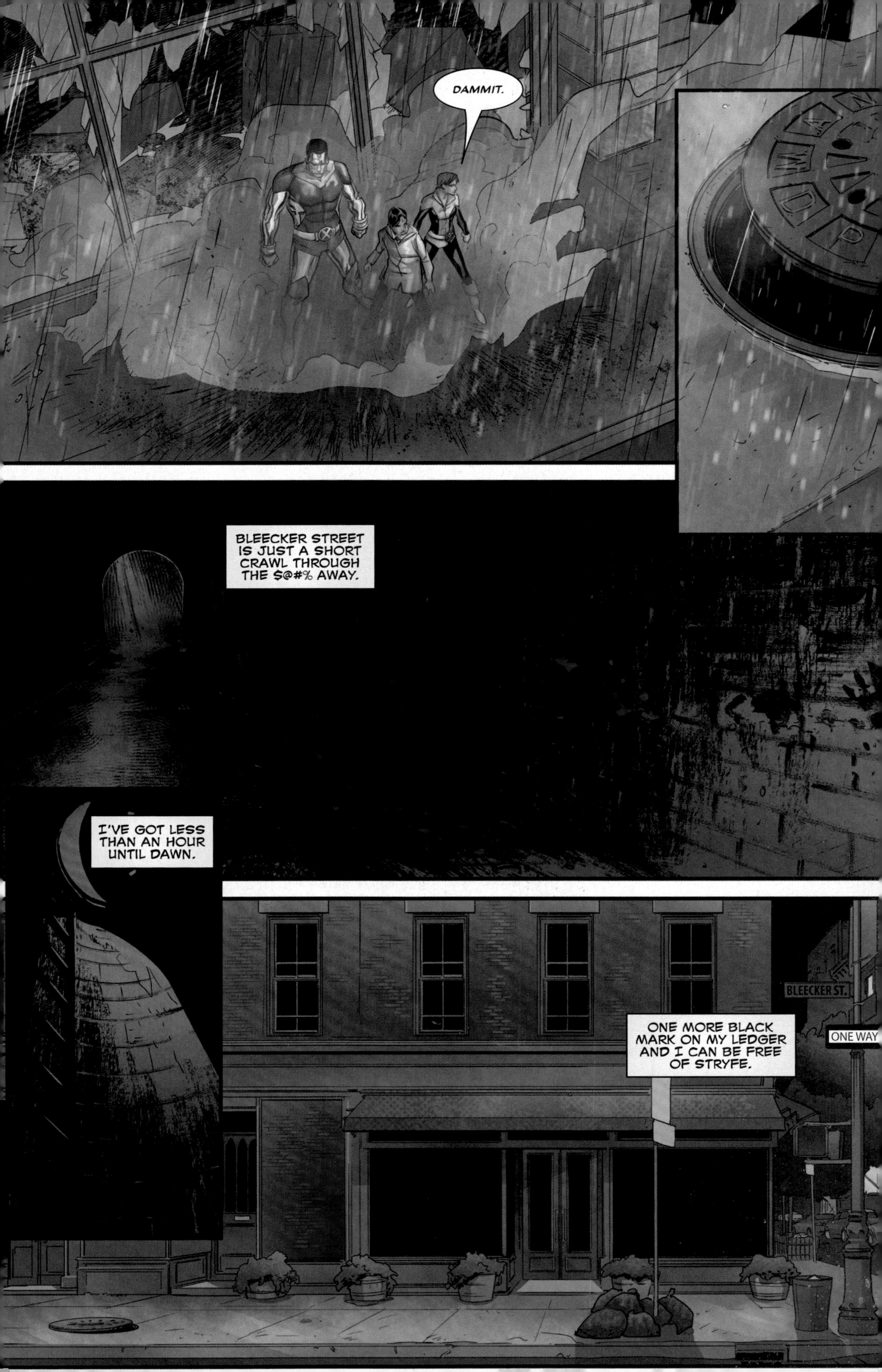
DAMMIT.
BLEECKER STREET IS JUST A SHORT CRAWL THROUGH THE $@#% AWAY.
I'VE GOT LESS THAN AN HOUR UNTIL DAWN.
BLEECKER ST.
ONE WAY
ONE MORE BLACK MARK ON MY LEDGER AND I CAN BE FREE OF STRYFE.

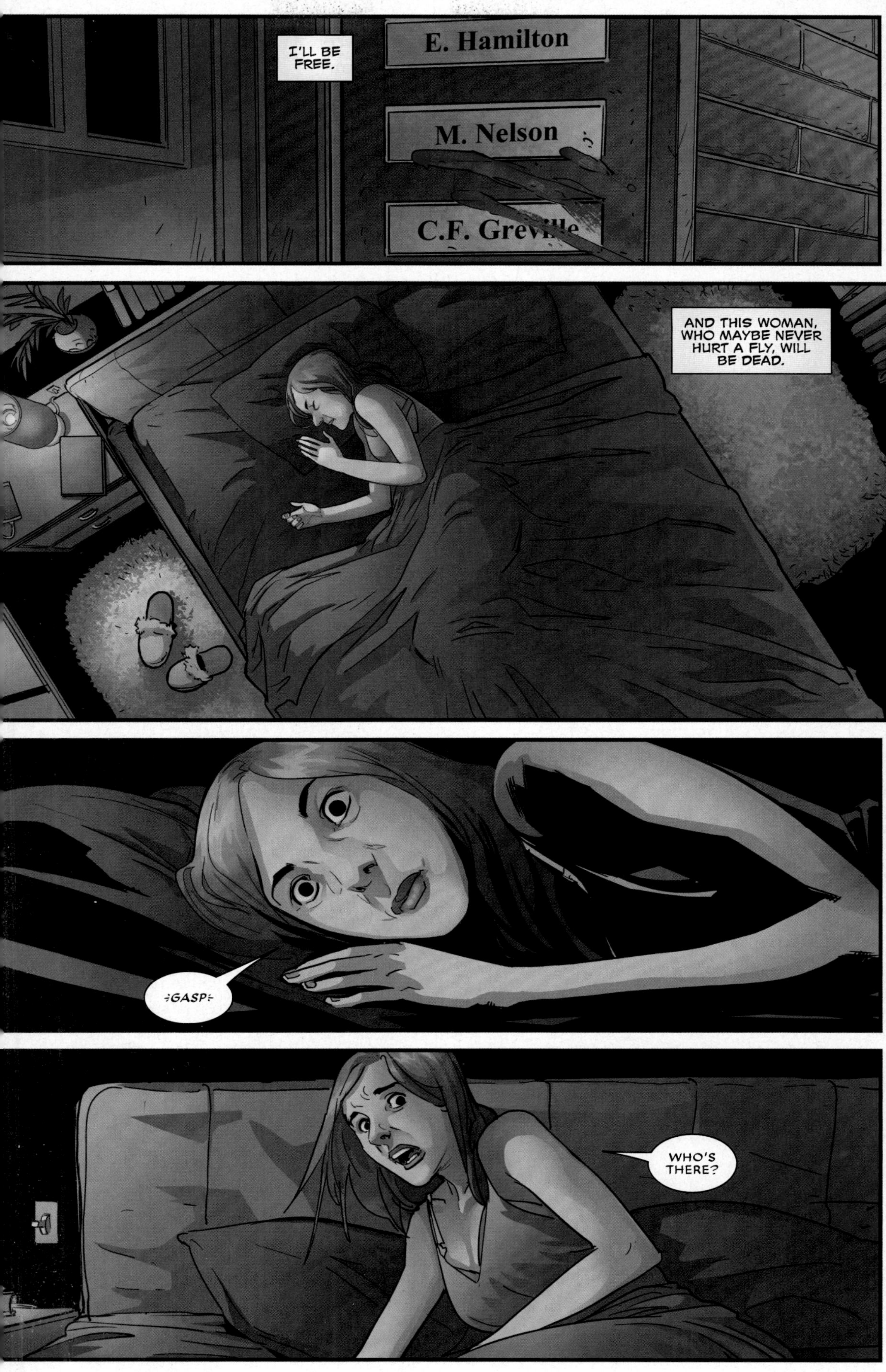
E. Hamilton
M. Nelson
C.F. Greville
I'LL BE FREE.
AND THIS WOMAN, WHO MAYBE NEVER HURT A FLY, WILL BE DEAD.
GASP
WHO'S THERE?

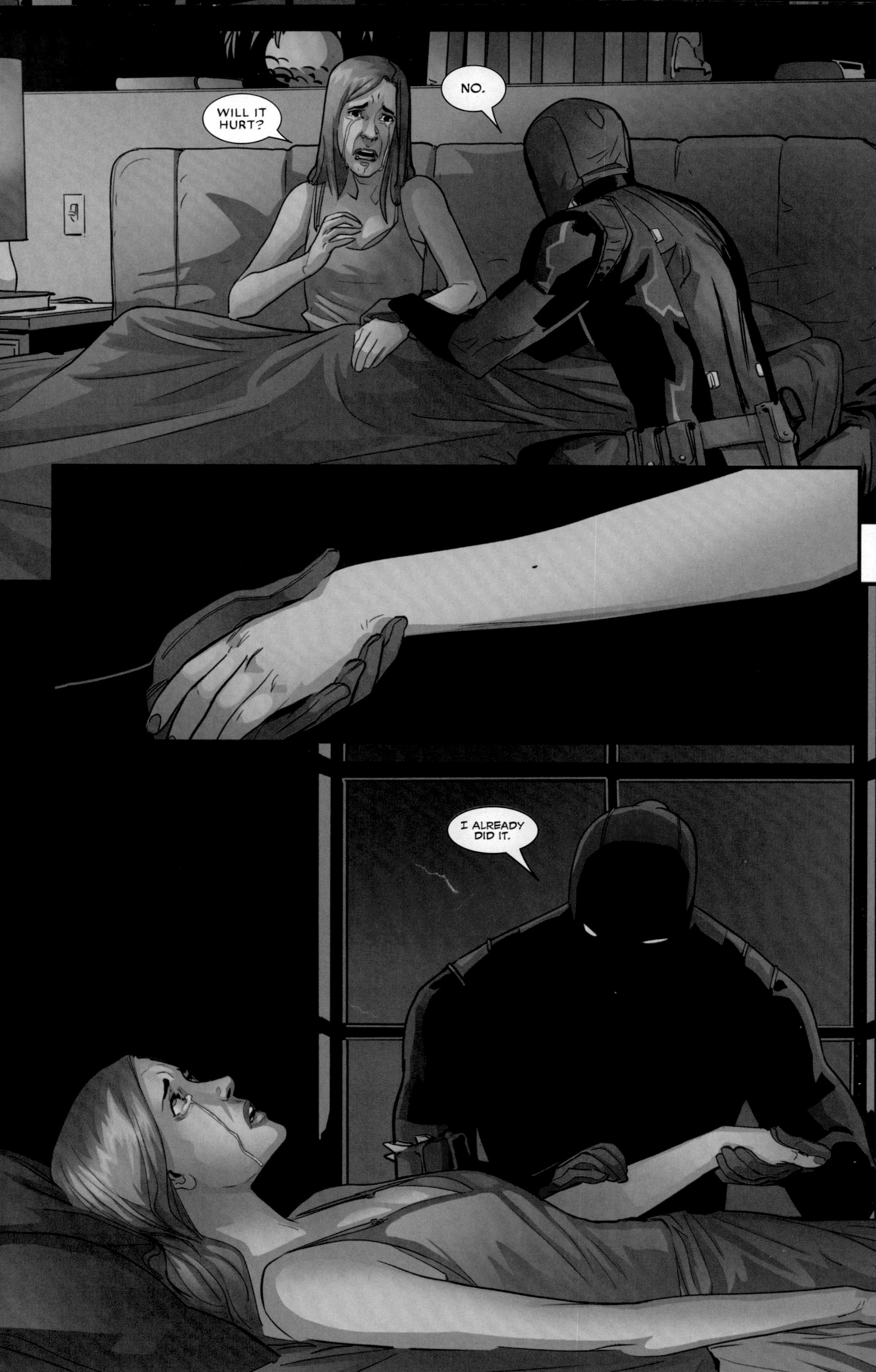
WILL IT HURT?
NO.
I ALREADY DID IT.

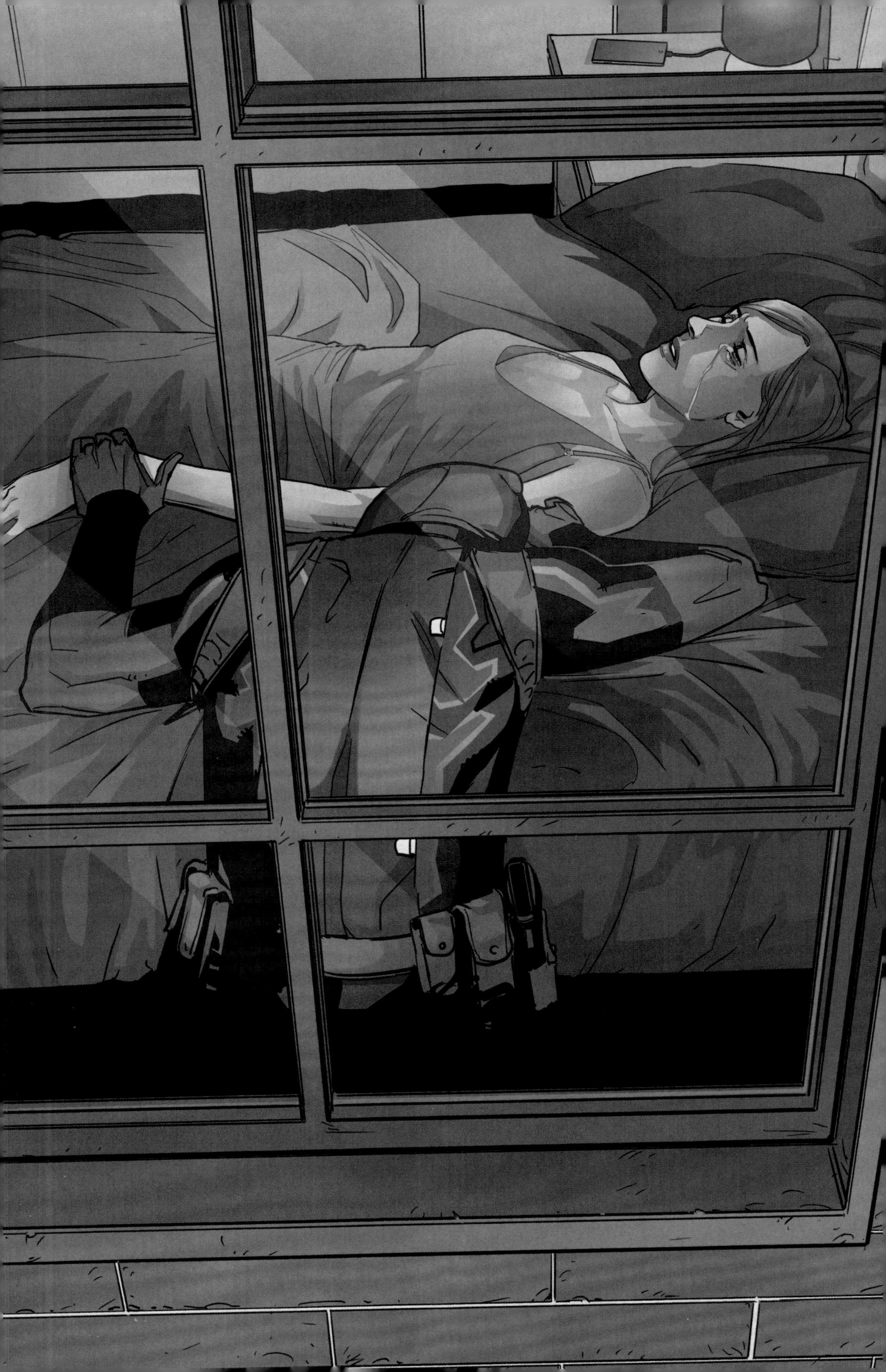

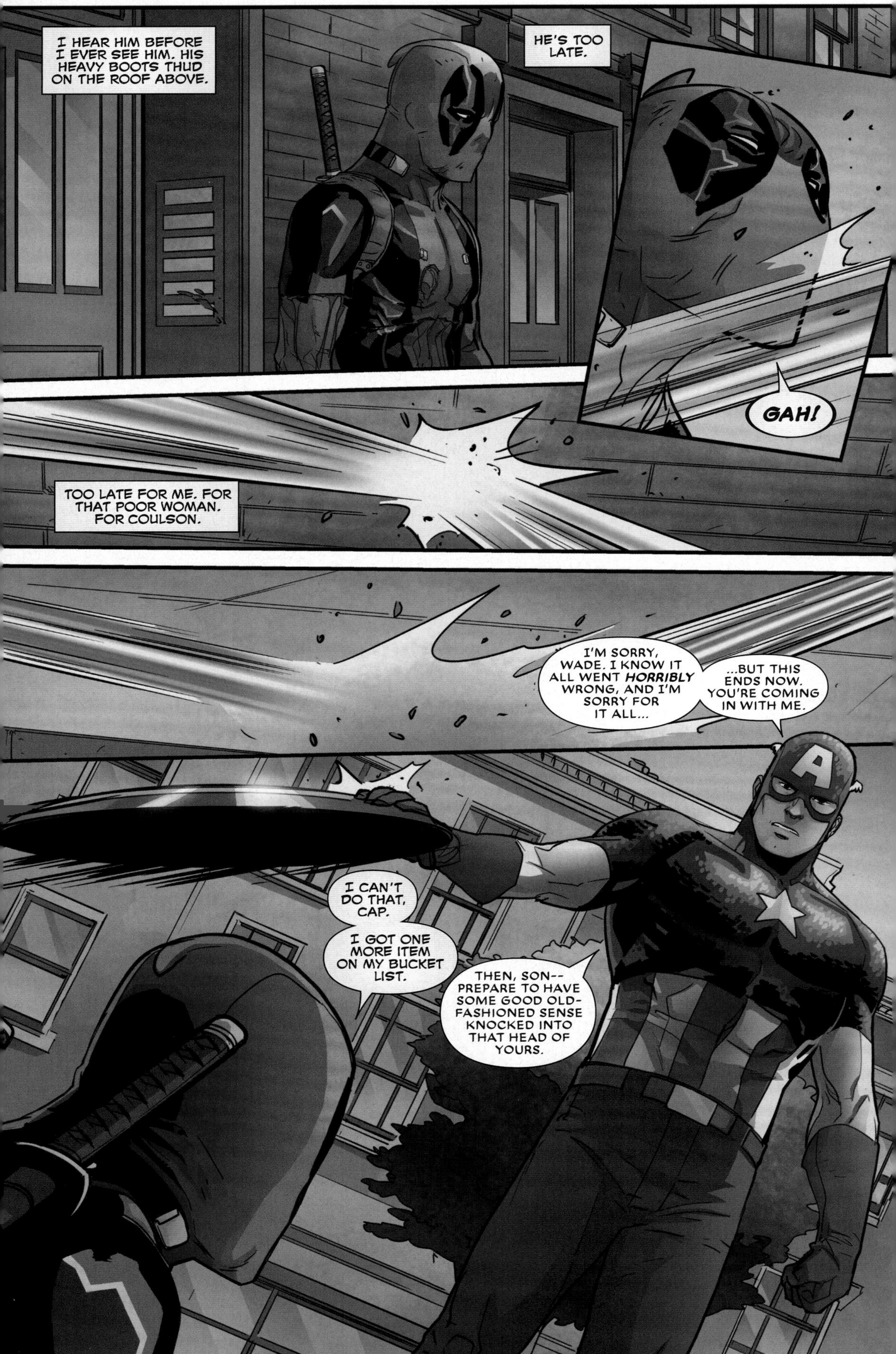
I HEAR HIM BEFORE I EVER SEE HIM. HIS HEAVY BOOTS THUD ON THE ROOF ABOVE.
HE'S TOO LATE.
GAH!
TOO LATE FOR ME. FOR THAT POOR WOMAN. FOR COULSON.
I'M SORRY, WADE. I KNOW IT ALL WENT HORRIBLY WRONG, AND I'M SORRY FOR IT ALL...
...BUT THIS ENDS NOW. YOU'RE COMING IN WITH ME.
I CAN'T DO THAT, CAP.
I GOT ONE MORE ITEM ON MY BUCKET LIST.
THEN, SON--PREPARE TO HAVE SOME GOOD OLD-FASHIONED SENSE KNOCKED INTO THAT HEAD OF YOURS.

296 – Part Five: "Steve & Wade & Kicking & Punching"

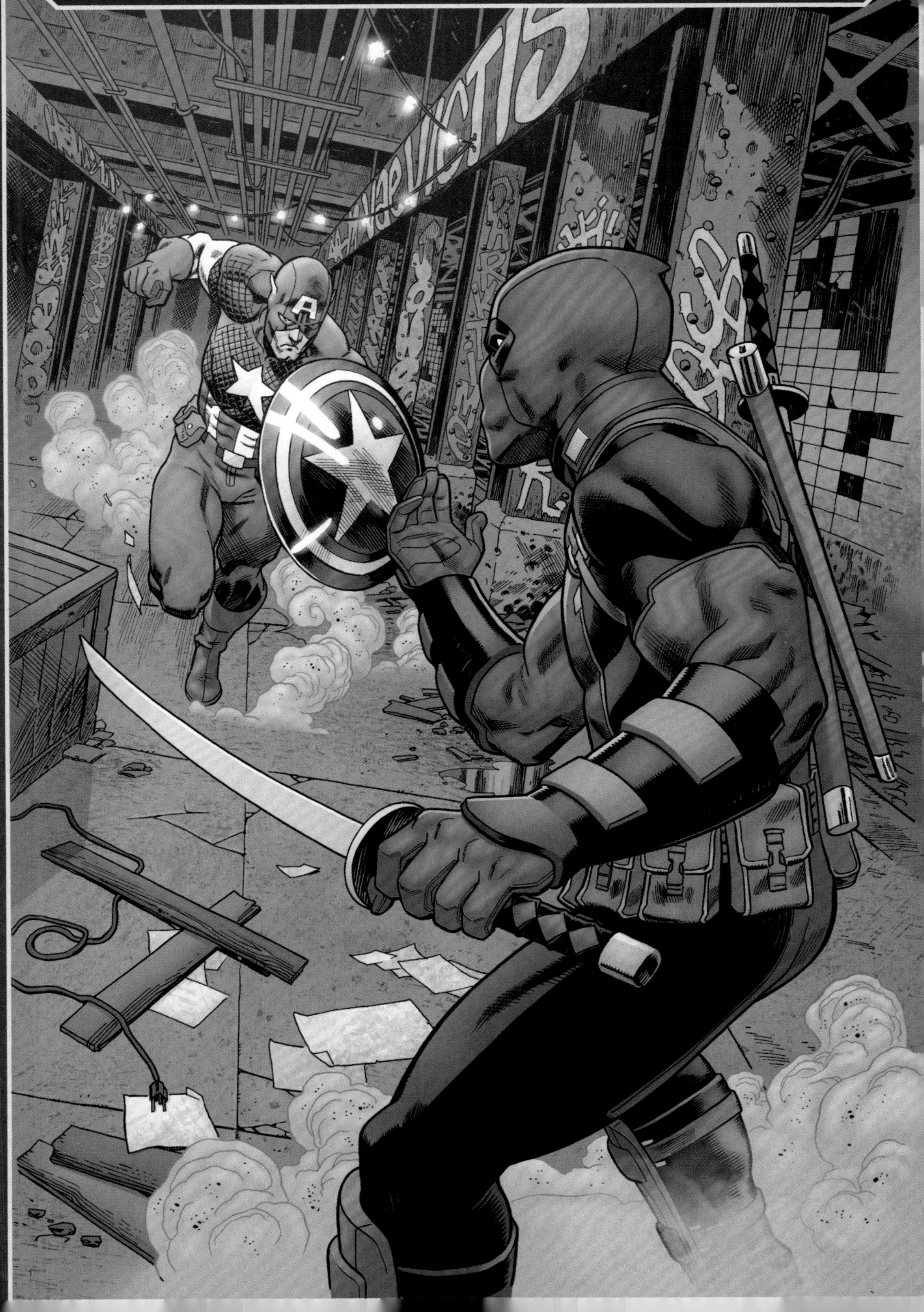
VICTIS

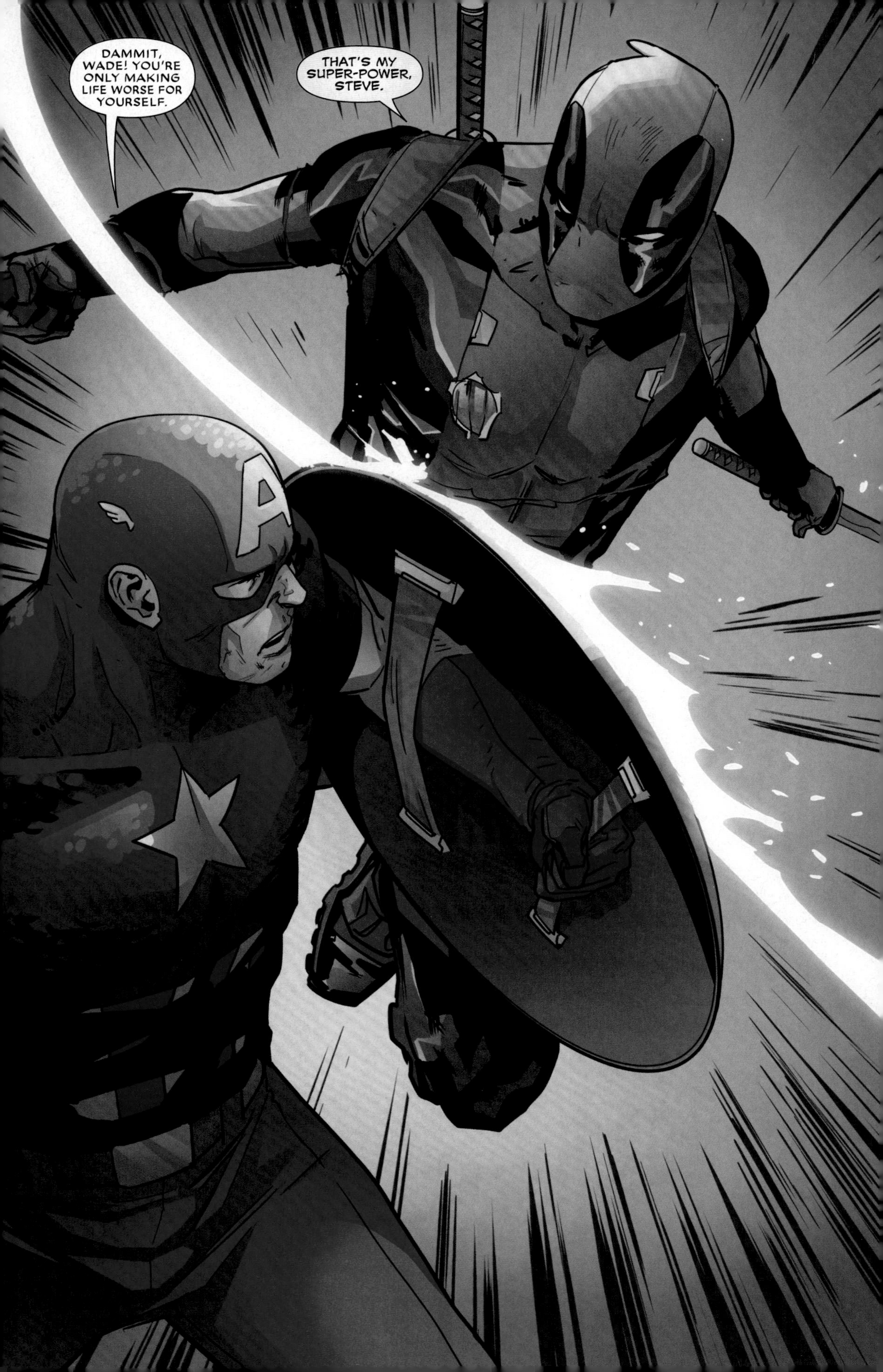
DAMMIT, WADE! YOU'RE ONLY MAKING LIFE WORSE FOR YOURSELF.
THAT'S MY SUPER-POWER, STEVE.

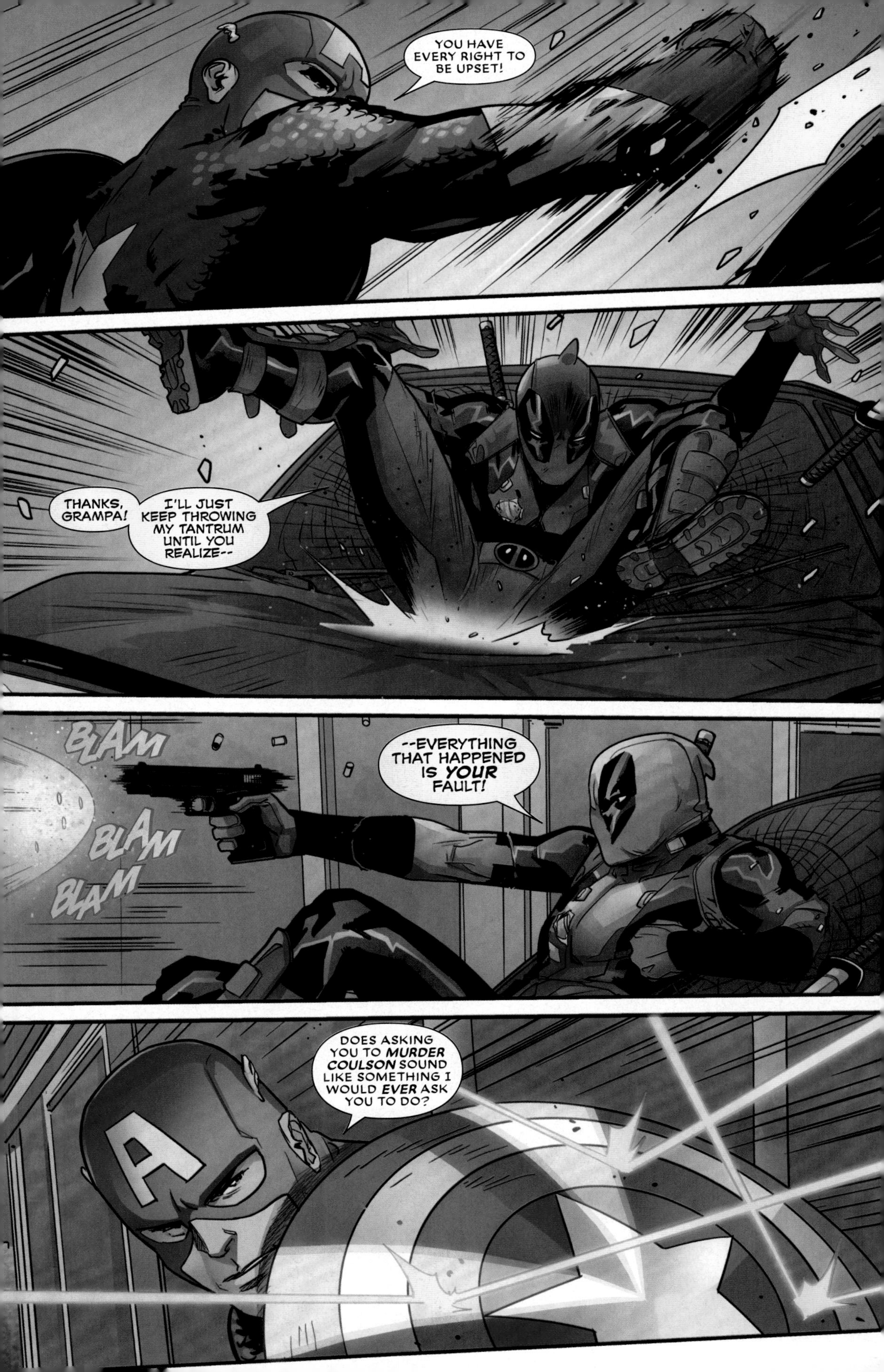
YOU HAVE EVERY RIGHT TO BE UPSET!
THANKS, GRAMPA!
I'LL JUST KEEP THROWING MY TANTRUM UNTIL YOU REALIZE--
BLAM
BLAM
BLAM
--EVERYTHING THAT HAPPENED IS YOUR FAULT!
DOES ASKING YOU TO MURDER COULSON SOUND LIKE SOMETHING I WOULD EVER ASK YOU TO DO?

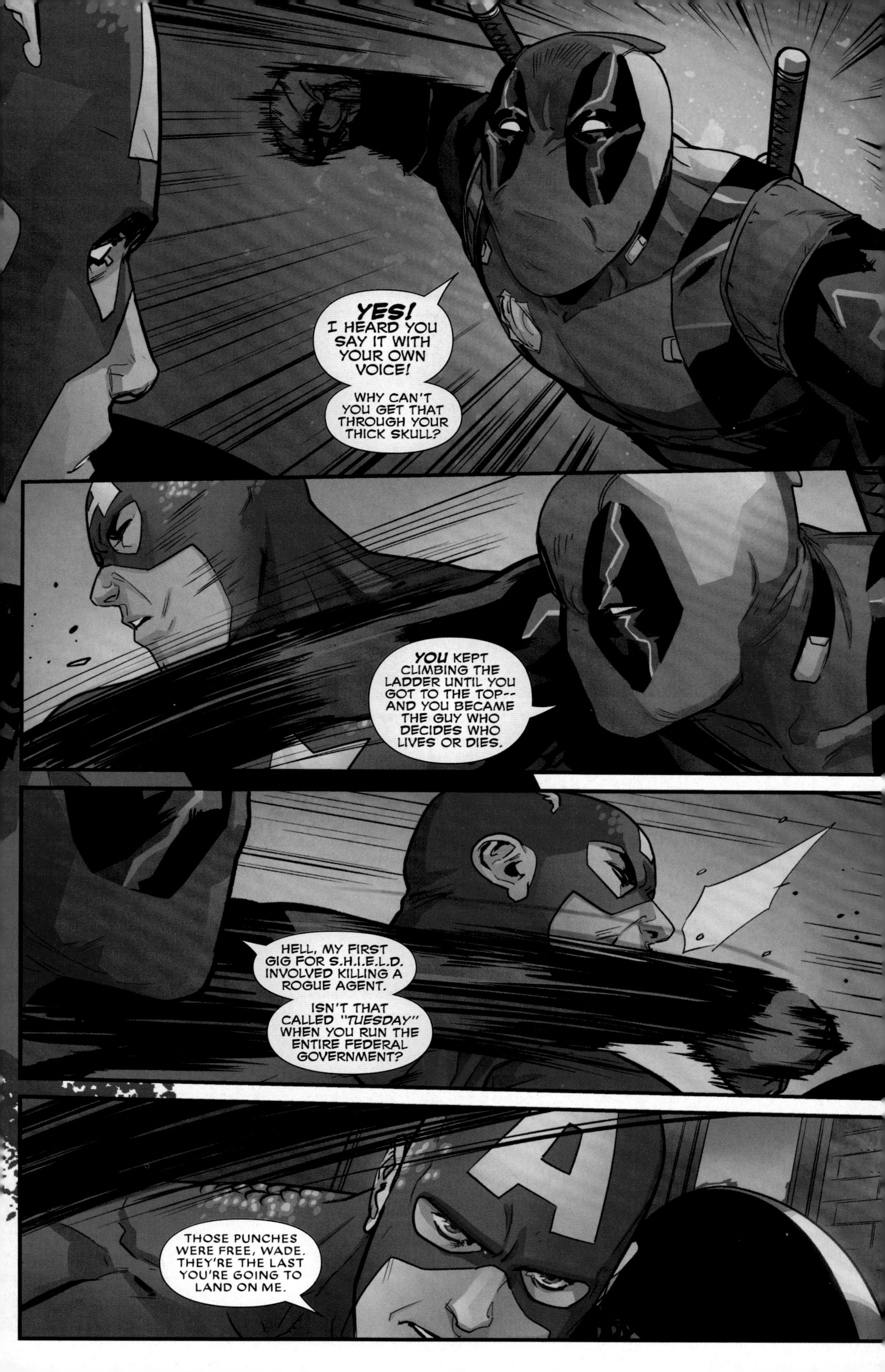
YES! I HEARD YOU SAY IT WITH YOUR OWN VOICE!
WHY CAN'T YOU GET THAT THROUGH YOUR THICK SKULL?
YOU KEPT CLIMBING THE LADDER UNTIL YOU GOT TO THE TOP-- AND YOU BECAME THE GUY WHO DECIDES WHO LIVES OR DIES.
HELL, MY FIRST GIG FOR S.H.I.E.L.D. INVOLVED KILLING A ROGUE AGENT.
ISN'T THAT CALLED "TUESDAY" WHEN YOU RUN THE ENTIRE FEDERAL GOVERNMENT?
THOSE PUNCHES WERE FREE, WADE. THEY'RE THE LAST YOU'RE GOING TO LAND ON ME.

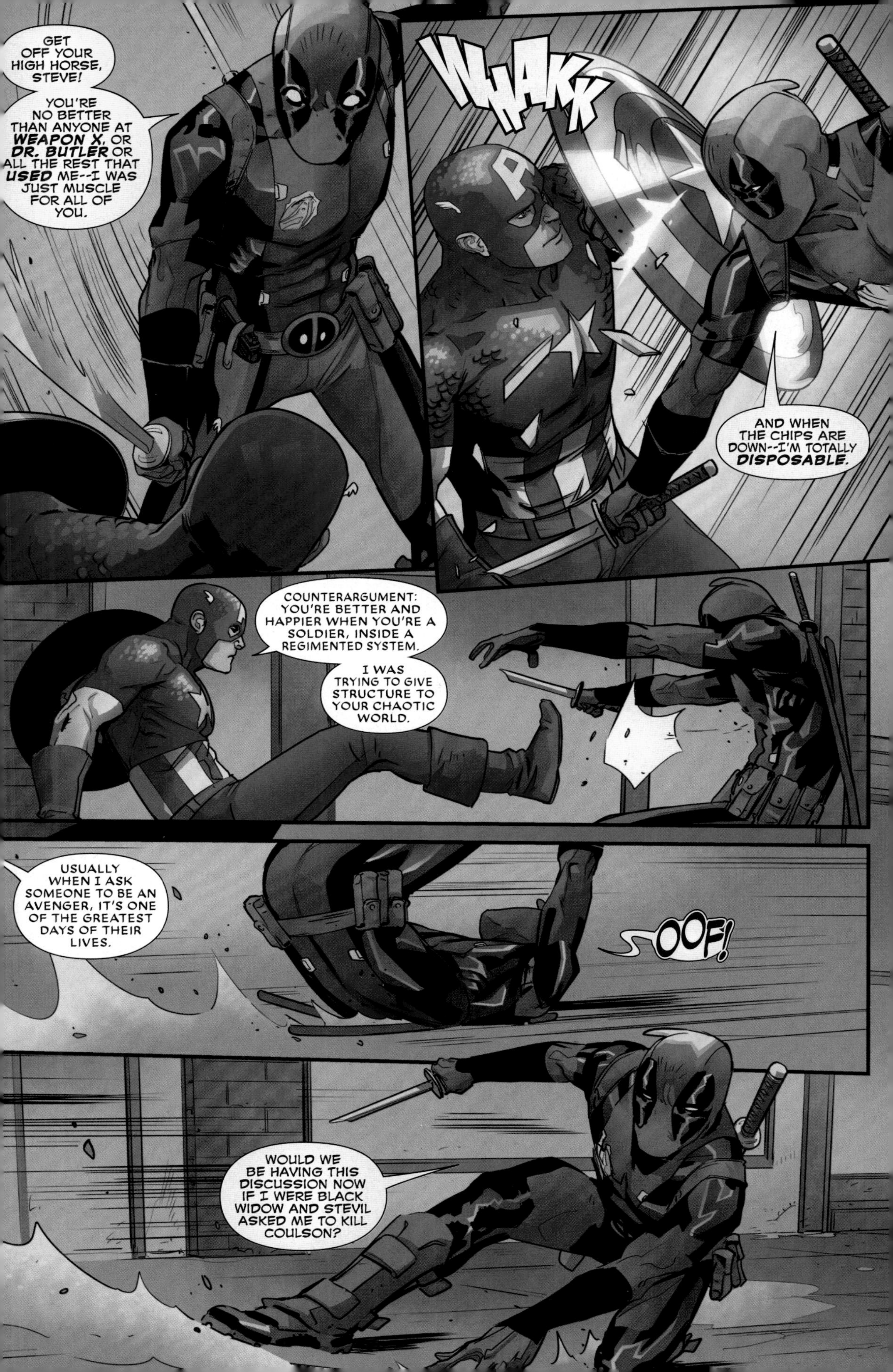

GET OFF YOUR HIGH HORSE, STEVE!
YOU'RE NO BETTER THAN ANYONE AT **WEAPON X**, OR **DR. BUTLER** OR ALL THE REST THAT **USED** ME--I WAS JUST MUSCLE FOR ALL OF YOU.
WHAKK
AND WHEN THE CHIPS ARE DOWN--I'M TOTALLY **DISPOSABLE.**
COUNTERARGUMENT: YOU'RE BETTER AND HAPPIER WHEN YOU'RE A SOLDIER, INSIDE A REGIMENTED SYSTEM.
I WAS TRYING TO GIVE STRUCTURE TO YOUR CHAOTIC WORLD.
USUALLY WHEN I ASK SOMEONE TO BE AN AVENGER, IT'S ONE OF THE GREATEST DAYS OF THEIR LIVES.
OOF!
WOULD WE BE HAVING THIS DISCUSSION NOW IF I WERE BLACK WIDOW AND STEVIL ASKED ME TO KILL COULSON?

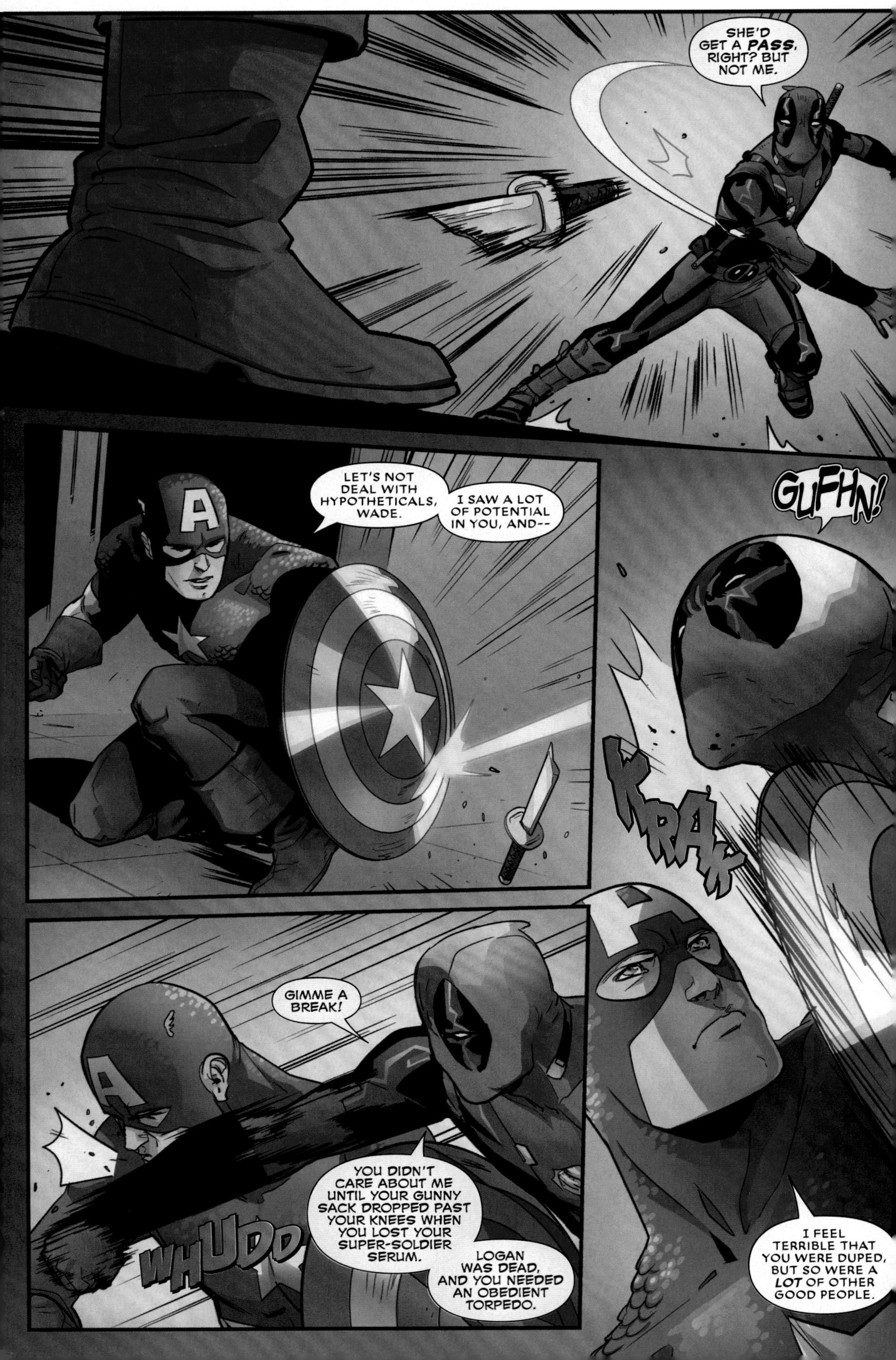
SHE'D GET A PASS, RIGHT? BUT NOT ME.
LET'S NOT DEAL WITH HYPOTHETICALS, WADE.
I SAW A LOT OF POTENTIAL IN YOU, AND--
GUFHN!
KRAK
GIMME A BREAK!
YOU DIDN'T CARE ABOUT ME UNTIL YOUR GUNNY SACK DROPPED PAST YOUR KNEES WHEN YOU LOST YOUR SUPER-SOLDIER SERUM.
LOGAN WAS DEAD, AND YOU NEEDED AN OBEDIENT TORPEDO.
WHUDD
I FEEL TERRIBLE THAT YOU WERE DUPED, BUT SO WERE A LOT OF OTHER GOOD PEOPLE.

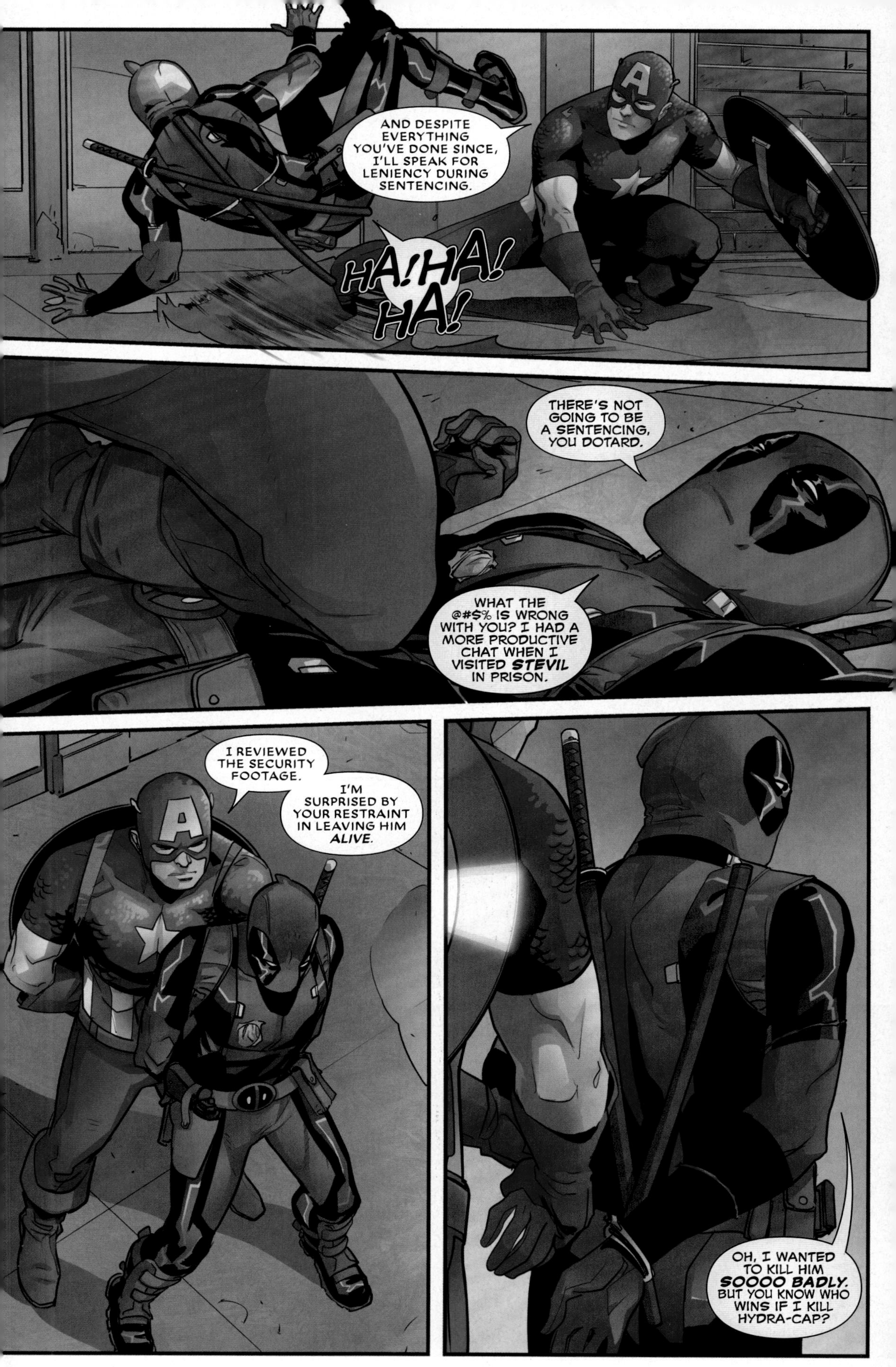
AND DESPITE EVERYTHING YOU'VE DONE SINCE, I'LL SPEAK FOR LENIENCY DURING SENTENCING.
HA!HA! HA!
THERE'S NOT GOING TO BE A SENTENCING, YOU DOTARD.
WHAT THE @#$% IS WRONG WITH YOU? I HAD A MORE PRODUCTIVE CHAT WHEN I VISITED STEVIL IN PRISON.
I REVIEWED THE SECURITY FOOTAGE.
I'M SURPRISED BY YOUR RESTRAINT IN LEAVING HIM ALIVE.
OH, I WANTED TO KILL HIM SOOOO BADLY. BUT YOU KNOW WHO WINS IF I KILL HYDRA-CAP?

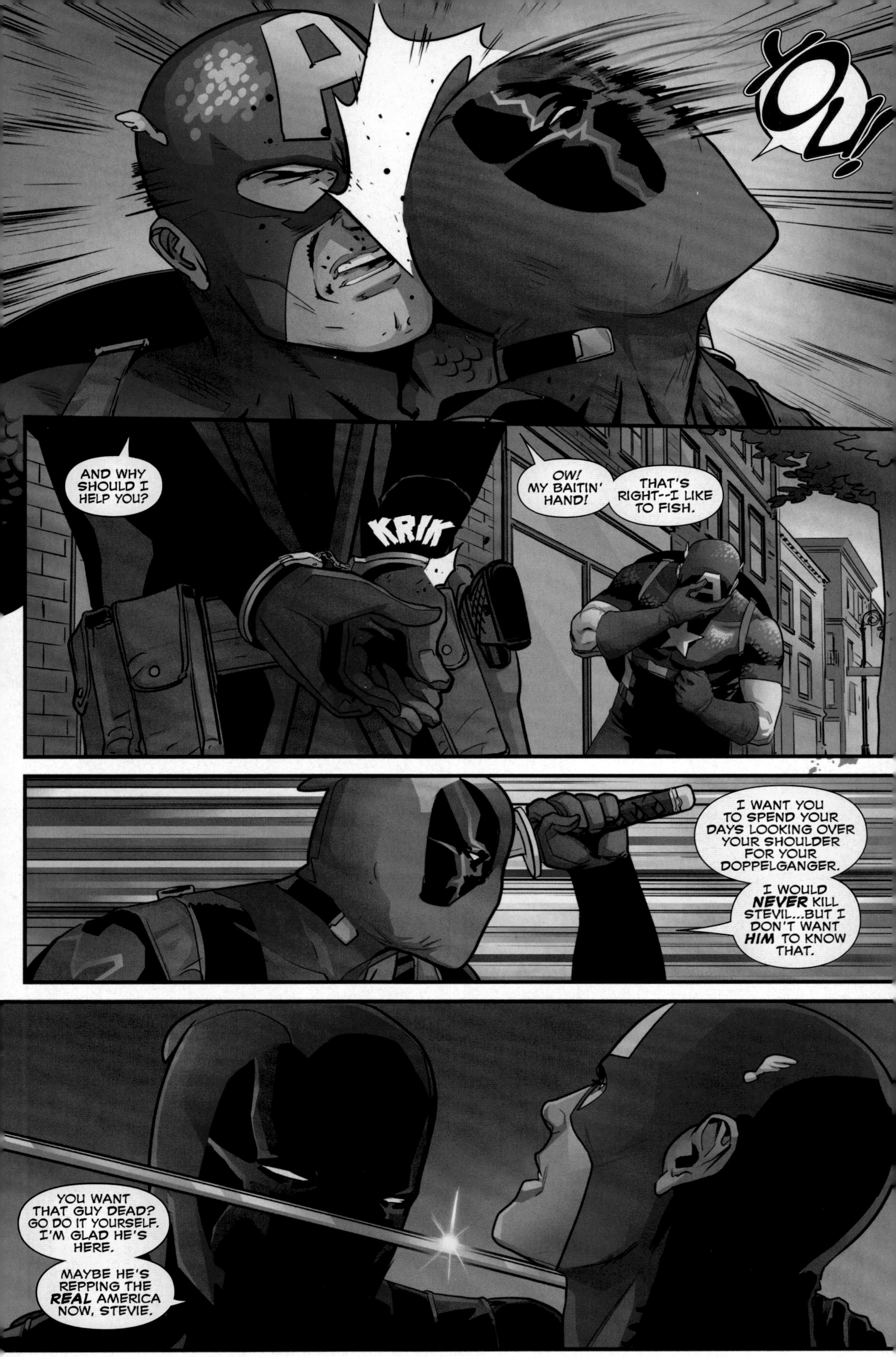
YOU!!
AND WHY SHOULD I HELP YOU?
KRIK
OW! MY BAITIN' HAND!
THAT'S RIGHT--I LIKE TO FISH.
I WANT YOU TO SPEND YOUR DAYS LOOKING OVER YOUR SHOULDER FOR YOUR DOPPELGANGER.
I WOULD NEVER KILL STEVIL...BUT I DON'T WANT HIM TO KNOW THAT.
YOU WANT THAT GUY DEAD? GO DO IT YOURSELF. I'M GLAD HE'S HERE.
MAYBE HE'S REPPING THE REAL AMERICA NOW, STEVIE.

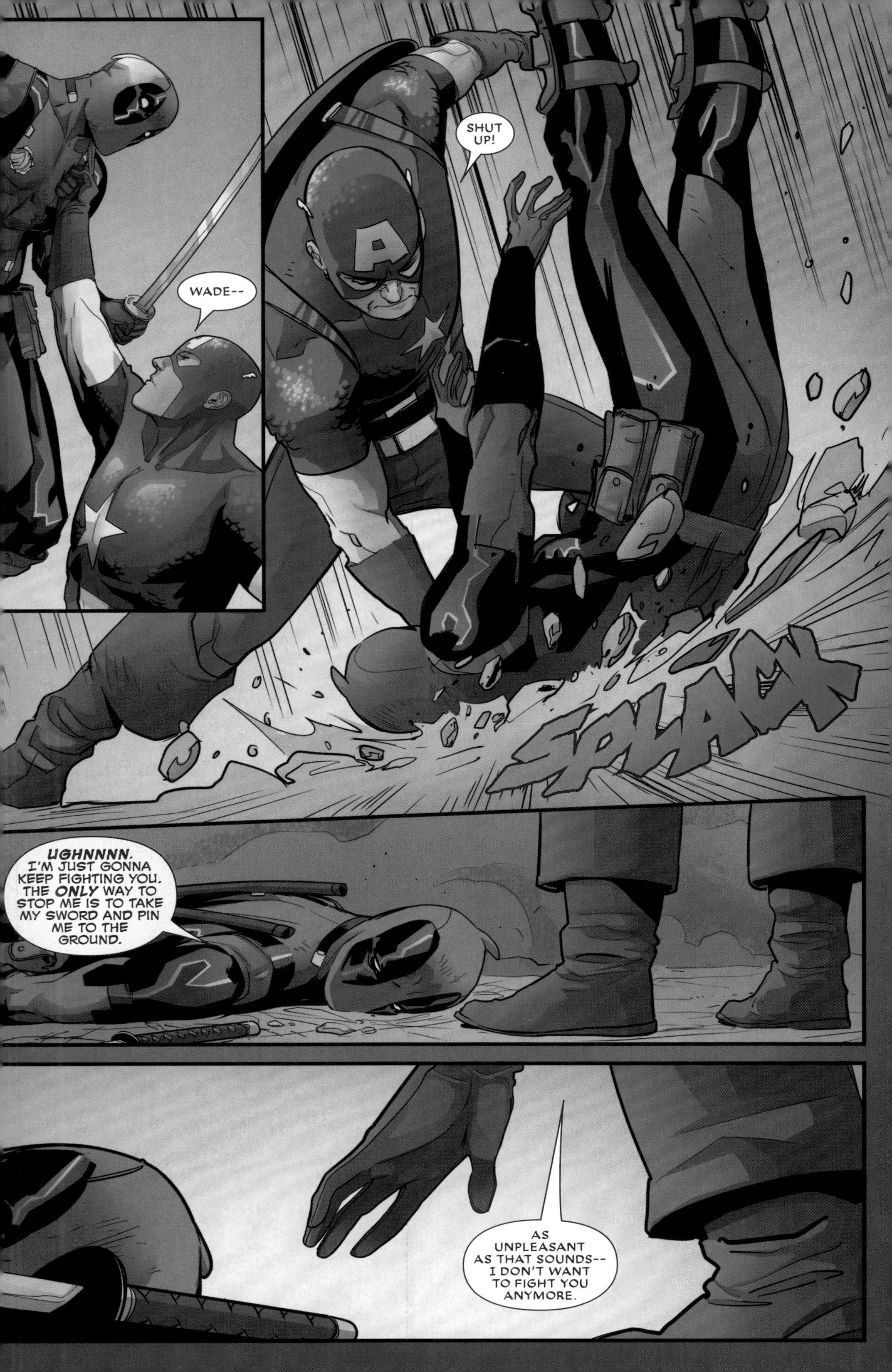
WADE--
SHUT UP!
SPLACK
UGHNNNN. I'M JUST GONNA KEEP FIGHTING YOU. THE ONLY WAY TO STOP ME IS TO TAKE MY SWORD AND PIN ME TO THE GROUND.
AS UNPLEASANT AS THAT SOUNDS-- I DON'T WANT TO FIGHT YOU ANYMORE.

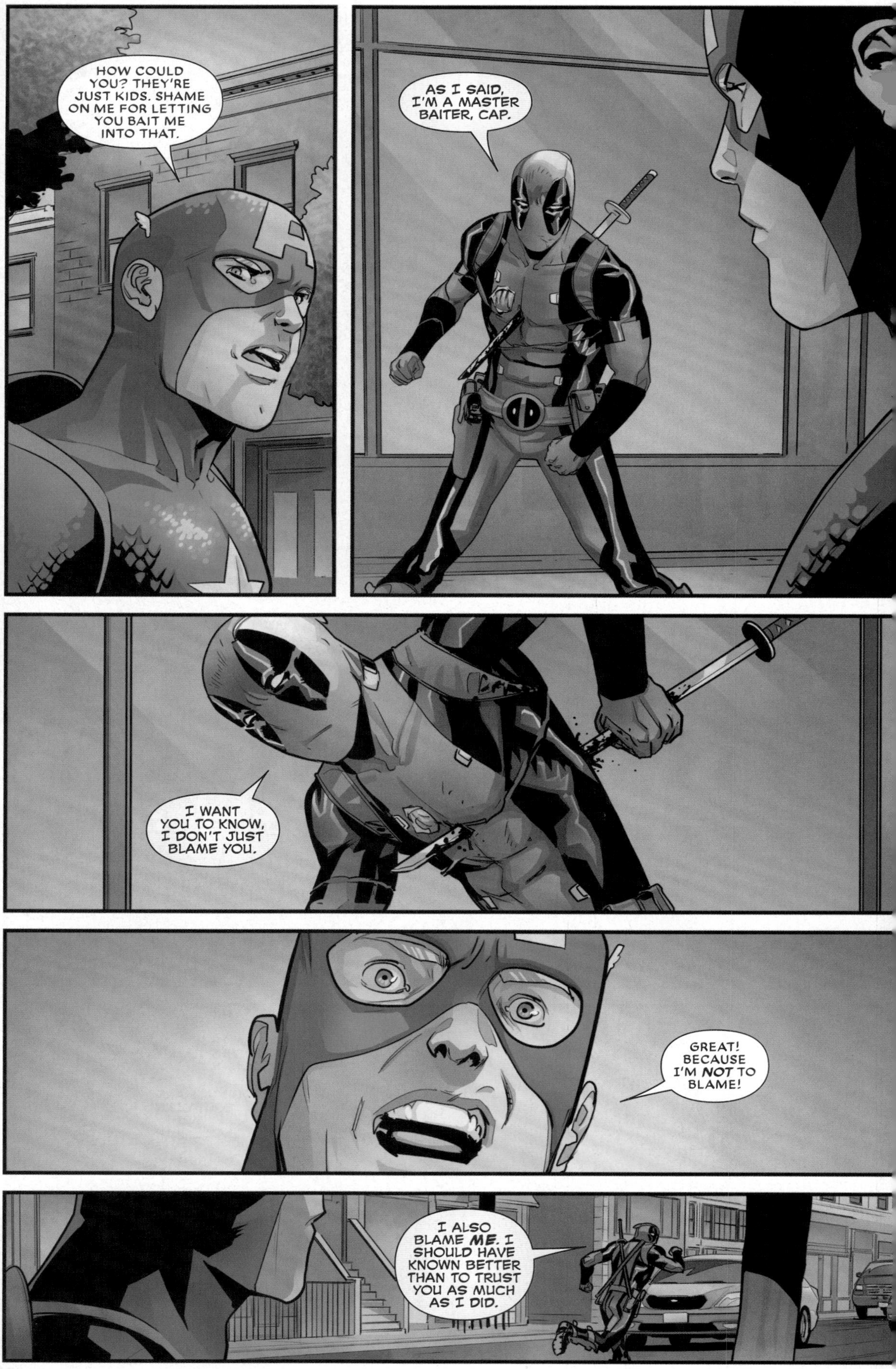
HOW COULD YOU? THEY'RE JUST KIDS. SHAME ON ME FOR LETTING YOU BAIT ME INTO THAT.
AS I SAID, I'M A MASTER BAITER, CAP.
I WANT YOU TO KNOW, I DON'T JUST BLAME YOU.
GREAT! BECAUSE I'M ***NOT*** TO BLAME!
I ALSO BLAME ***ME***. I SHOULD HAVE KNOWN BETTER THAN TO TRUST YOU AS MUCH AS I DID.

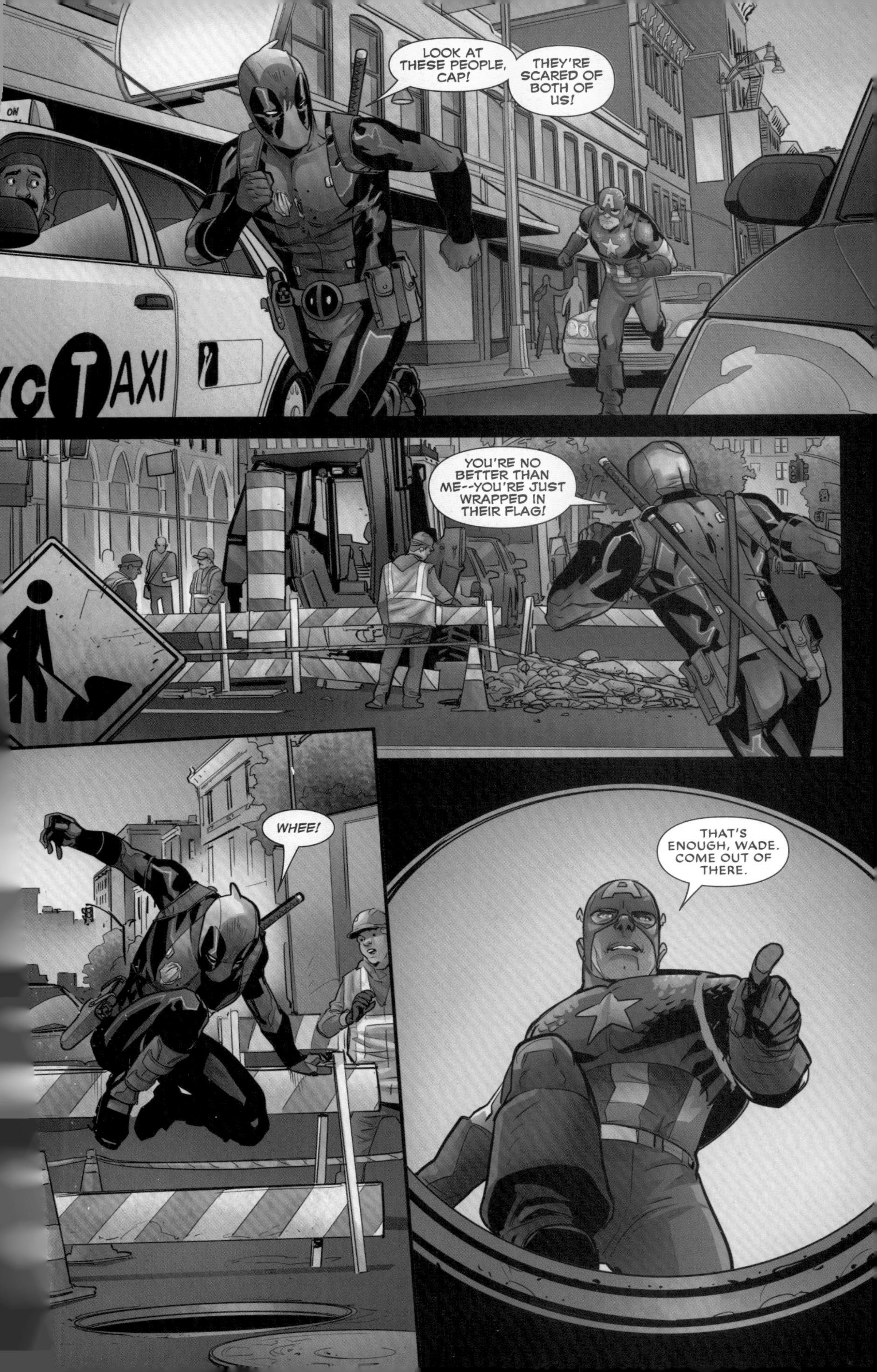

ON
LOOK AT THESE PEOPLE, CAP!
THEY'RE SCARED OF BOTH OF US!
YC TAXI
YOU'RE NO BETTER THAN ME--YOU'RE JUST WRAPPED IN THEIR FLAG!
WHEE!
THAT'S ENOUGH, WADE. COME OUT OF THERE.

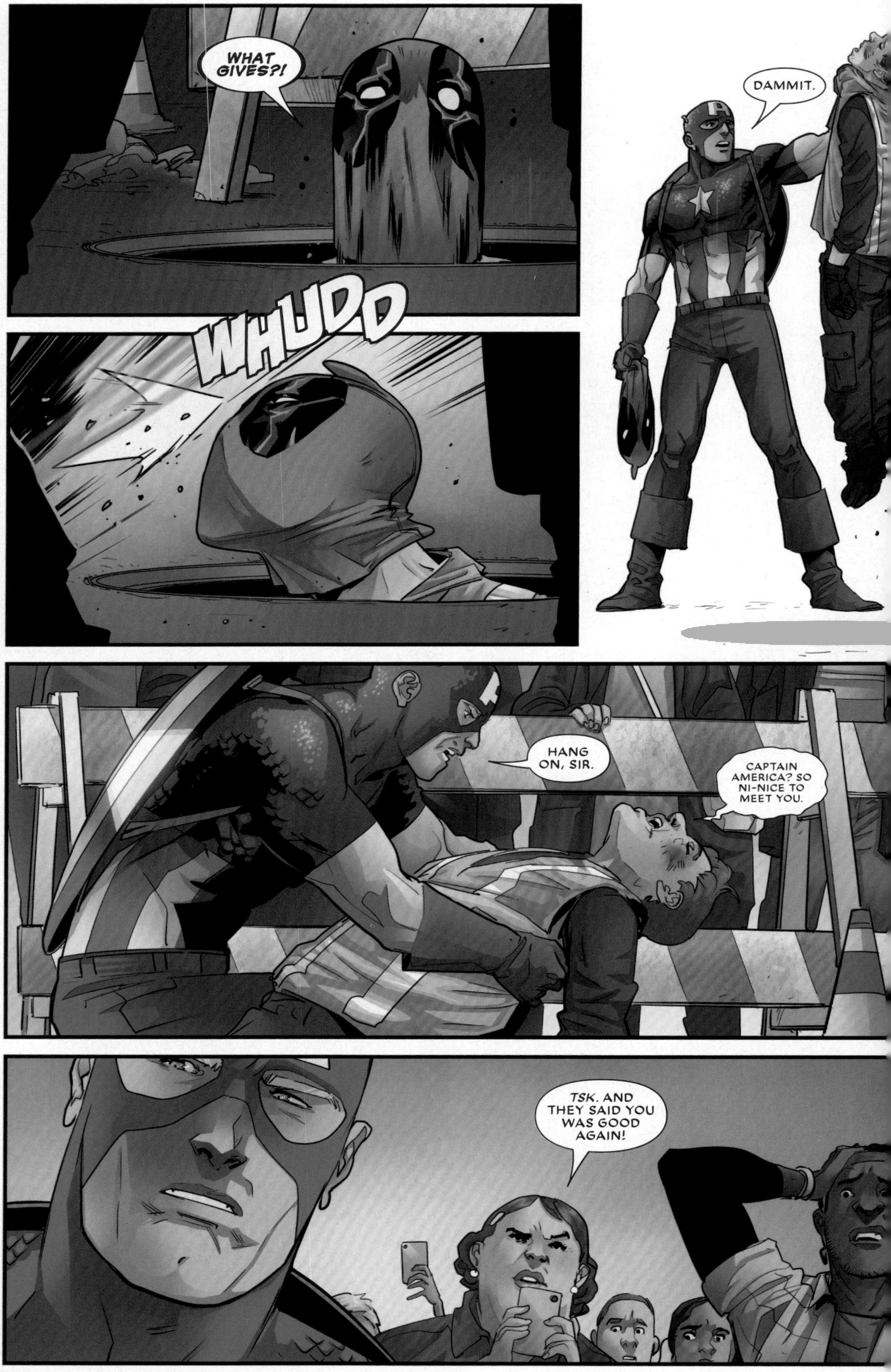
WHAT GIVES?!
DAMMIT.
WHUDD
HANG ON, SIR.
CAPTAIN AMERICA? SO NI-NICE TO MEET YOU.
TSK. AND THEY SAID YOU WAS GOOD AGAIN!

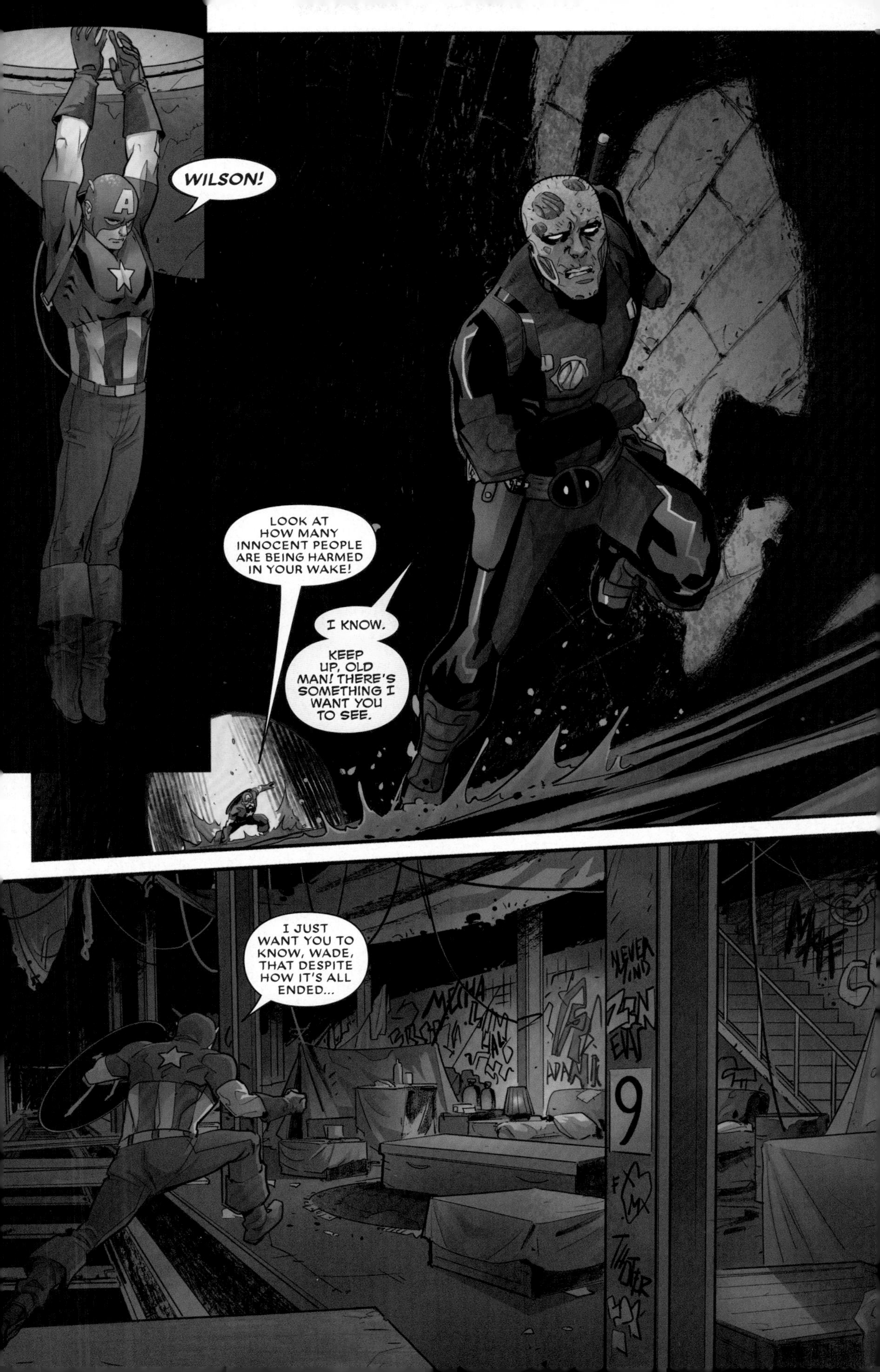
WILSON!
LOOK AT HOW MANY INNOCENT PEOPLE ARE BEING HARMED IN YOUR WAKE!
I KNOW.
KEEP UP, OLD MAN! THERE'S SOMETHING I WANT YOU TO SEE.
I JUST WANT YOU TO KNOW, WADE, THAT DESPITE HOW IT'S ALL ENDED...
9

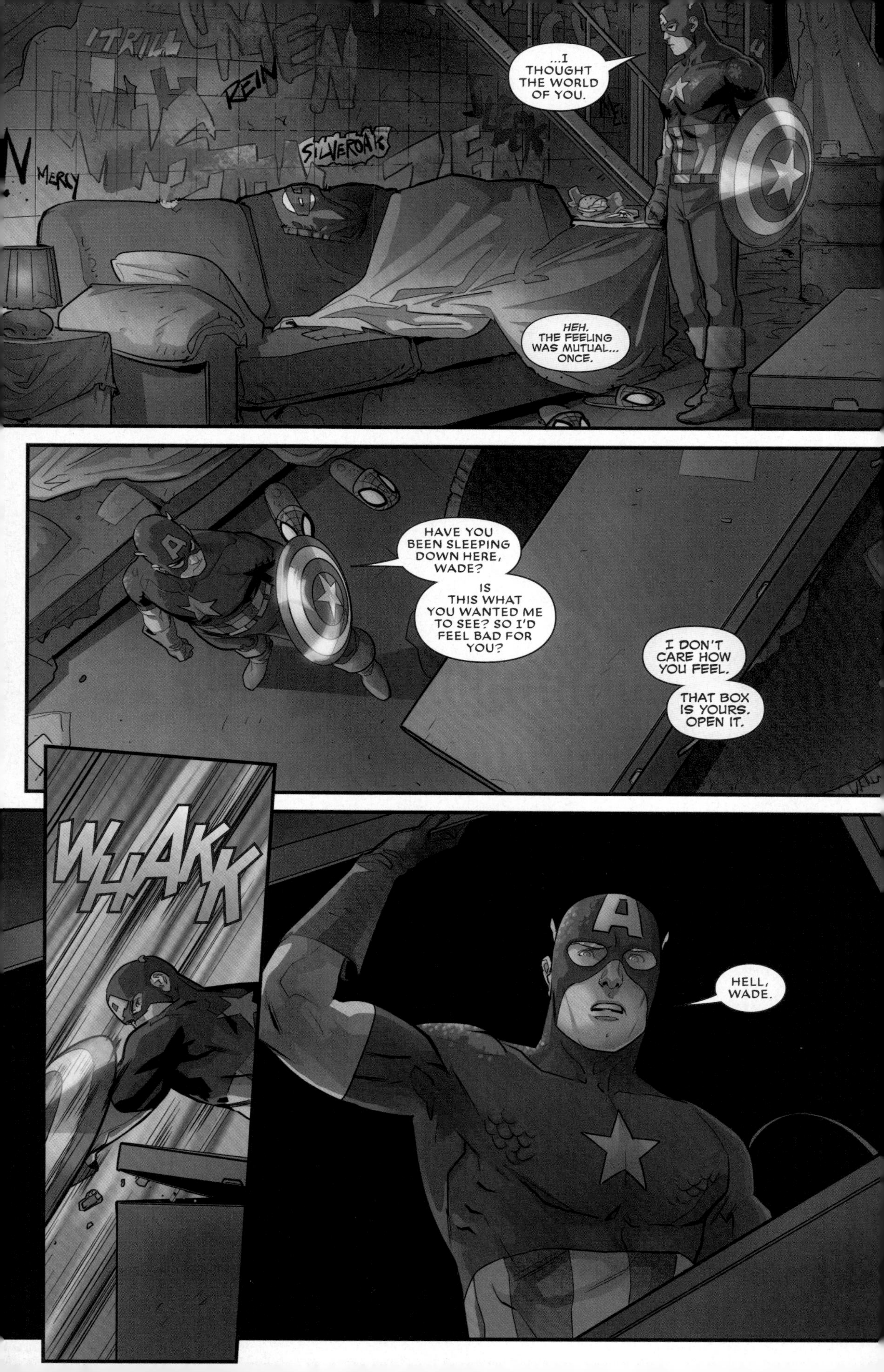
ITRILL
REIN
SILVEROAKS
MERCY
...I THOUGHT THE WORLD OF YOU.
HEH. THE FEELING WAS MUTUAL... ONCE.
HAVE YOU BEEN SLEEPING DOWN HERE, WADE?
IS THIS WHAT YOU WANTED ME TO SEE? SO I'D FEEL BAD FOR YOU?
I DON'T CARE HOW YOU FEEL.
THAT BOX IS YOURS. OPEN IT.
WHAKK
HELL, WADE.

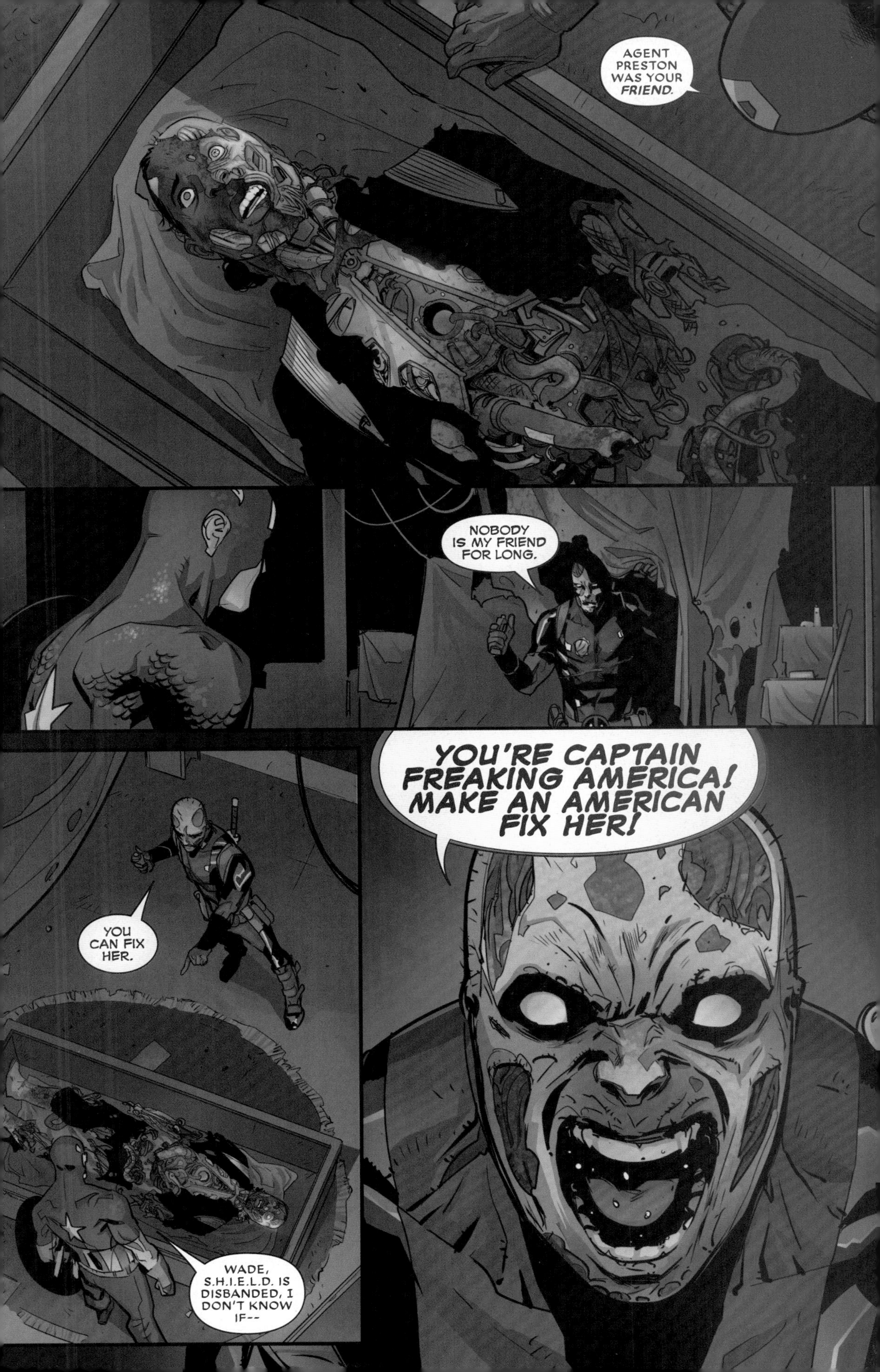
AGENT PRESTON WAS YOUR *FRIEND.*
NOBODY IS MY FRIEND FOR LONG.
YOU CAN FIX HER.
WADE, S.H.I.E.L.D. IS DISBANDED, I DON'T KNOW IF--
YOU'RE CAPTAIN FREAKING AMERICA! MAKE AN AMERICAN FIX HER!

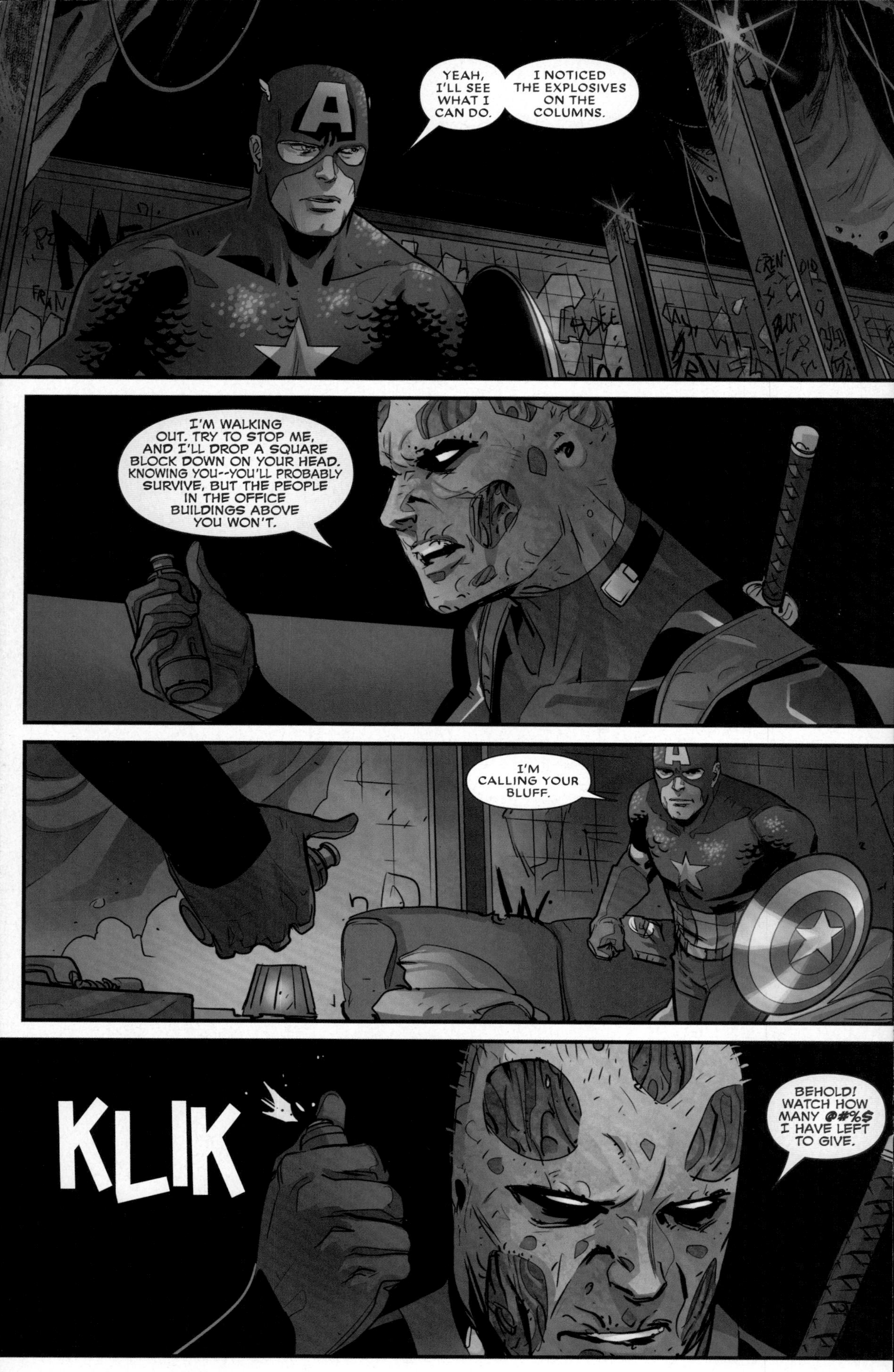
YEAH, I'LL SEE WHAT I CAN DO.
I NOTICED THE EXPLOSIVES ON THE COLUMNS.
I'M WALKING OUT. TRY TO STOP ME, AND I'LL DROP A SQUARE BLOCK DOWN ON YOUR HEAD. KNOWING YOU--YOU'LL PROBABLY SURVIVE, BUT THE PEOPLE IN THE OFFICE BUILDINGS ABOVE YOU WON'T.
I'M CALLING YOUR BLUFF.
KLIK
BEHOLD! WATCH HOW MANY @#%$ I HAVE LEFT TO GIVE.

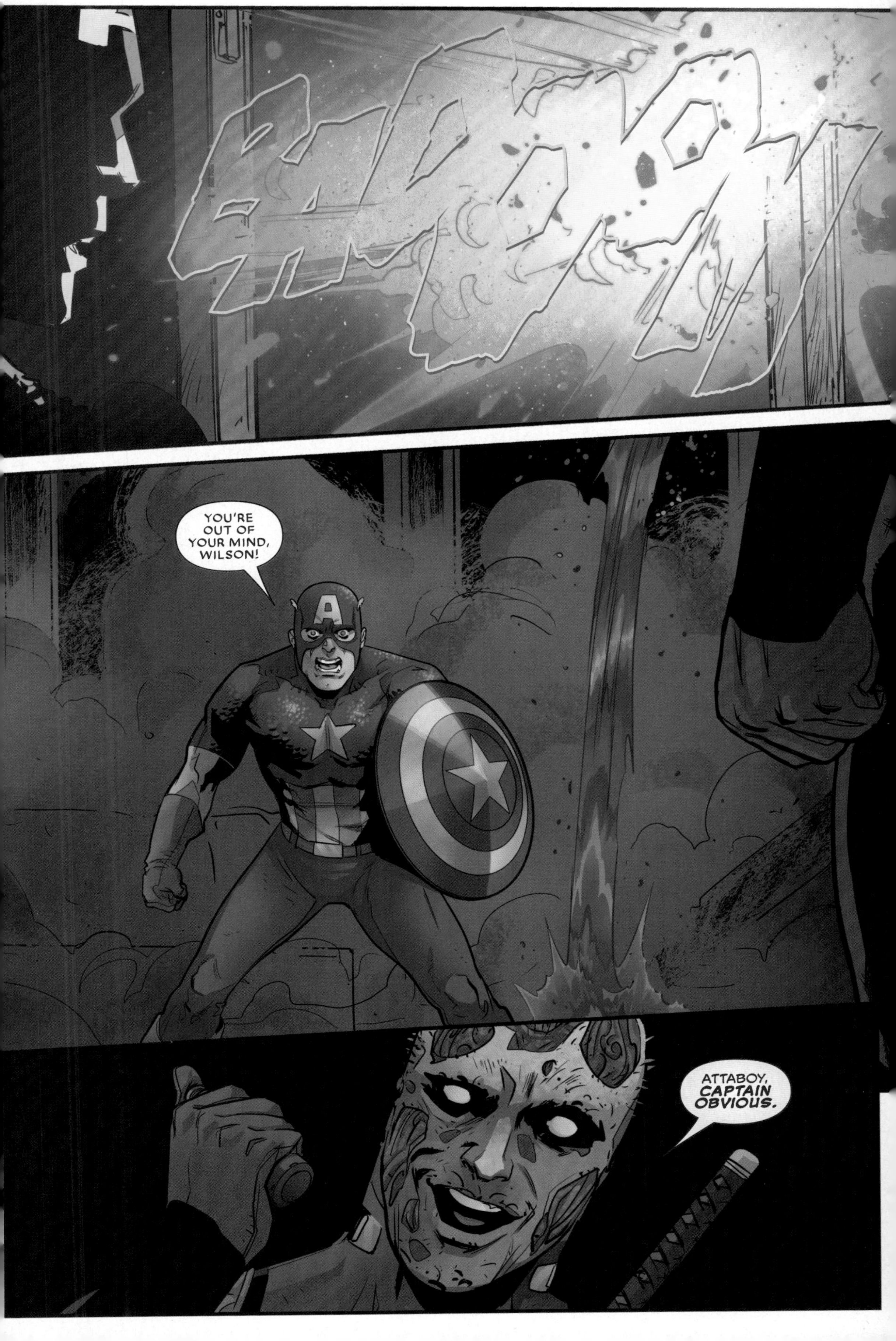
YOU'RE OUT OF YOUR MIND, WILSON!
ATTABOY, *CAPTAIN OBVIOUS.*

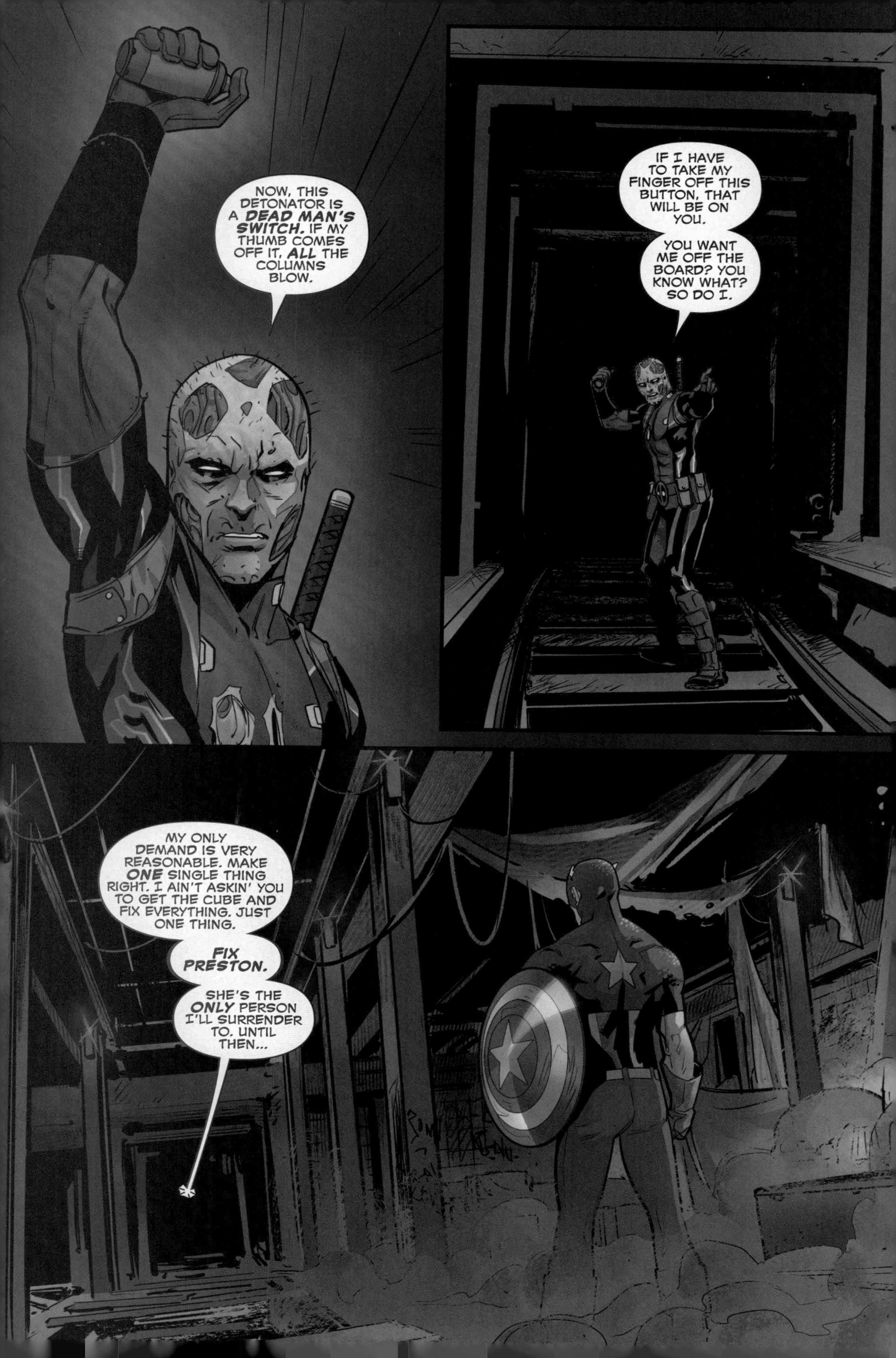
NOW, THIS DETONATOR IS A **DEAD MAN'S SWITCH.** IF MY THUMB COMES OFF IT, **ALL** THE COLUMNS BLOW.
IF I HAVE TO TAKE MY FINGER OFF THIS BUTTON, THAT WILL BE ON YOU.
YOU WANT ME OFF THE BOARD? YOU KNOW WHAT? SO DO I.
MY ONLY DEMAND IS VERY REASONABLE. MAKE **ONE** SINGLE THING RIGHT. I AIN'T ASKIN' YOU TO GET THE CUBE AND FIX EVERYTHING. JUST ONE THING.
FIX PRESTON.
SHE'S THE **ONLY** PERSON I'LL SURRENDER TO. UNTIL THEN...

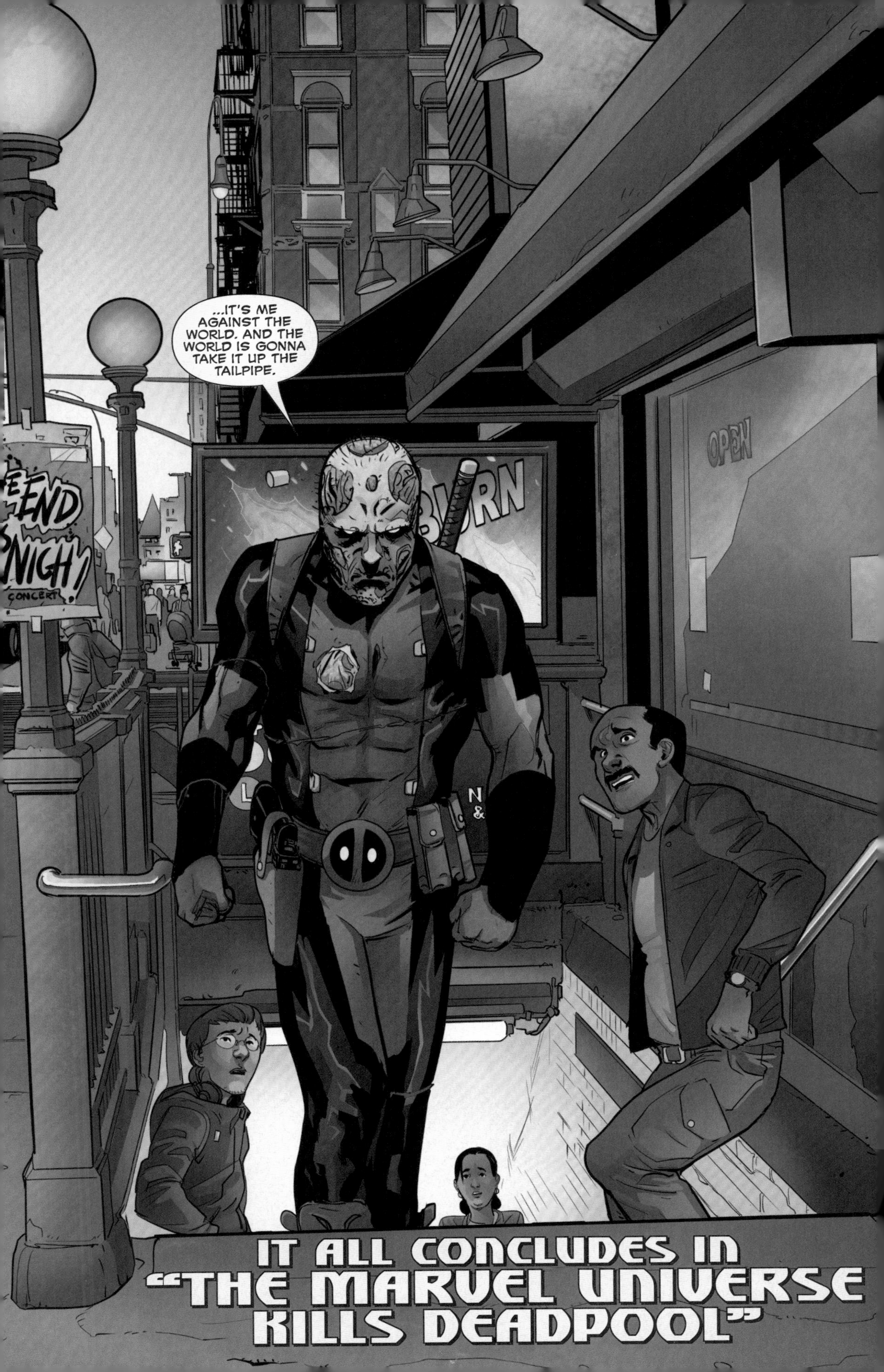
...IT'S ME AGAINST THE WORLD. AND THE WORLD IS GONNA TAKE IT UP THE TAILPIPE.
OPEN
IT ALL CONCLUDES IN "THE MARVEL UNIVERSE KILLS DEADPOOL"

Hey there, 'Pool Partiers!

Welcome to the madness that is the *Deadpool* #SecretComic Variant covers! As you may know, variant covers are a pretty common thing in the comics industry right now — special additional covers usually created by top-tier artists that sometimes end up being more rare than the main cover of the series. We in the Deadpool office wanted to get into this variant cover game...but we decided to turn the whole thing on its head.

The following 20 pages of comic book were originally printed as 20 variant covers over 20 issues of the ongoing *Deadpool* series. Each issue, those intrepid fans who sought out these extra-special issues got one page more of the ongoing story of Deadpool's cover adventure, along with the chance to meet one of the most important characters in Marvel history — one who affects every single issue we've published for the last number of years.

This is the first time that "Issue #2" of our #SecretComic tales has been collected in one place! Never before has one page of the tale immediately followed the last, unless some collector tore off all the covers and stitched them together into some sort of unnatural Frankenstein comic. If you read "Issue #1" of the #SecretComic, [collected in *Deadpool, World's Greatest Vol 9 — Deadpool in Space*] you know that Deadpool went on a crazy journey into the world of comic book covers and met the aforementioned important character: UPC-PO, the UPC on every cover of Marvel's comics! In the end, Deadpool freed UPC-PO, leaving a sham replacement in his stead, and the two of them retired to the Marvel Comics Universe of the 1970s. That's where we find them now...deep in that groovy era...

And yeah, this story is super in-continuity, and don't let anyone tell you otherwise.

Be seeing you!

Deadpool's Pal,
Jordan D. White

WRITER	ARTIST	COLOR ARTIST
Gerry Duggan	*Scott Koblish*	*Guru-eFX*

LETTERER	ASSISTANT EDITOR	EDITOR
VC's Joe Sabino	*Heather Antos*	*Jordan D. White*

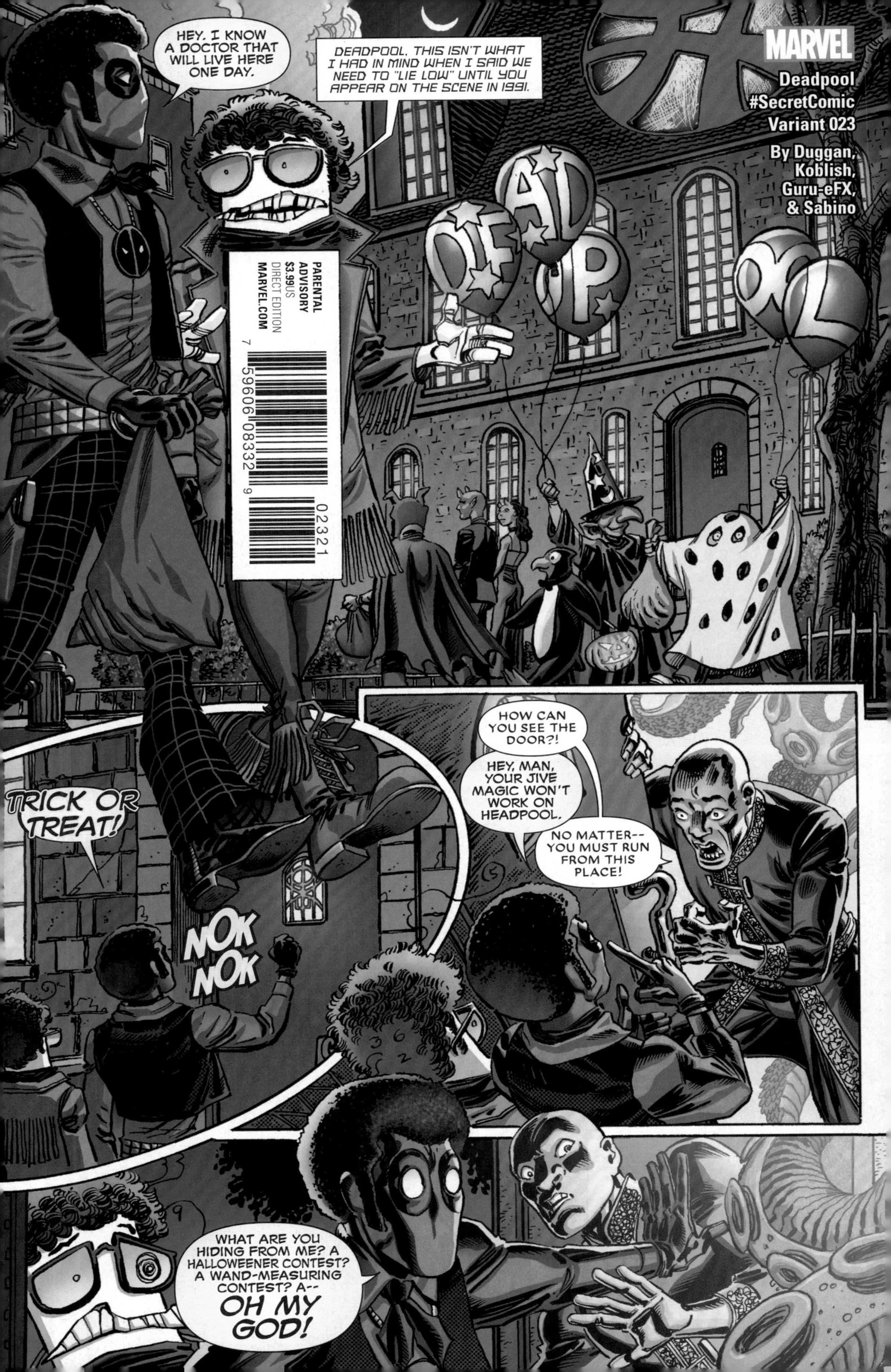
MARVEL
Deadpool
#SecretComic
Variant 023
By Duggan,
Koblish,
Guru-eFX,
& Sabino
HEY. I KNOW A DOCTOR THAT WILL LIVE HERE ONE DAY.
DEADPOOL. THIS ISN'T WHAT I HAD IN MIND WHEN I SAID WE NEED TO "LIE LOW" UNTIL YOU APPEAR ON THE SCENE IN 1991.
PARENTAL ADVISORY
$3.99US
DIRECT EDITION
MARVEL.COM
TRICK OR TREAT!
NOK NOK
HOW CAN YOU SEE THE DOOR?!
HEY, MAN, YOUR JIVE MAGIC WON'T WORK ON HEADPOOL.
NO MATTER-- YOU MUST RUN FROM THIS PLACE!
WHAT ARE YOU HIDING FROM ME? A HALLOWEENER CONTEST? A WAND-MEASURING CONTEST? A--
OH MY GOD!

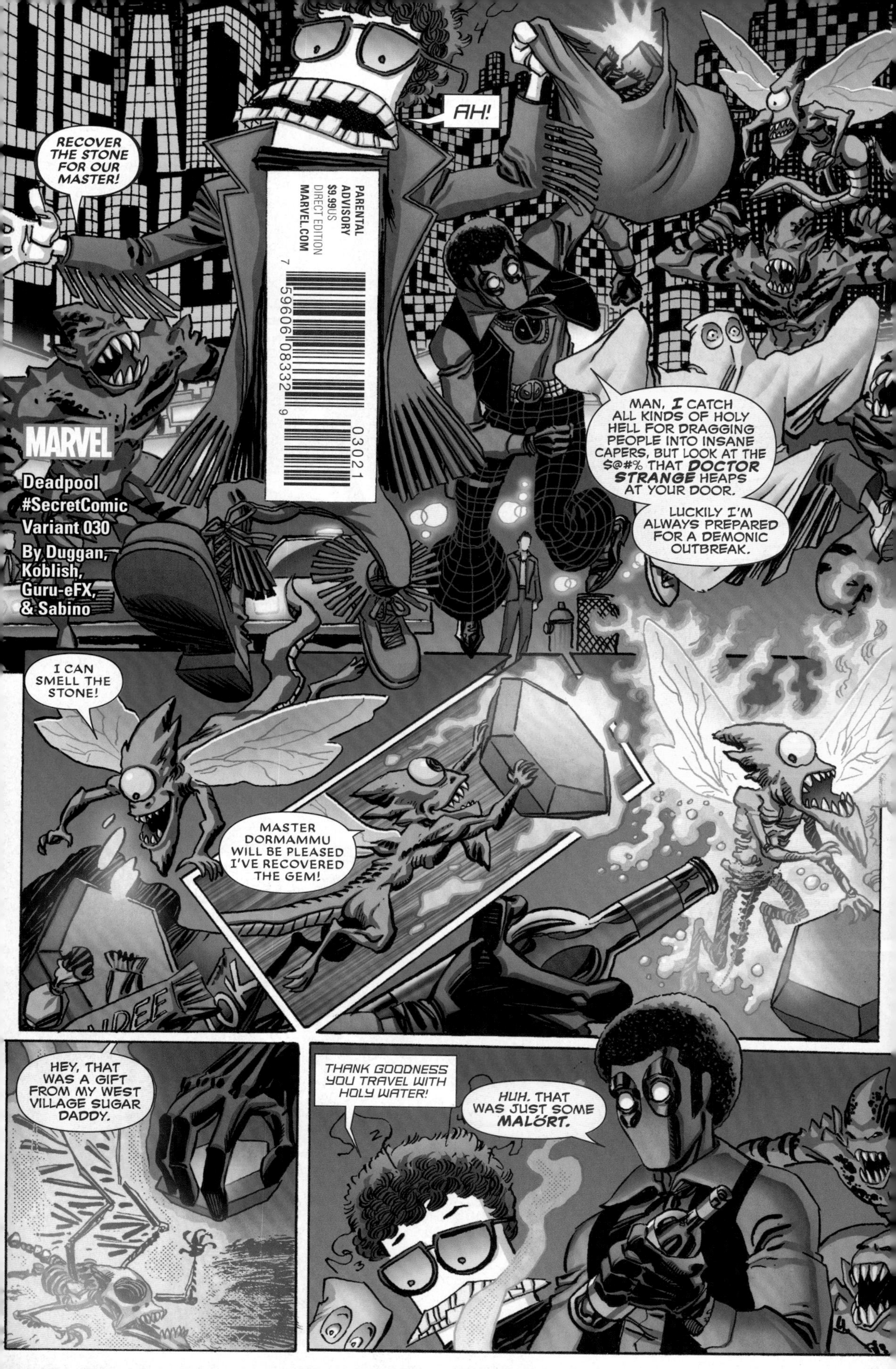

PARENTAL ADVISORY
$9.99US
DIRECT EDITION
MARVEL.COM
7 59606 08332 9 03021
Deadpool #SecretComic Variant 030
By Duggan, Koblish, Guru-eFX, & Sabino
RECOVER THE STONE FOR OUR MASTER!
AH!
MAN, I CATCH ALL KINDS OF HOLY HELL FOR DRAGGING PEOPLE INTO INSANE CAPERS, BUT LOOK AT THE $@#% THAT DOCTOR STRANGE HEAPS AT YOUR DOOR.
LUCKILY I'M ALWAYS PREPARED FOR A DEMONIC OUTBREAK.
I CAN SMELL THE STONE!
MASTER DORMAMMU WILL BE PLEASED I'VE RECOVERED THE GEM!
HEY, THAT WAS A GIFT FROM MY WEST VILLAGE SUGAR DADDY.
THANK GOODNESS YOU TRAVEL WITH HOLY WATER!
HUH. THAT WAS JUST SOME MALÖRT.

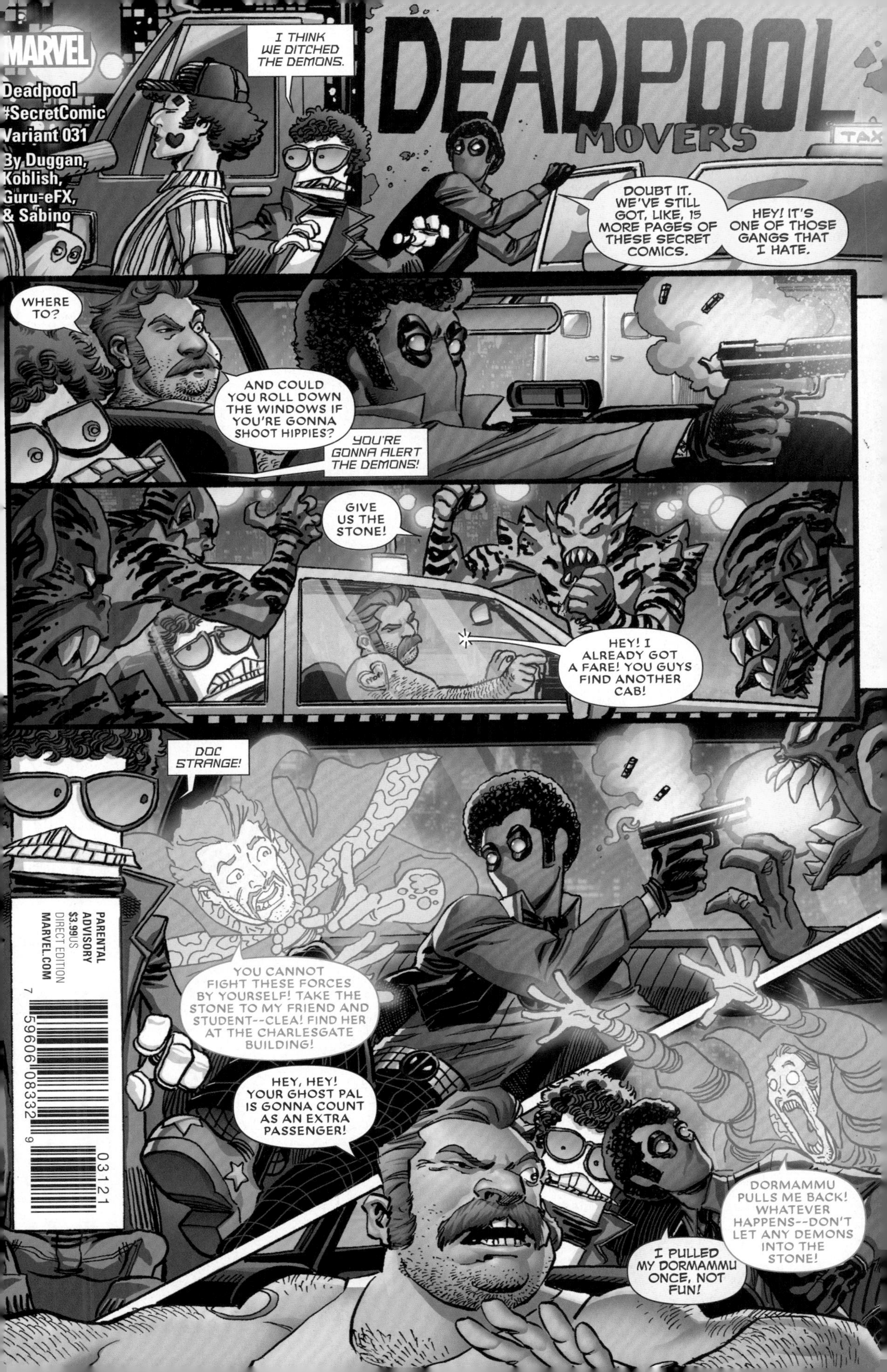
MARVEL
Deadpool
#SecretComic
Variant 031
By Duggan,
Koblish,
Guru-eFX,
& Sabino
DEADPOOL
MOVERS
TAXI
I THINK WE DITCHED THE DEMONS.
DOUBT IT. WE'VE STILL GOT, LIKE, 15 MORE PAGES OF THESE SECRET COMICS.
HEY! IT'S ONE OF THOSE GANGS THAT I HATE.
WHERE TO?
AND COULD YOU ROLL DOWN THE WINDOWS IF YOU'RE GONNA SHOOT HIPPIES?
YOU'RE GONNA ALERT THE DEMONS!
GIVE US THE STONE!
HEY! I ALREADY GOT A FARE! YOU GUYS FIND ANOTHER CAB!
DOC STRANGE!
YOU CANNOT FIGHT THESE FORCES BY YOURSELF! TAKE THE STONE TO MY FRIEND AND STUDENT--CLEA! FIND HER AT THE CHARLESGATE BUILDING!
HEY, HEY! YOUR GHOST PAL IS GONNA COUNT AS AN EXTRA PASSENGER!
DORMAMMU PULLS ME BACK! WHATEVER HAPPENS--DON'T LET ANY DEMONS INTO THE STONE!
I PULLED MY DORMAMMU ONCE, NOT FUN!
PARENTAL ADVISORY
$3.99US
DIRECT EDITION
MARVEL.COM

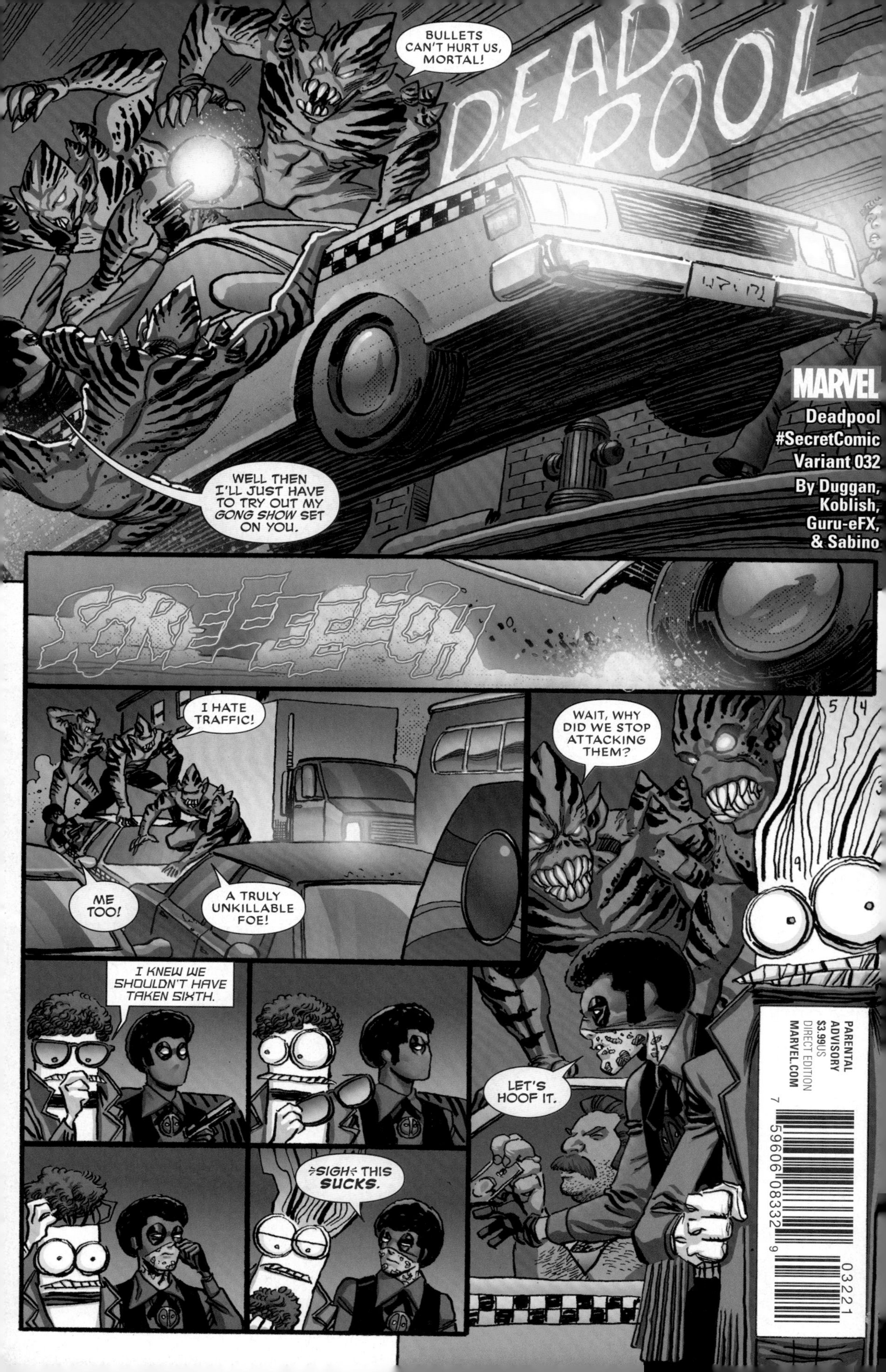
BULLETS CAN'T HURT US, MORTAL!
DEADPOOL
MARVEL
Deadpool #SecretComic Variant 032
By Duggan, Koblish, Guru-eFX, & Sabino
WELL THEN I'LL JUST HAVE TO TRY OUT MY GONG SHOW SET ON YOU.
SKREEEEECH
I HATE TRAFFIC!
ME TOO!
A TRULY UNKILLABLE FOE!
WAIT, WHY DID WE STOP ATTACKING THEM?
I KNEW WE SHOULDN'T HAVE TAKEN SIXTH.
LET'S HOOF IT.
SIGH THIS SUCKS.
PARENTAL ADVISORY
$3.99US
DIRECT EDITION
MARVEL.COM

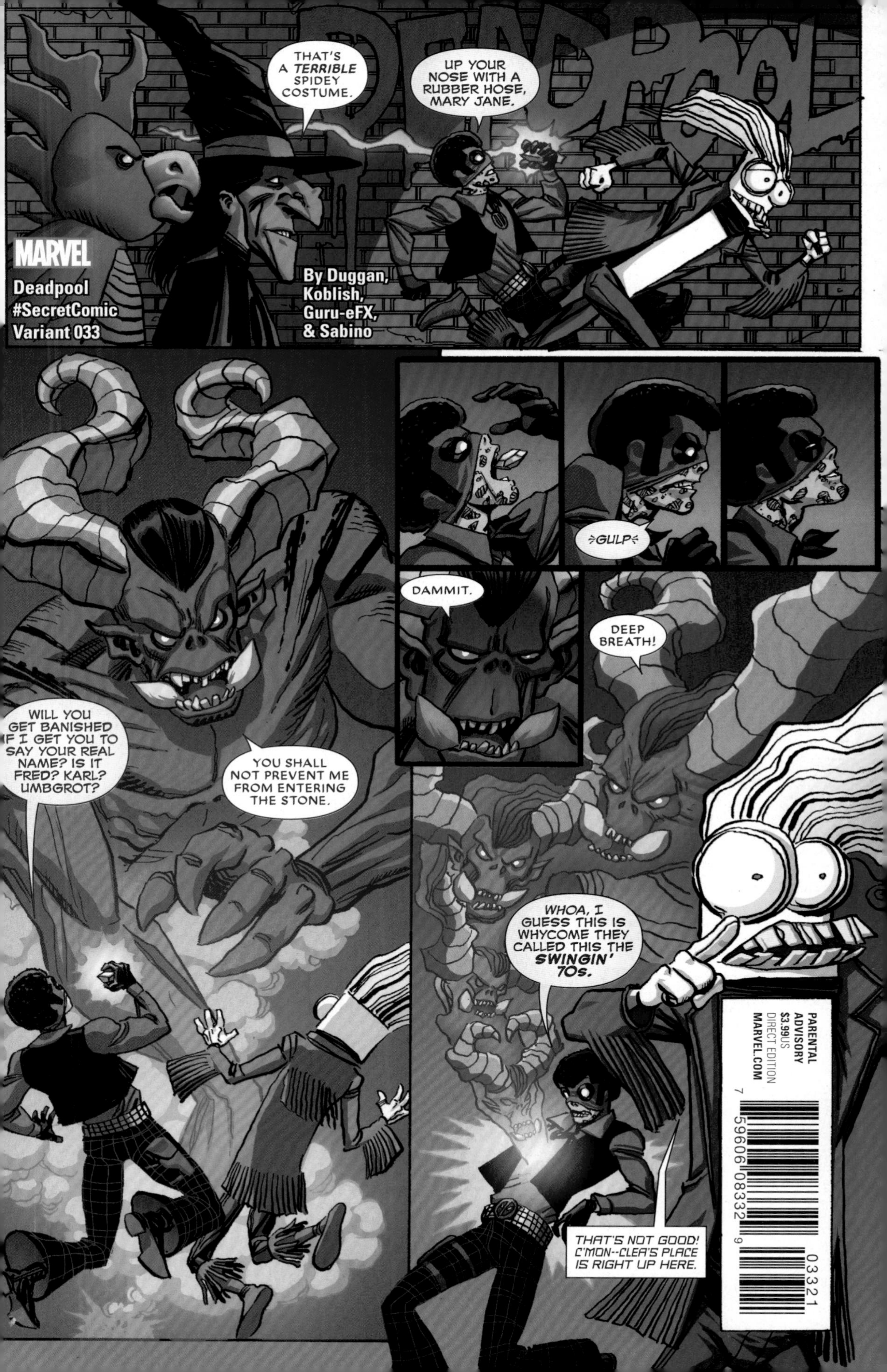
MARVEL
Deadpool #SecretComic Variant 033
By Duggan, Koblish, Guru-eFX, & Sabino
THAT'S A *TERRIBLE* SPIDEY COSTUME.
UP YOUR NOSE WITH A RUBBER HOSE, MARY JANE.
WILL YOU GET BANISHED IF I GET YOU TO SAY YOUR REAL NAME? IS IT FRED? KARL? UMBGROT?
YOU SHALL NOT PREVENT ME FROM ENTERING THE STONE.
GULP
DAMMIT.
DEEP BREATH!
WHOA, I GUESS THIS IS WHYCOME THEY CALLED THIS THE ***SWINGIN' 70s.***
THAT'S NOT GOOD! C'MON--CLEA'S PLACE IS RIGHT UP HERE.
PARENTAL ADVISORY
$3.99US
DIRECT EDITION
MARVEL.COM

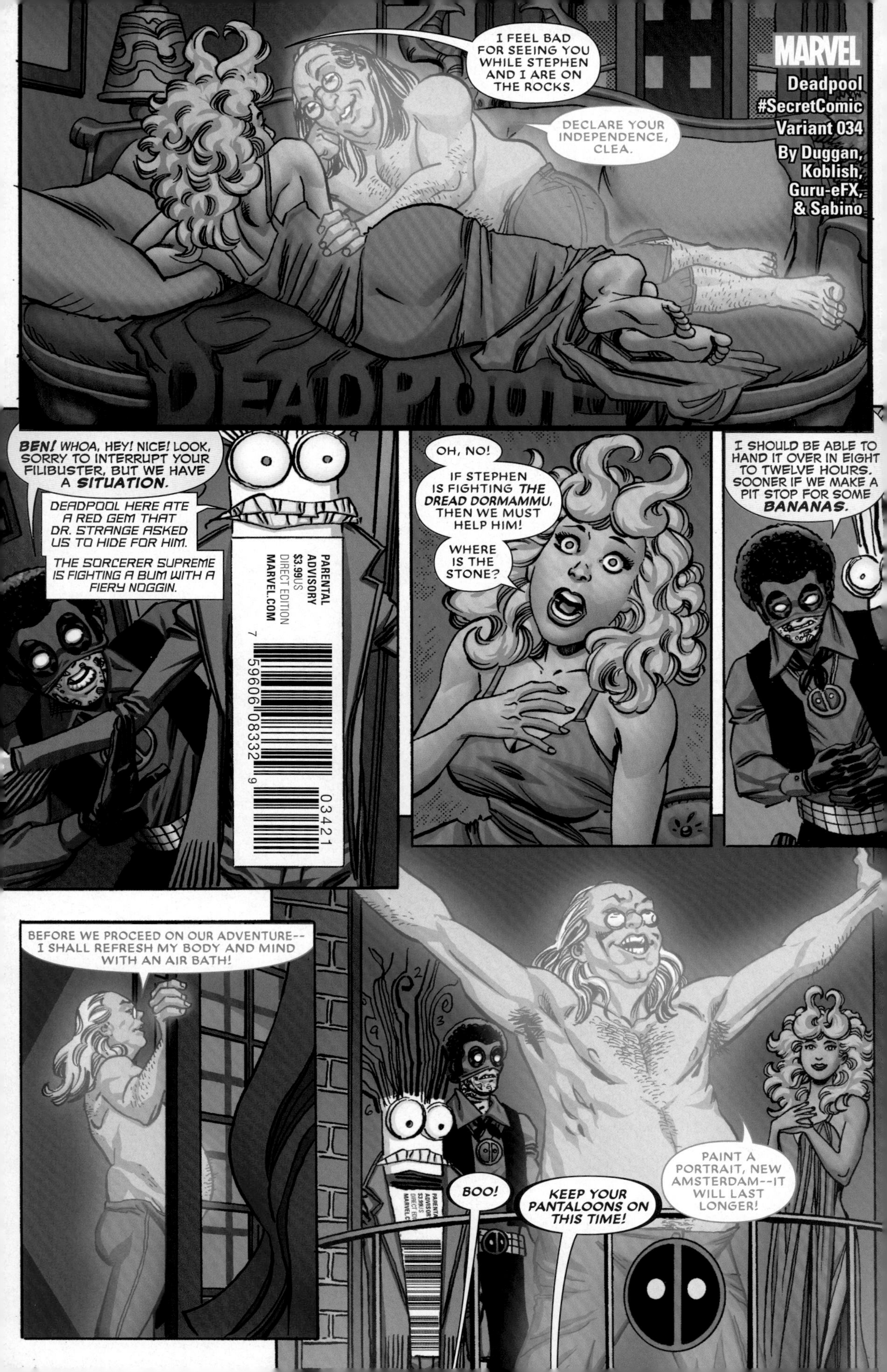
MARVEL
Deadpool #SecretComic Variant 034
By Duggan, Koblish, Guru-eFX, & Sabino
I FEEL BAD FOR SEEING YOU WHILE STEPHEN AND I ARE ON THE ROCKS.
DECLARE YOUR INDEPENDENCE, CLEA.
DEADPOOL
BEN! WHOA, HEY! NICE! LOOK, SORRY TO INTERRUPT YOUR FILIBUSTER, BUT WE HAVE A SITUATION.
DEADPOOL HERE ATE A RED GEM THAT DR. STRANGE ASKED US TO HIDE FOR HIM.
THE SORCERER SUPREME IS FIGHTING A BUM WITH A FIERY NOGGIN.
PARENTAL ADVISORY
$3.99US
DIRECT EDITION
MARVEL.COM
OH, NO!
IF STEPHEN IS FIGHTING THE DREAD DORMAMMU, THEN WE MUST HELP HIM!
WHERE IS THE STONE?
I SHOULD BE ABLE TO HAND IT OVER IN EIGHT TO TWELVE HOURS. SOONER IF WE MAKE A PIT STOP FOR SOME BANANAS.
BEFORE WE PROCEED ON OUR ADVENTURE-- I SHALL REFRESH MY BODY AND MIND WITH AN AIR BATH!
BOO!
KEEP YOUR PANTALOONS ON THIS TIME!
PAINT A PORTRAIT, NEW AMSTERDAM--IT WILL LAST LONGER!

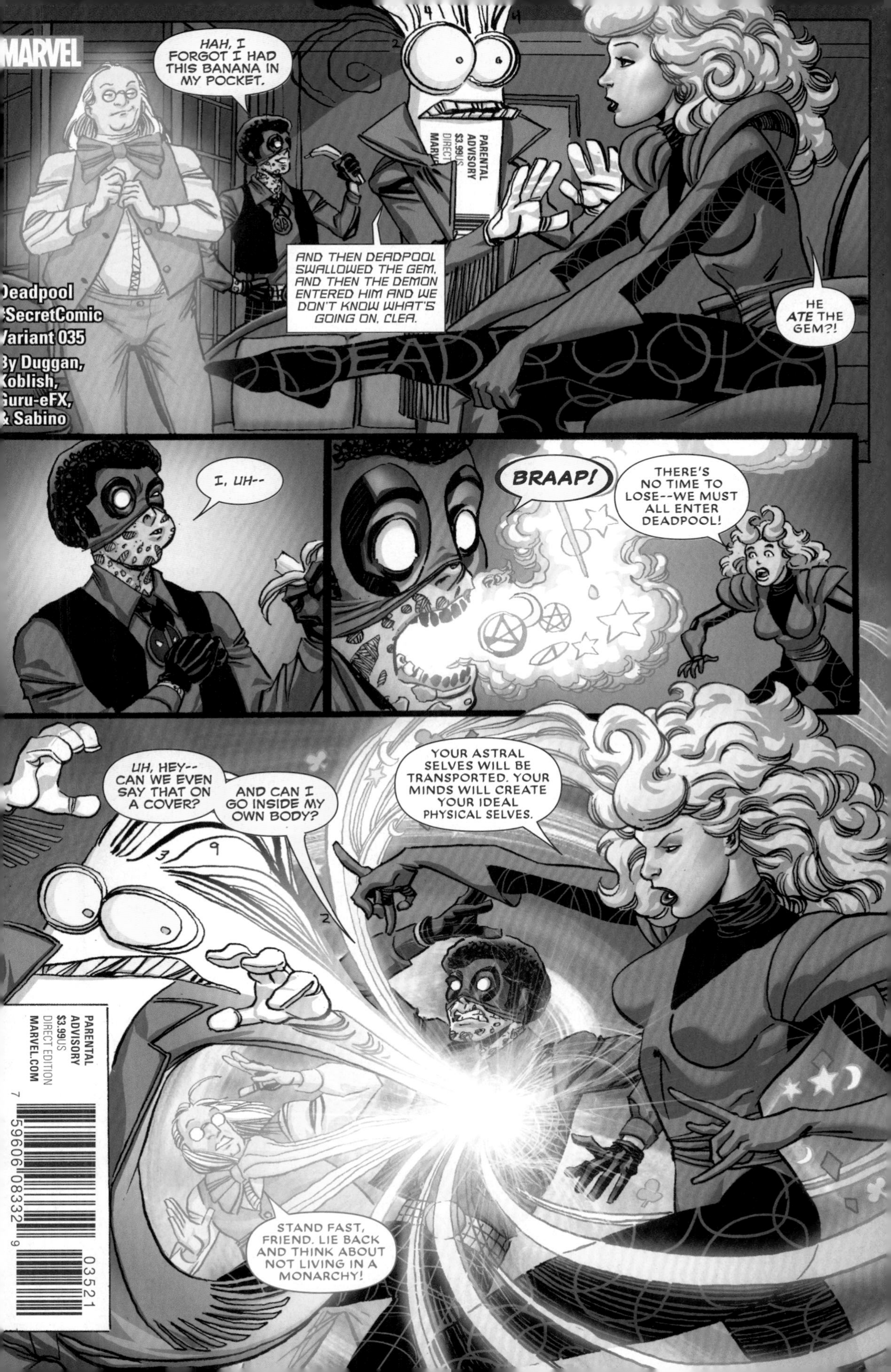

MARVEL
HAH, I FORGOT I HAD THIS BANANA IN MY POCKET.
AND THEN DEADPOOL SWALLOWED THE GEM, AND THEN THE DEMON ENTERED HIM AND WE DON'T KNOW WHAT'S GOING ON, CLEA.
HE ATE THE GEM?!
Deadpool
#SecretComic
Variant 035
By Duggan, Koblish, Guru-eFX, & Sabino
I, UH--
BRAAP!
THERE'S NO TIME TO LOSE--WE MUST ALL ENTER DEADPOOL!
UH, HEY-- CAN WE EVEN SAY THAT ON A COVER?
AND CAN I GO INSIDE MY OWN BODY?
YOUR ASTRAL SELVES WILL BE TRANSPORTED. YOUR MINDS WILL CREATE YOUR IDEAL PHYSICAL SELVES.
STAND FAST, FRIEND. LIE BACK AND THINK ABOUT NOT LIVING IN A MONARCHY!
PARENTAL ADVISORY $3.99US DIRECT EDITION MARVEL.COM

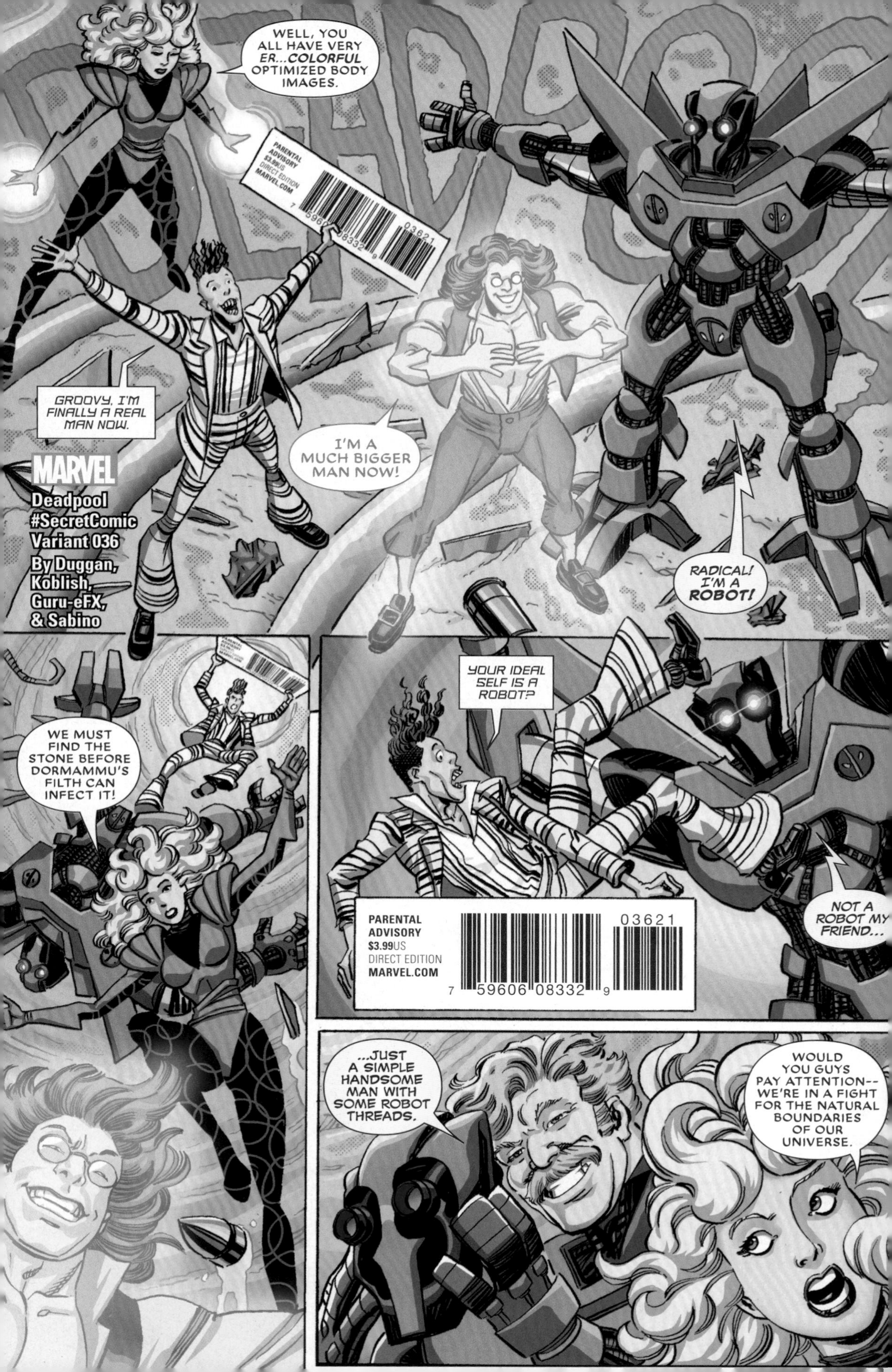
WELL, YOU ALL HAVE VERY ER...COLORFUL OPTIMIZED BODY IMAGES.
GROOVY, I'M FINALLY A REAL MAN NOW.
I'M A MUCH BIGGER MAN NOW!
RADICAL! I'M A ROBOT!
MARVEL
Deadpool #SecretComic Variant 036
By Duggan, Koblish, Guru-eFX, & Sabino
WE MUST FIND THE STONE BEFORE DORMAMMU'S FILTH CAN INFECT IT!
YOUR IDEAL SELF IS A ROBOT?
NOT A ROBOT MY FRIEND...
PARENTAL ADVISORY
$3.99US
DIRECT EDITION
MARVEL.COM
...JUST A SIMPLE HANDSOME MAN WITH SOME ROBOT THREADS.
WOULD YOU GUYS PAY ATTENTION-- WE'RE IN A FIGHT FOR THE NATURAL BOUNDARIES OF OUR UNIVERSE.

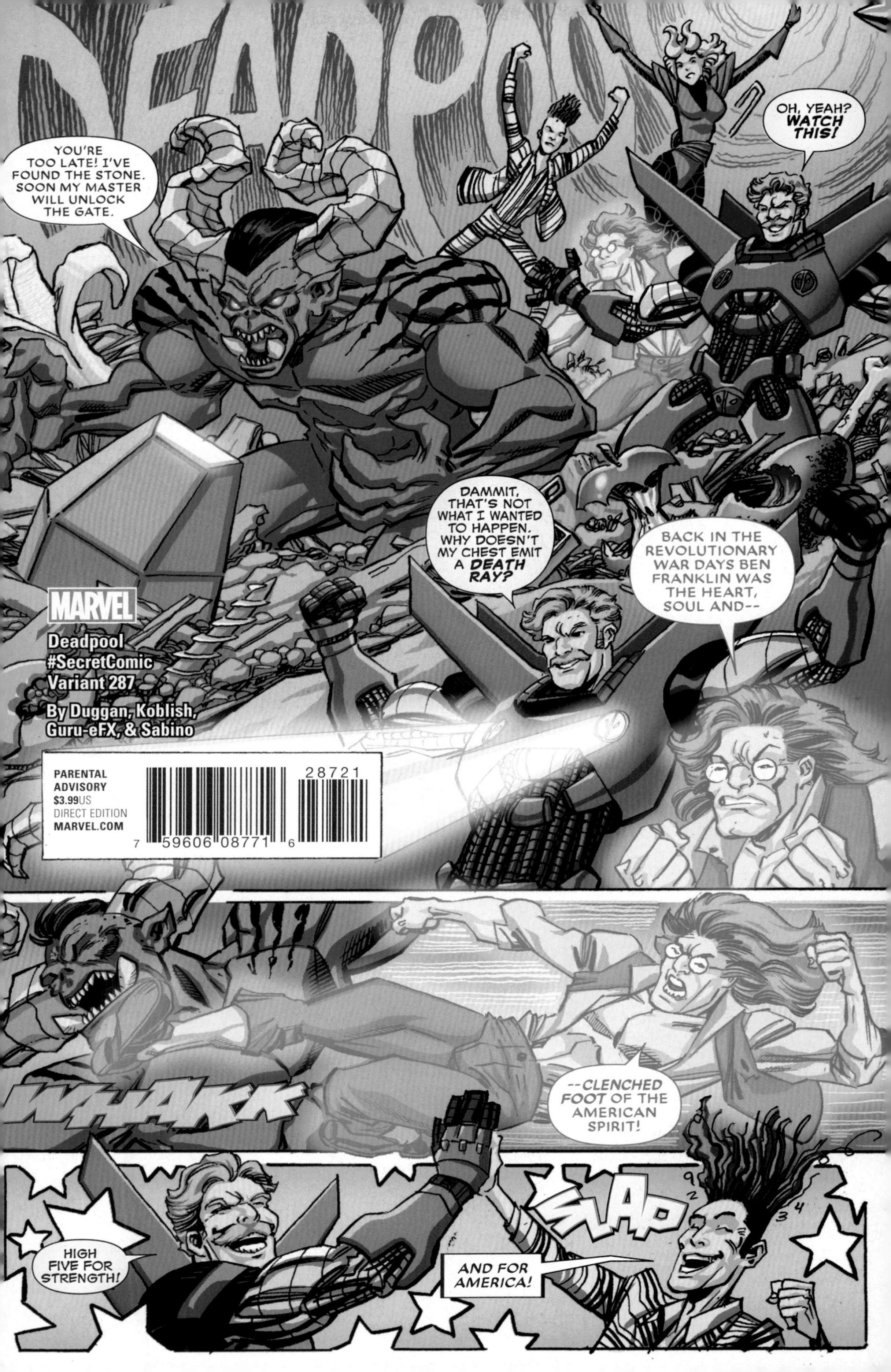
YOU'RE TOO LATE! I'VE FOUND THE STONE. SOON MY MASTER WILL UNLOCK THE GATE.
OH, YEAH? WATCH THIS!
DAMMIT, THAT'S NOT WHAT I WANTED TO HAPPEN. WHY DOESN'T MY CHEST EMIT A DEATH RAY?
BACK IN THE REVOLUTIONARY WAR DAYS BEN FRANKLIN WAS THE HEART, SOUL AND--
MARVEL
Deadpool
#SecretComic
Variant 287
By Duggan, Koblish, Guru-eFX, & Sabino
PARENTAL ADVISORY
$3.99US
DIRECT EDITION
MARVEL.COM
WHAKK
--CLENCHED FOOT OF THE AMERICAN SPIRIT!
HIGH FIVE FOR STRENGTH!
AND FOR AMERICA!

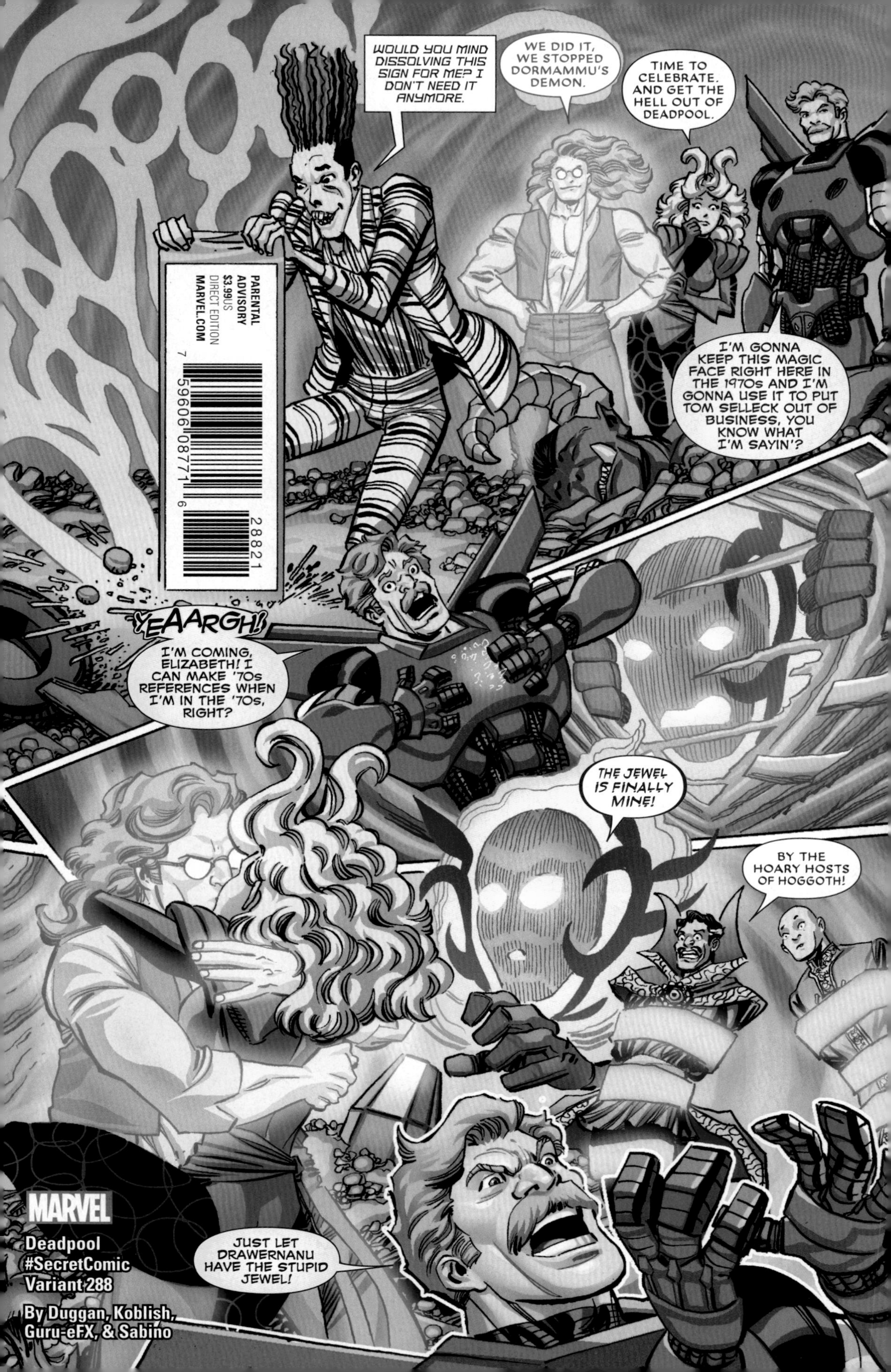

WOULD YOU MIND DISSOLVING THIS SIGN FOR ME? I DON'T NEED IT ANYMORE.
WE DID IT, WE STOPPED DORMAMMU'S DEMON.
TIME TO CELEBRATE. AND GET THE HELL OUT OF DEADPOOL.
I'M GONNA KEEP THIS MAGIC FACE RIGHT HERE IN THE 1970s AND I'M GONNA USE IT TO PUT TOM SELLECK OUT OF BUSINESS, YOU KNOW WHAT I'M SAYIN'?
PARENTAL ADVISORY
$3.99US
DIRECT EDITION
MARVEL.COM
YEAARGH!
I'M COMING, ELIZABETH! I CAN MAKE '70s REFERENCES WHEN I'M IN THE '70s, RIGHT?
THE JEWEL IS FINALLY MINE!
BY THE HOARY HOSTS OF HOGGOTH!
JUST LET DRAWERNANU HAVE THE STUPID JEWEL!
MARVEL
Deadpool
#SecretComic
Variant 288
By Duggan, Koblish, Guru-eFX, & Sabino

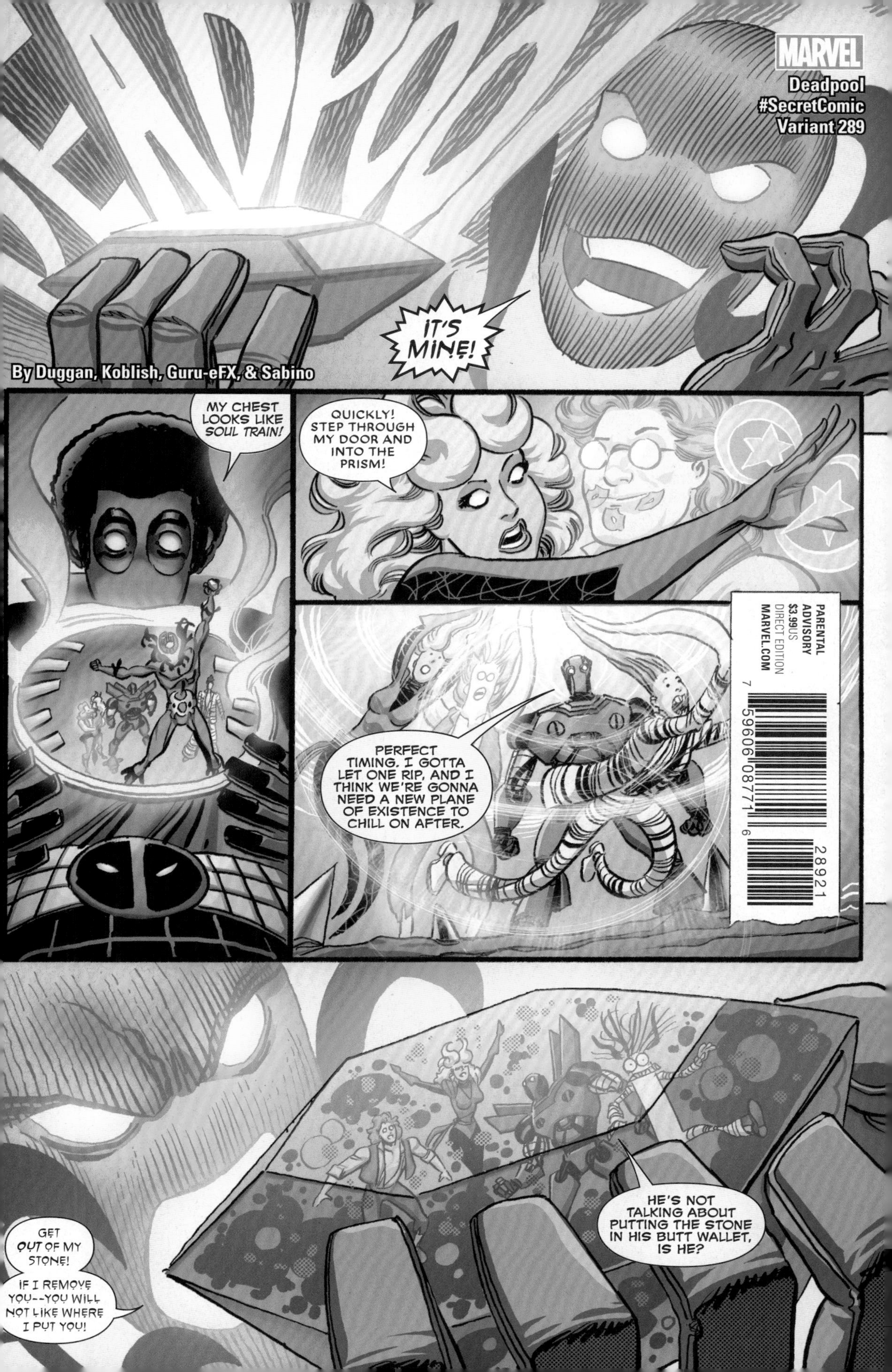

MARVEL
Deadpool
#SecretComic
Variant 289
IT'S MINE!
By Duggan, Koblish, Guru-eFX, & Sabino
MY CHEST LOOKS LIKE SOUL TRAIN!
QUICKLY! STEP THROUGH MY DOOR AND INTO THE PRISM!
PERFECT TIMING. I GOTTA LET ONE RIP, AND I THINK WE'RE GONNA NEED A NEW PLANE OF EXISTENCE TO CHILL ON AFTER.
PARENTAL ADVISORY
$3.99US
DIRECT EDITION
MARVEL.COM
7 59606 08771 6 28921
GET OUT OF MY STONE!
IF I REMOVE YOU--YOU WILL NOT LIKE WHERE I PUT YOU!
HE'S NOT TALKING ABOUT PUTTING THE STONE IN HIS BUTT WALLET, IS HE?

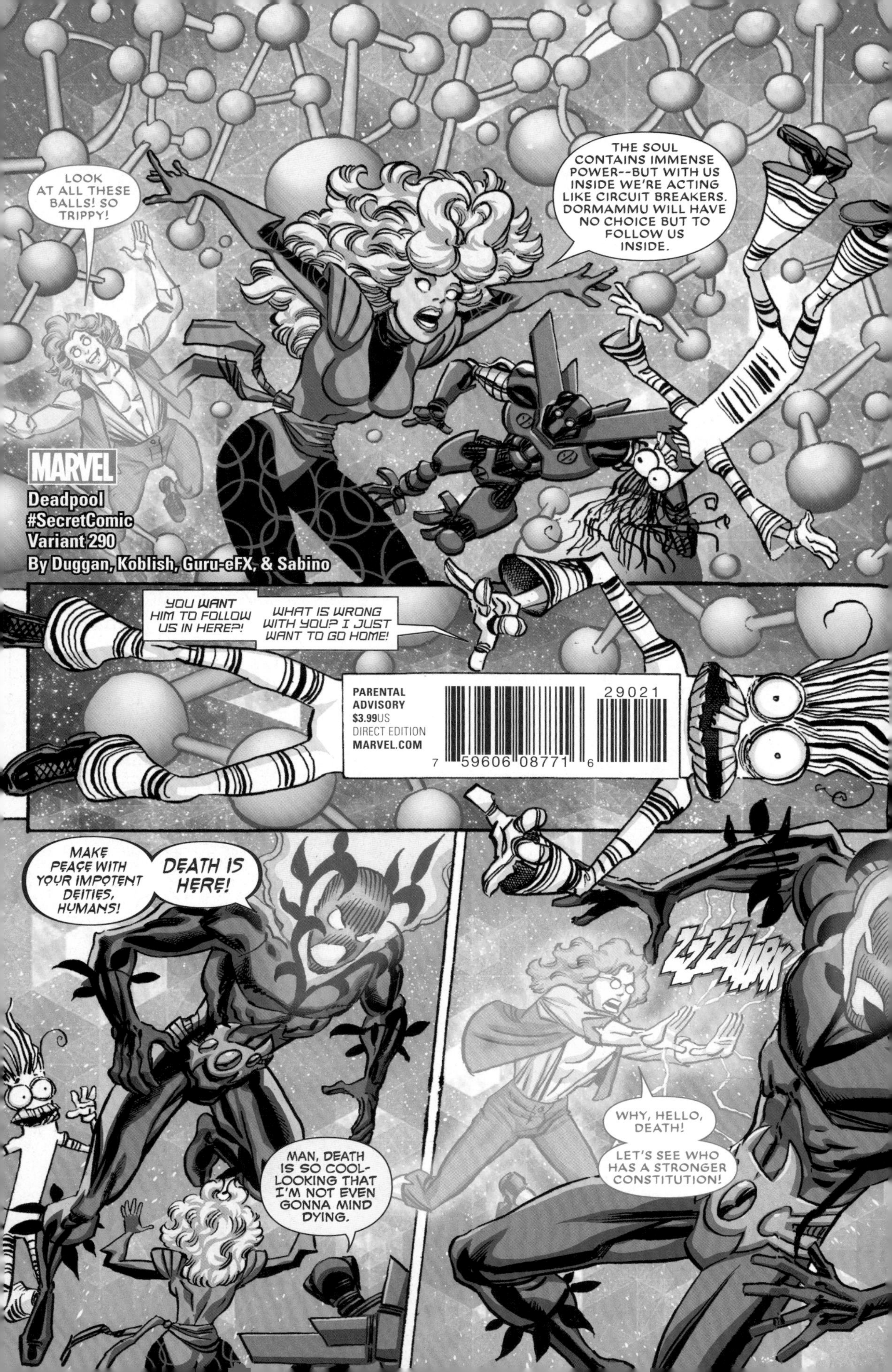
LOOK AT ALL THESE BALLS! SO TRIPPY!
THE SOUL CONTAINS IMMENSE POWER--BUT WITH US INSIDE WE'RE ACTING LIKE CIRCUIT BREAKERS. DORMAMMU WILL HAVE NO CHOICE BUT TO FOLLOW US INSIDE.
MARVEL
Deadpool
#SecretComic
Variant 290
By Duggan, Koblish, Guru-eFX, & Sabino
YOU WANT HIM TO FOLLOW US IN HERE?!
WHAT IS WRONG WITH YOU? I JUST WANT TO GO HOME!
PARENTAL ADVISORY
$3.99US
DIRECT EDITION
MARVEL.COM
MAKE PEACE WITH YOUR IMPOTENT DEITIES, HUMANS!
DEATH IS HERE!
ZZZZAARK
MAN, DEATH IS SO COOL-LOOKING THAT I'M NOT EVEN GONNA MIND DYING.
WHY, HELLO, DEATH!
LET'S SEE WHO HAS A STRONGER CONSTITUTION!

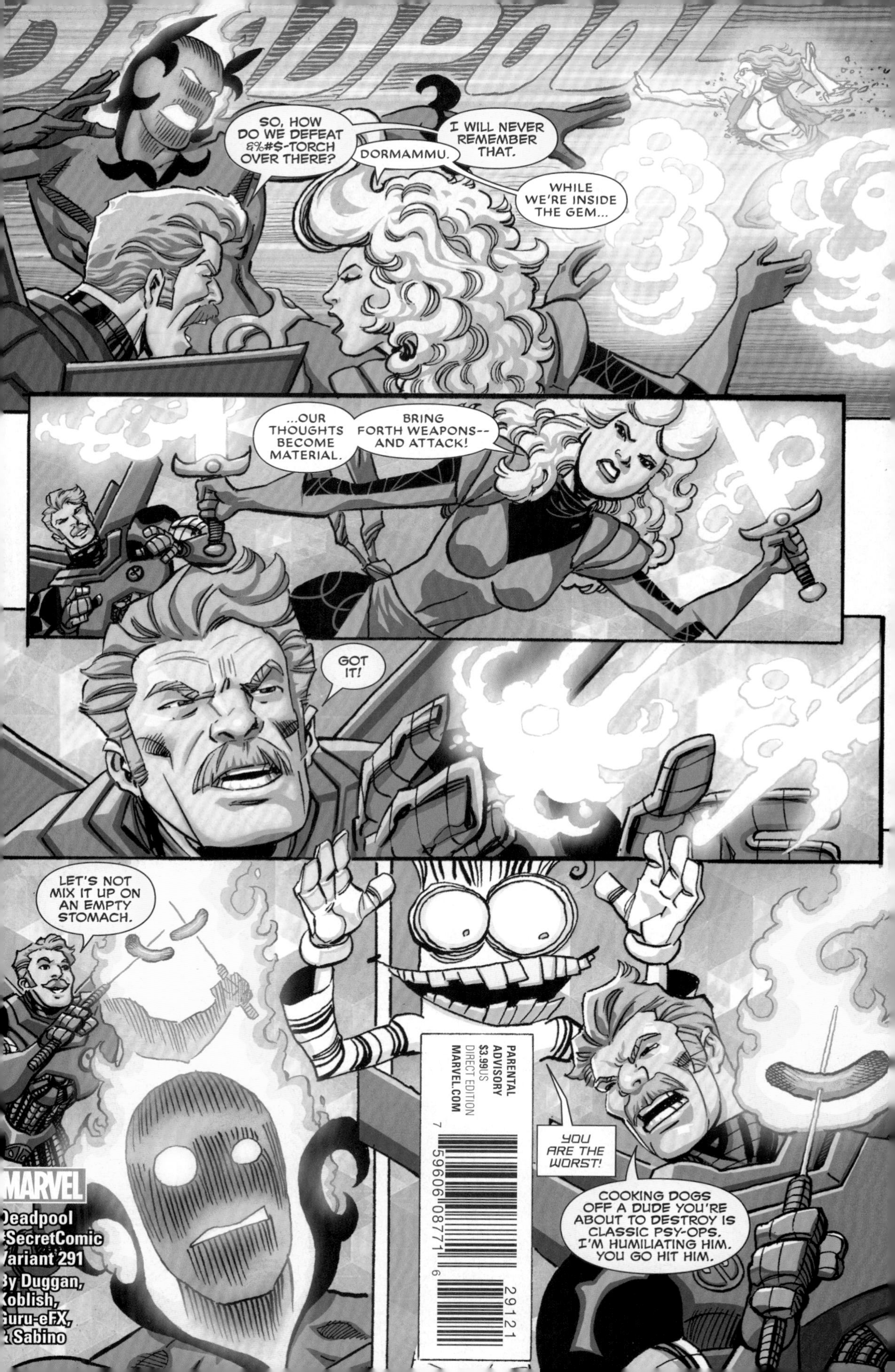
SO, HOW DO WE DEFEAT &%#$-TORCH OVER THERE?
DORMAMMU.
I WILL NEVER REMEMBER THAT.
WHILE WE'RE INSIDE THE GEM...
...OUR THOUGHTS BECOME MATERIAL.
BRING FORTH WEAPONS-- AND ATTACK!
GOT IT!
LET'S NOT MIX IT UP ON AN EMPTY STOMACH.
YOU ARE THE WORST!
COOKING DOGS OFF A DUDE YOU'RE ABOUT TO DESTROY IS CLASSIC PSY-OPS. I'M HUMILIATING HIM. YOU GO HIT HIM.
PARENTAL ADVISORY
$3.99US
DIRECT EDITION
MARVEL.COM
MARVEL
Deadpool
#SecretComic
Variant 291
By Duggan,
Koblish,
Guru-eFX,
& Sabino

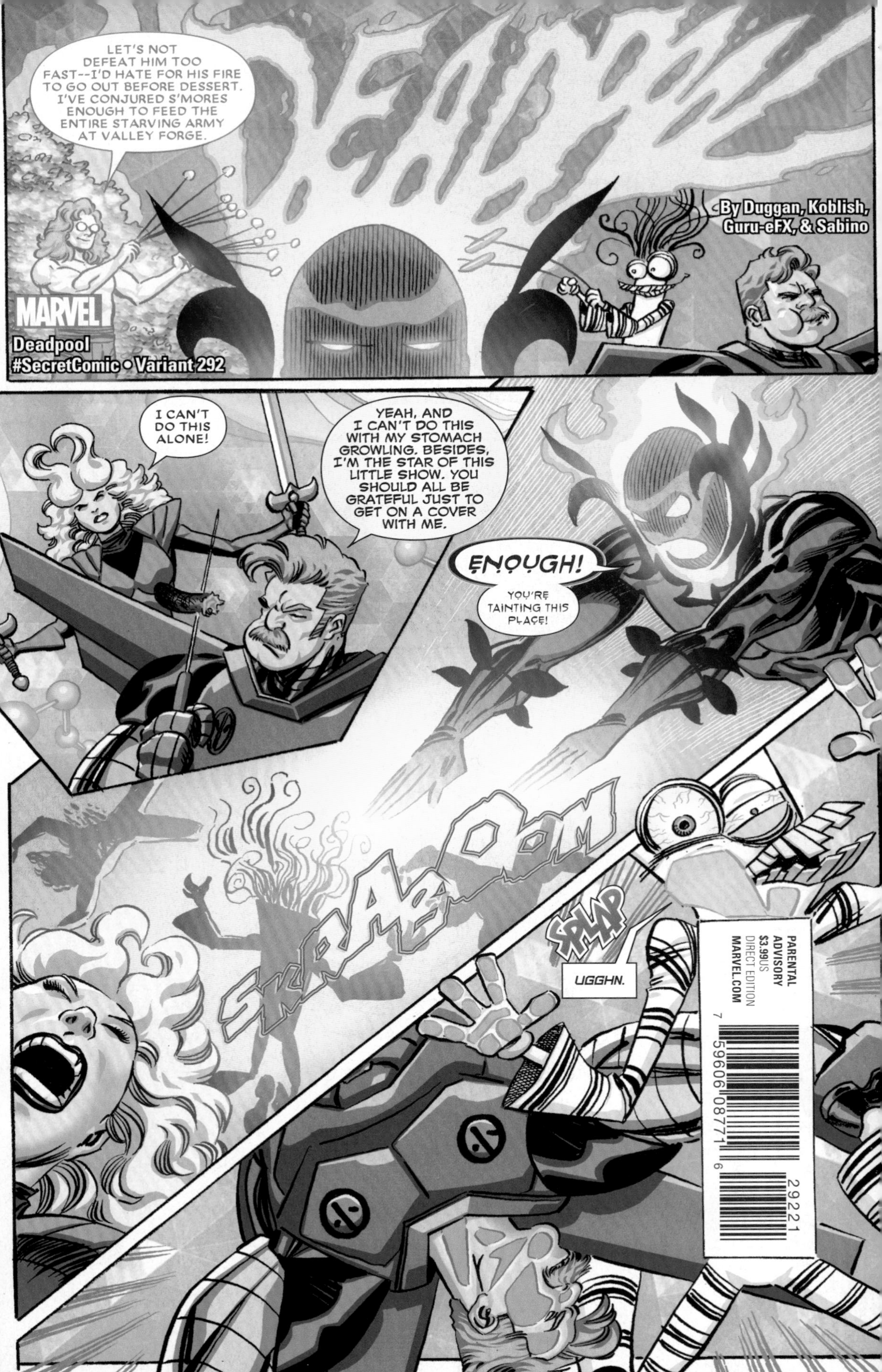
LET'S NOT DEFEAT HIM TOO FAST--I'D HATE FOR HIS FIRE TO GO OUT BEFORE DESSERT. I'VE CONJURED S'MORES ENOUGH TO FEED THE ENTIRE STARVING ARMY AT VALLEY FORGE.
By Duggan, Koblish, Guru-eFX, & Sabino
MARVEL
Deadpool
#SecretComic • Variant 292
I CAN'T DO THIS ALONE!
YEAH, AND I CAN'T DO THIS WITH MY STOMACH GROWLING. BESIDES, I'M THE STAR OF THIS LITTLE SHOW. YOU SHOULD ALL BE GRATEFUL JUST TO GET ON A COVER WITH ME.
ENOUGH!
YOU'RE TAINTING THIS PLACE!
SKRA-BOOM
SPLAP
UGGHN.
PARENTAL ADVISORY
$3.99US
DIRECT EDITION
MARVEL.COM

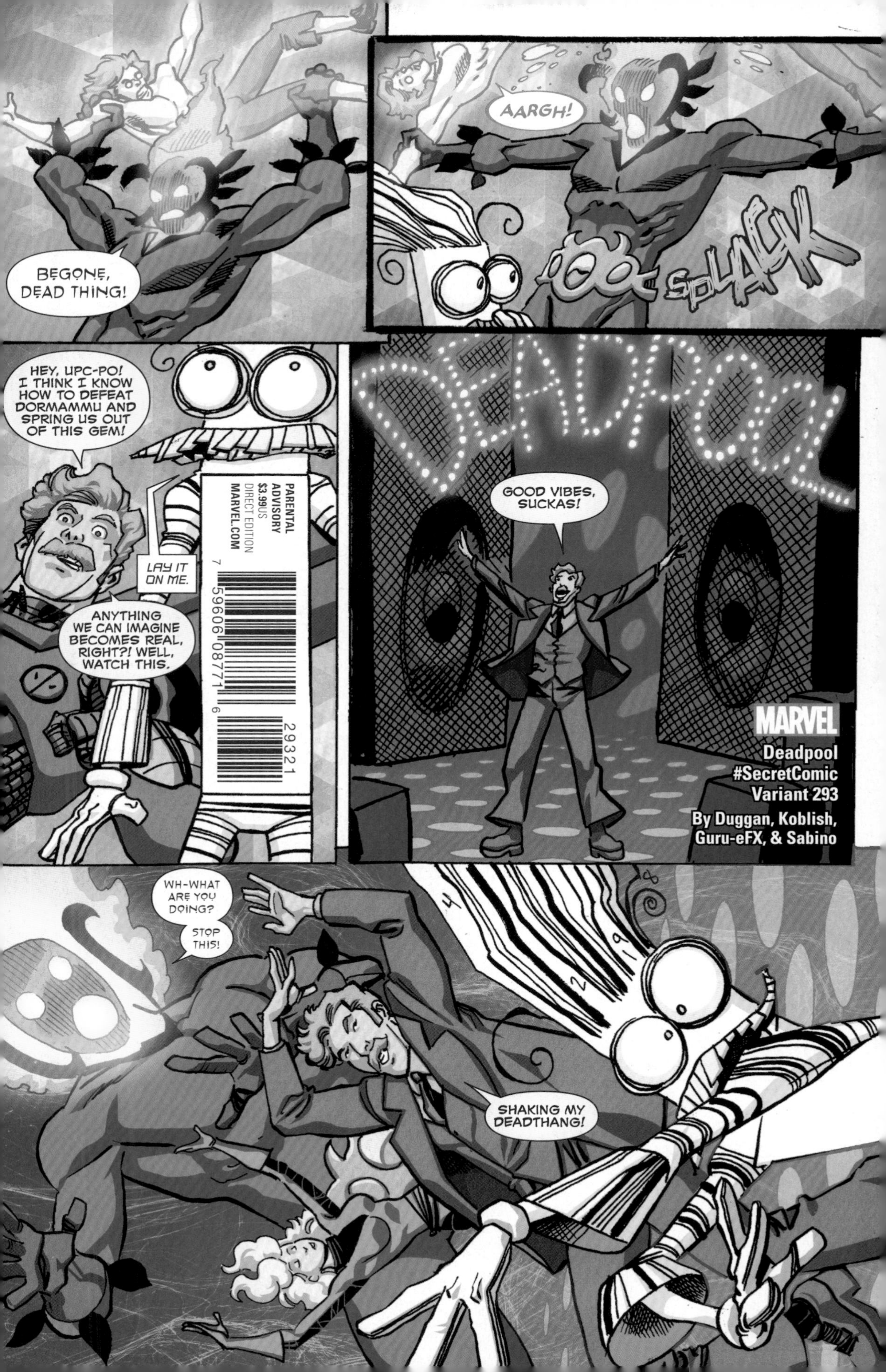

BEGONE, DEAD THING!
AARGH!
SPLAK
HEY, UPC-PO! I THINK I KNOW HOW TO DEFEAT DORMAMMU AND SPRING US OUT OF THIS GEM!
LAY IT ON ME.
ANYTHING WE CAN IMAGINE BECOMES REAL, RIGHT?! WELL, WATCH THIS.
PARENTAL ADVISORY
$3.99US
DIRECT EDITION
MARVEL.COM
7 59606 08771 6 29321
DEADPOOL
GOOD VIBES, SUCKAS!
MARVEL
Deadpool #SecretComic Variant 293
By Duggan, Koblish, Guru-eFX, & Sabino
WH-WHAT ARE YOU DOING?
STOP THIS!
SHAKING MY DEADTHANG!

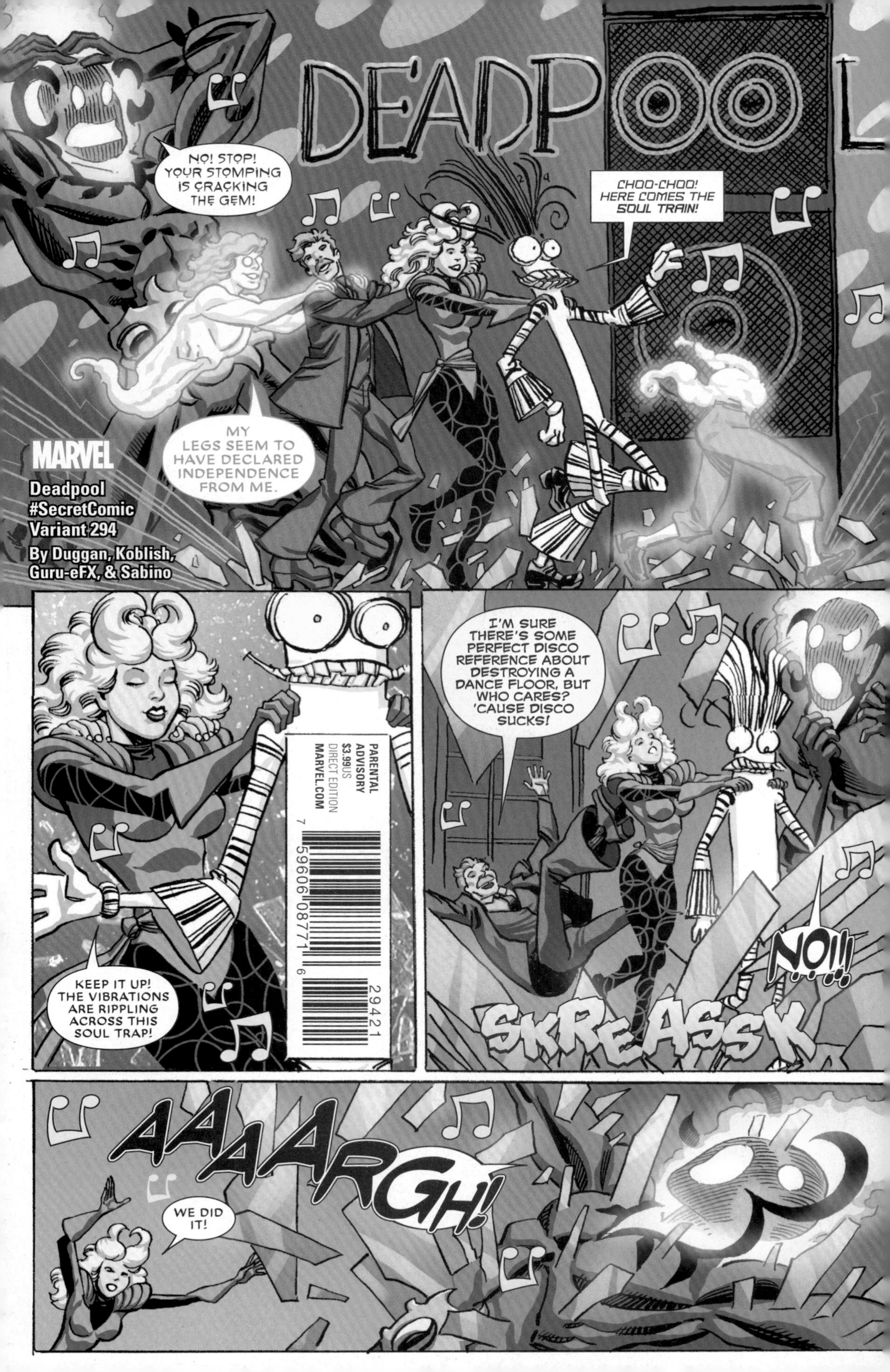
DEADPOOL
NO! STOP! YOUR STOMPING IS CRACKING THE GEM!
CHOO-CHOO! HERE COMES THE SOUL TRAIN!
MY LEGS SEEM TO HAVE DECLARED INDEPENDENCE FROM ME.
MARVEL
Deadpool #SecretComic Variant 294
By Duggan, Koblish, Guru-eFX, & Sabino
PARENTAL ADVISORY
$3.99US
DIRECT EDITION
MARVEL.COM
KEEP IT UP! THE VIBRATIONS ARE RIPPLING ACROSS THIS SOUL TRAP!
I'M SURE THERE'S SOME PERFECT DISCO REFERENCE ABOUT DESTROYING A DANCE FLOOR, BUT WHO CARES? 'CAUSE DISCO SUCKS!
NO!!!
SKREASSK
AAAAARGH!
WE DID IT!

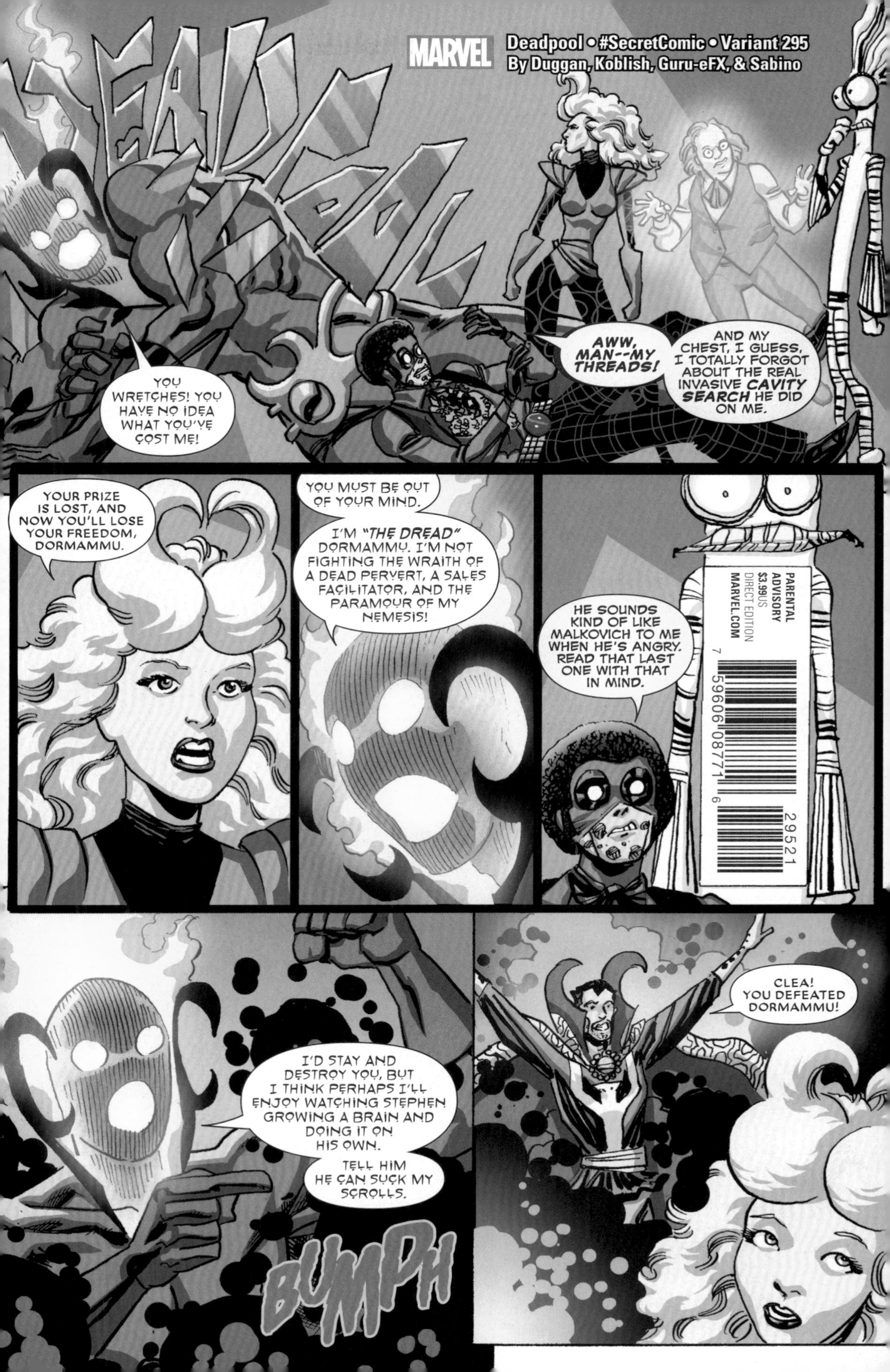
MARVEL
Deadpool • #SecretComic • Variant 295
By Duggan, Koblish, Guru-eFX, & Sabino
YOU WRETCHES! YOU HAVE NO IDEA WHAT YOU'VE COST ME!
AWW, MAN--MY THREADS!
AND MY CHEST, I GUESS. I TOTALLY FORGOT ABOUT THE REAL INVASIVE CAVITY SEARCH HE DID ON ME.
YOUR PRIZE IS LOST, AND NOW YOU'LL LOSE YOUR FREEDOM, DORMAMMU.
YOU MUST BE OUT OF YOUR MIND.
I'M "THE DREAD" DORMAMMU. I'M NOT FIGHTING THE WRAITH OF A DEAD PERVERT, A SALES FACILITATOR, AND THE PARAMOUR OF MY NEMESIS!
PARENTAL ADVISORY
$3.99US
DIRECT EDITION
MARVEL.COM
HE SOUNDS KIND OF LIKE MALKOVICH TO ME WHEN HE'S ANGRY. READ THAT LAST ONE WITH THAT IN MIND.
I'D STAY AND DESTROY YOU, BUT I THINK PERHAPS I'LL ENJOY WATCHING STEPHEN GROWING A BRAIN AND DOING IT ON HIS OWN.
TELL HIM HE CAN SUCK MY SCROLLS.
BUMPH
CLEA! YOU DEFEATED DORMAMMU!

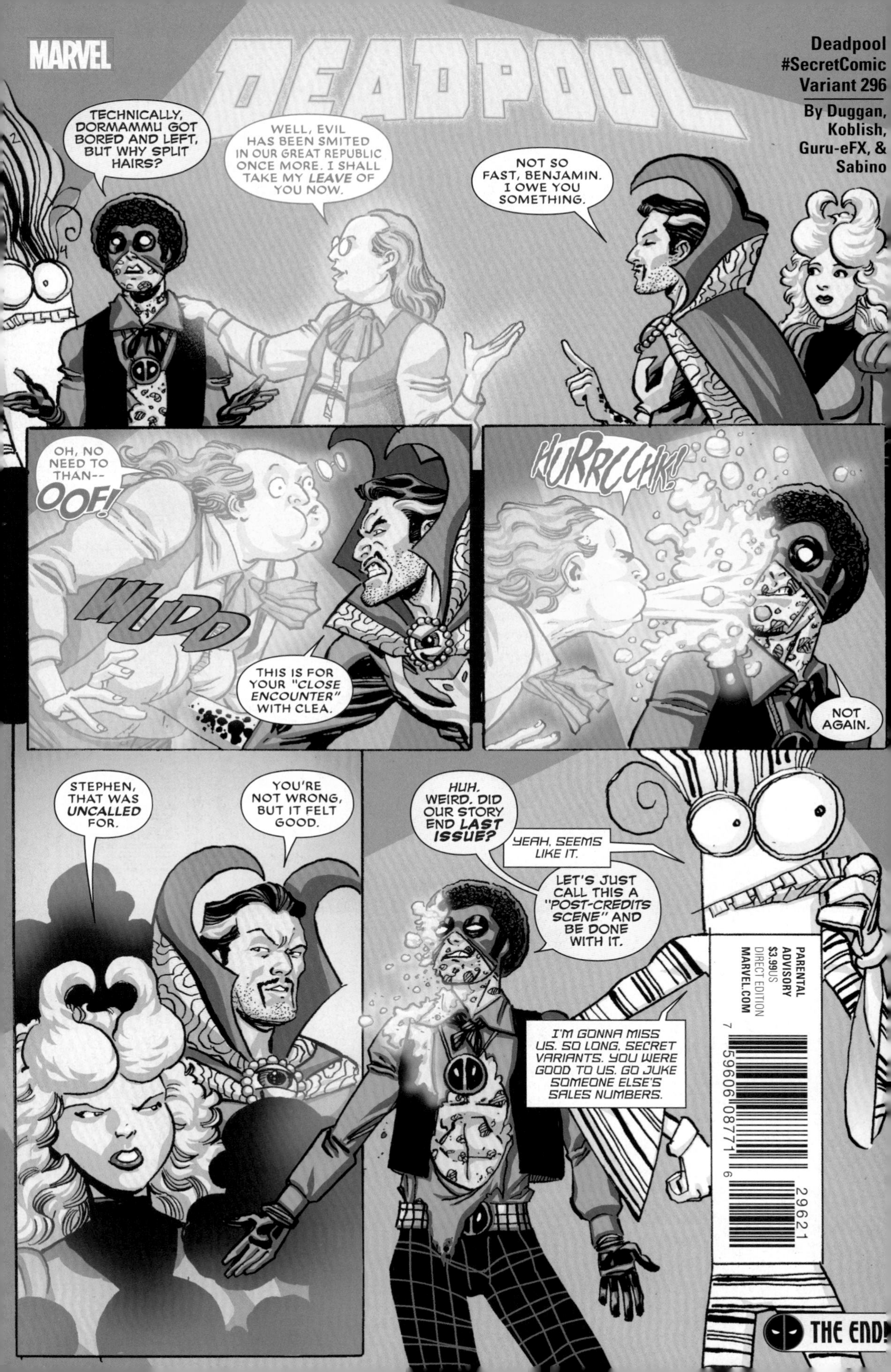
MARVEL
DEADPOOL
Deadpool #SecretComic Variant 296
By Duggan, Koblish, Guru-eFX, & Sabino
TECHNICALLY, DORMAMMU GOT BORED AND LEFT, BUT WHY SPLIT HAIRS?
WELL, EVIL HAS BEEN SMITED IN OUR GREAT REPUBLIC ONCE MORE. I SHALL TAKE MY LEAVE OF YOU NOW.
NOT SO FAST, BENJAMIN. I OWE YOU SOMETHING.
OH, NO NEED TO THAN-- OOF!
WUDD
THIS IS FOR YOUR "CLOSE ENCOUNTER" WITH CLEA.
HURRCCHK!
NOT AGAIN.
STEPHEN, THAT WAS UNCALLED FOR.
YOU'RE NOT WRONG, BUT IT FELT GOOD.
HUH. WEIRD. DID OUR STORY END LAST ISSUE?
YEAH, SEEMS LIKE IT.
LET'S JUST CALL THIS A "POST-CREDITS SCENE" AND BE DONE WITH IT.
I'M GONNA MISS US. SO LONG, SECRET VARIANTS. YOU WERE GOOD TO US. GO JUKE SOMEONE ELSE'S SALES NUMBERS.
PARENTAL ADVISORY
$3.99US
DIRECT EDITION
MARVEL.COM
THE END!

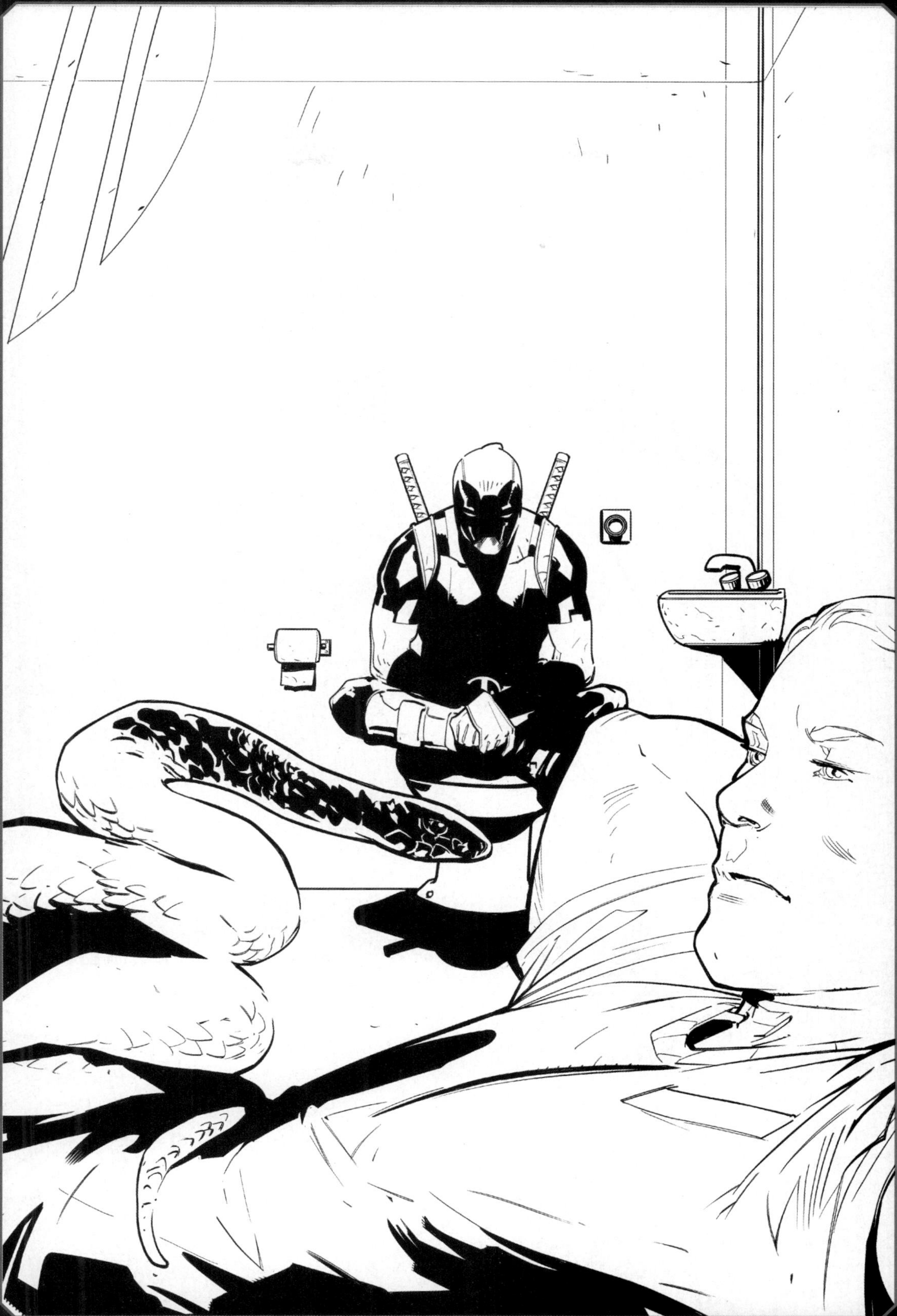

#292, PAGE 7 ART BY **MATTEO LOLLI**

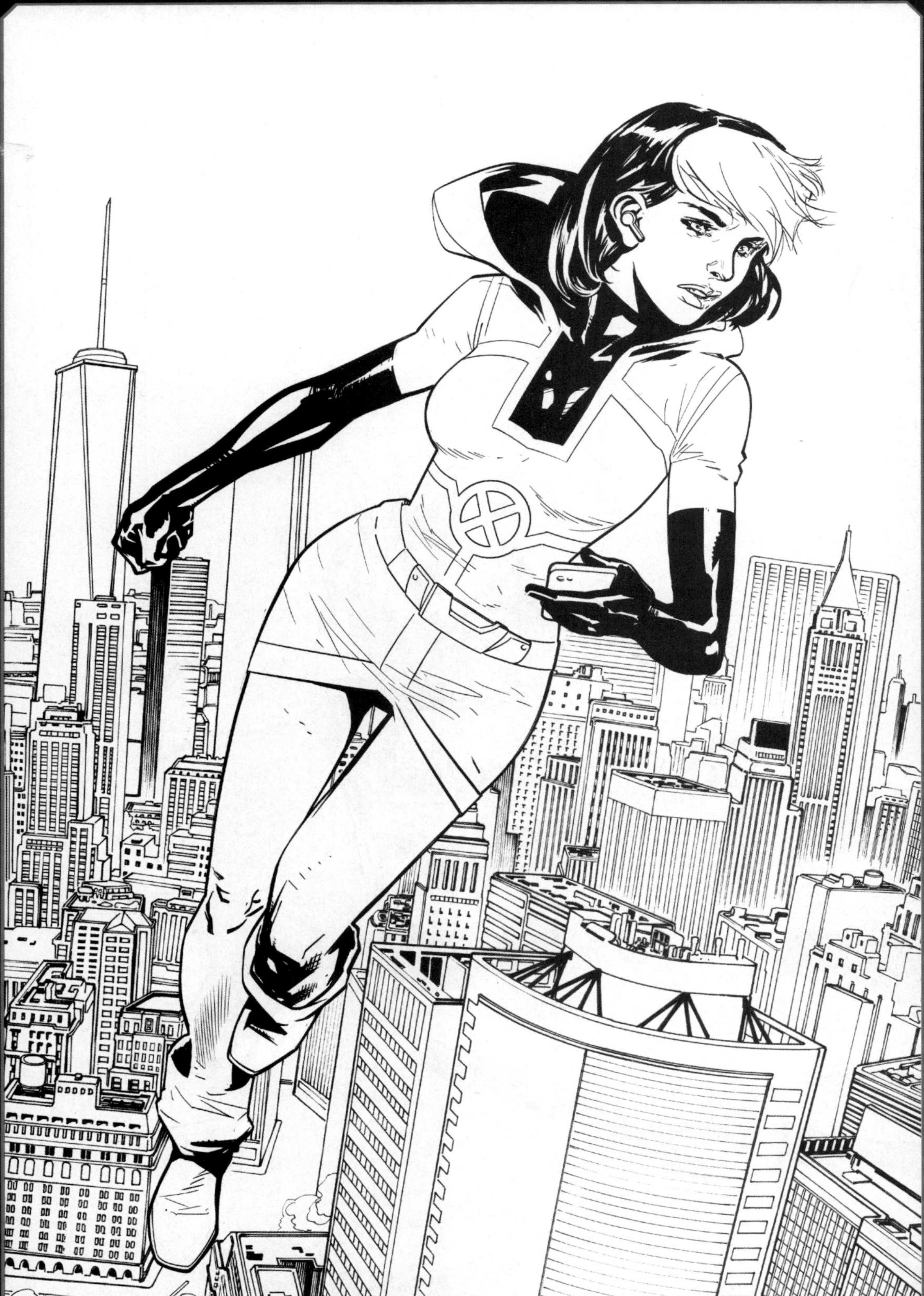

#292, PAGE 20 ART BY MATTEO LOLLI

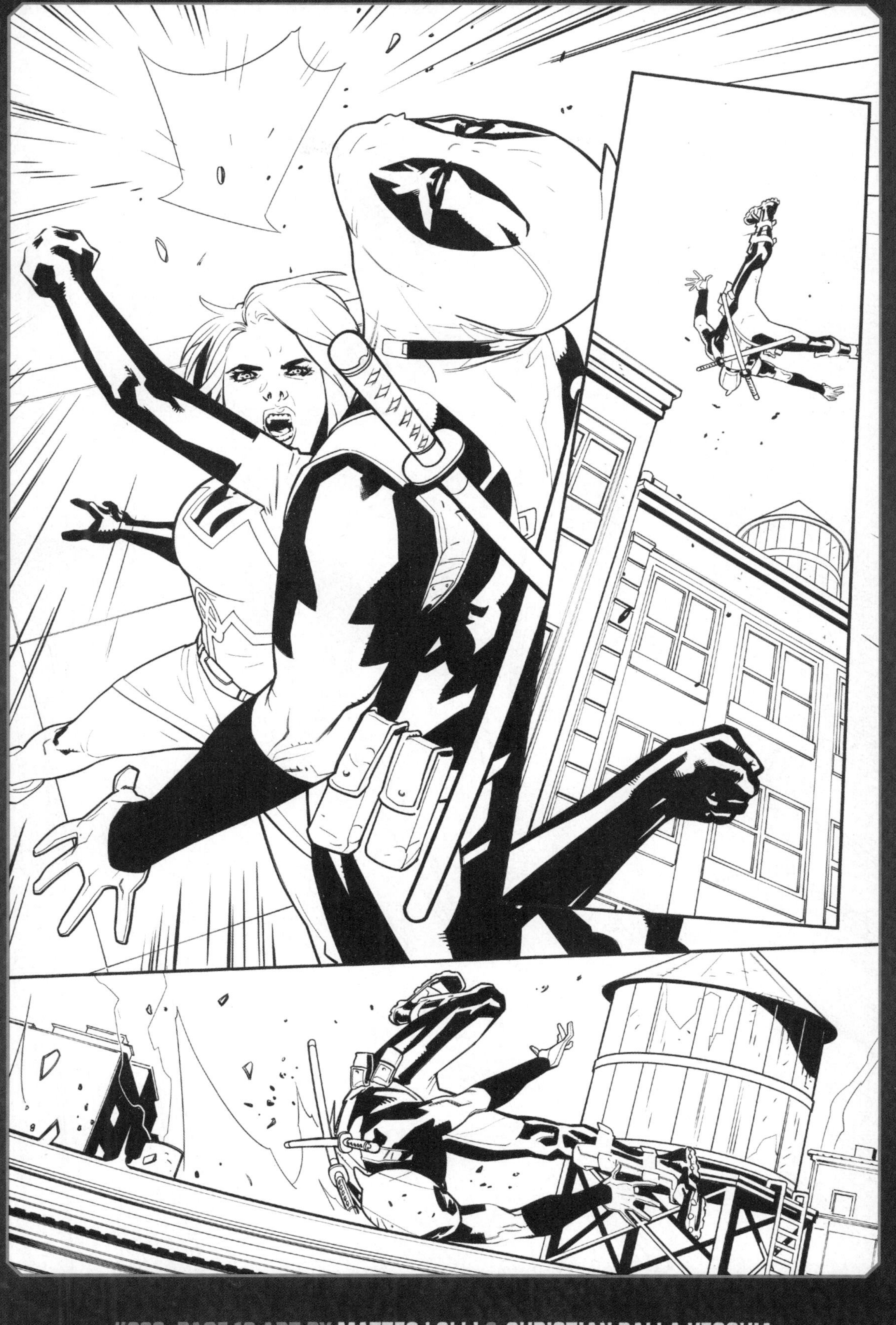

#293, PAGE 12 ART BY **MATTEO LOLLI & CHRISTIAN DALLA VECCHIA**

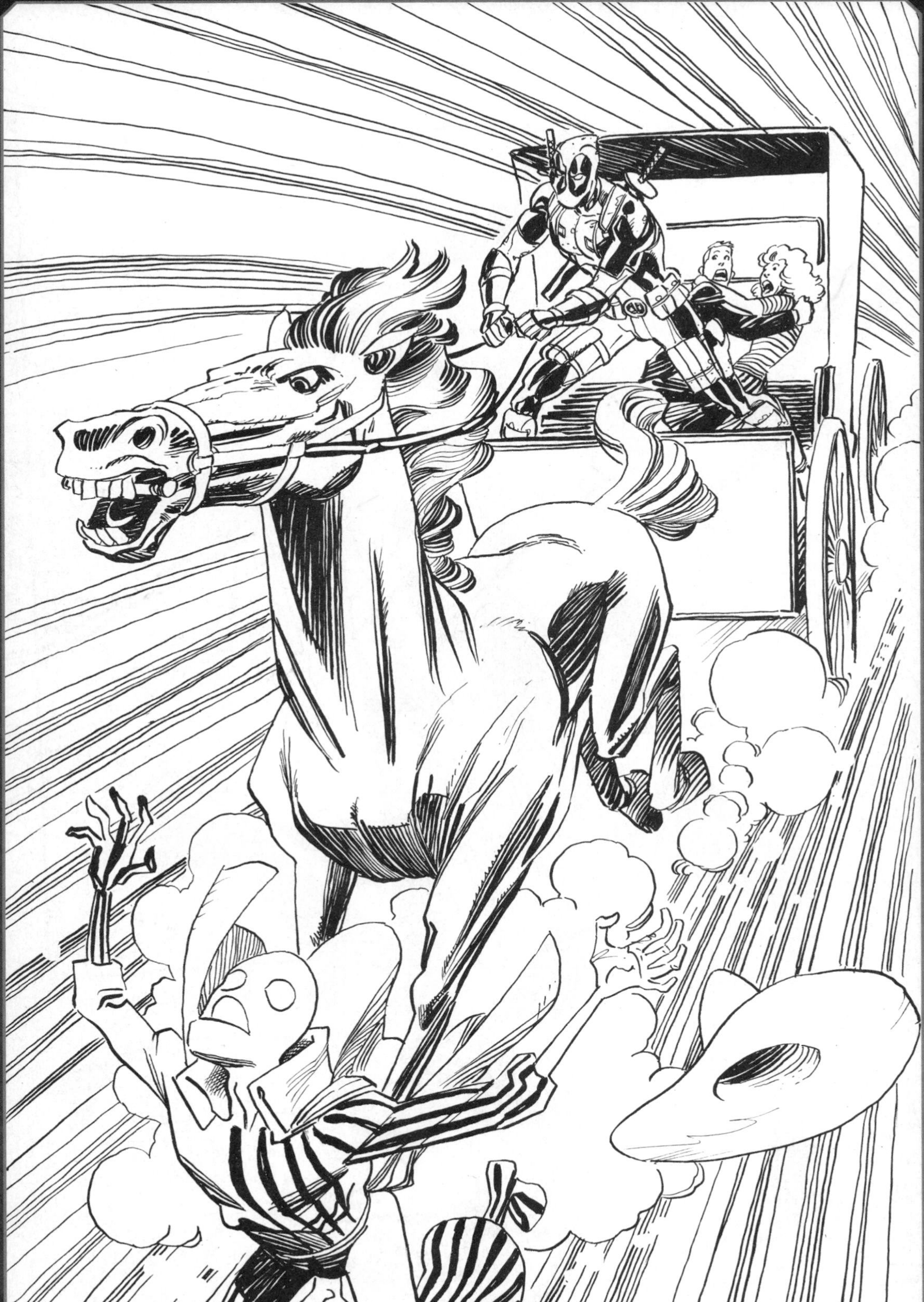

#294, PAGE 6 ART BY **SCOTT KOBLISH**

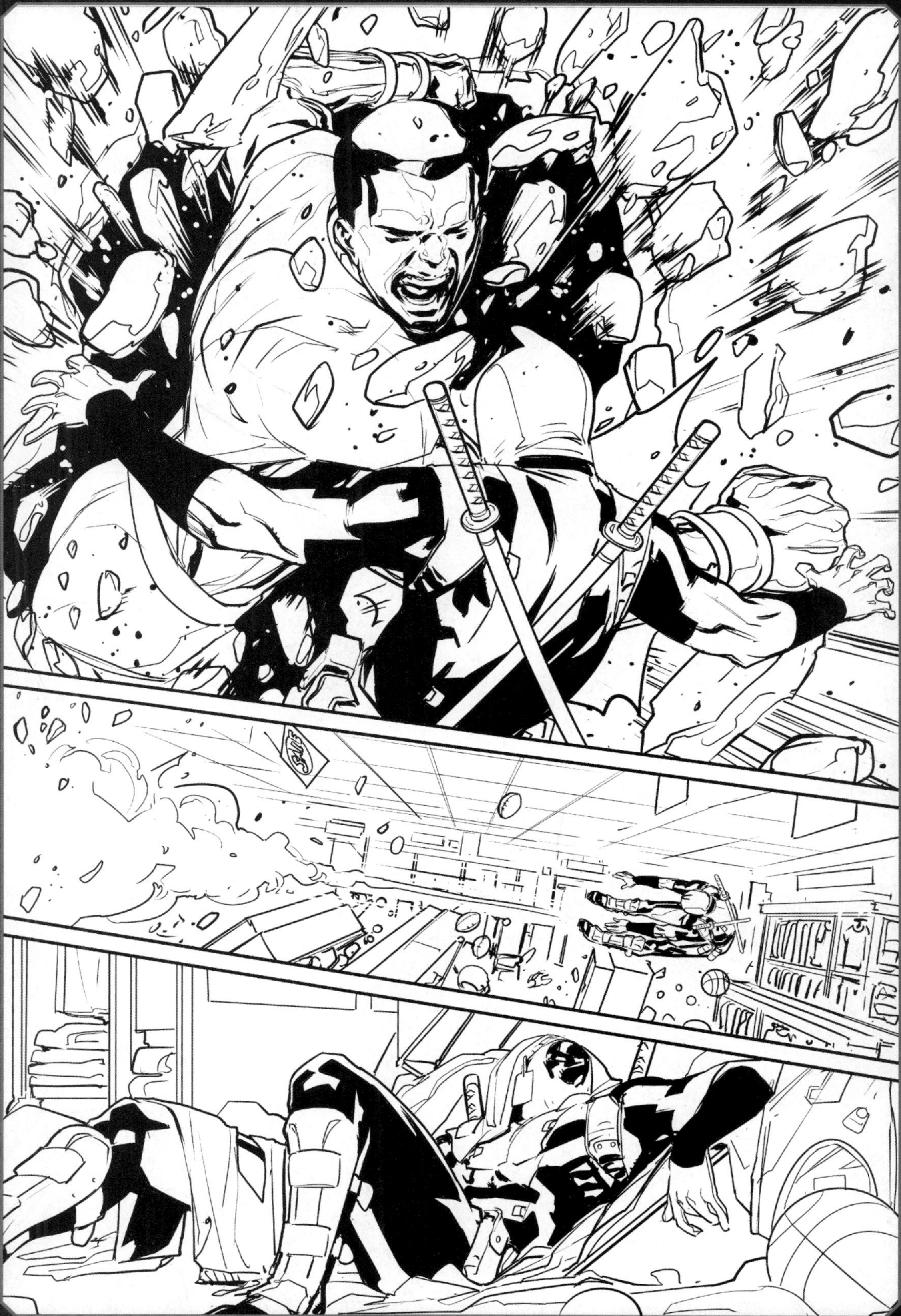

#295, PAGE 8 ART BY **MATTEO LOLLI**

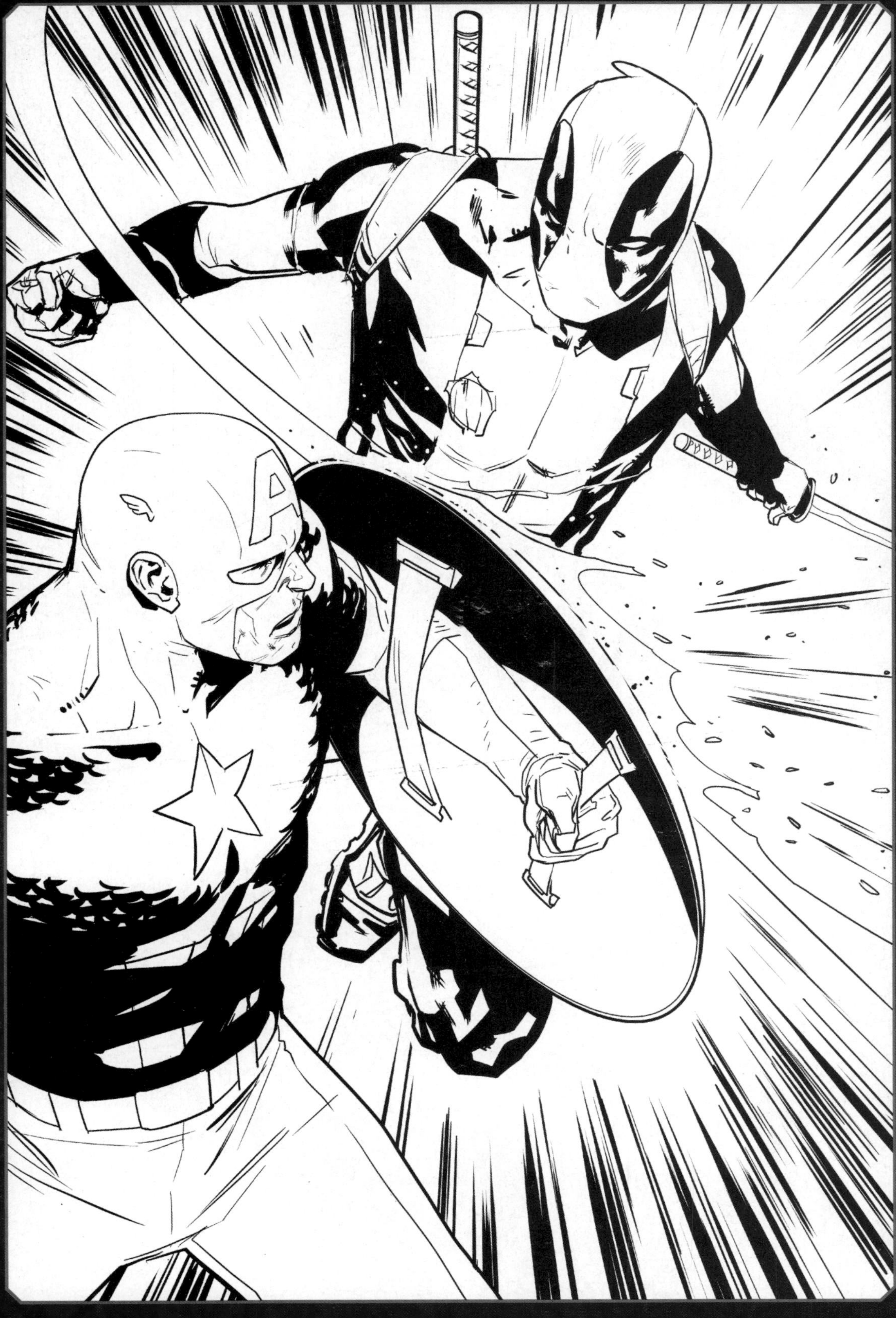

#296, PAGE 1 ART BY MATTEO LOLLI